Praise for *Building Fires in the Snow*

Not so long ago an anthology of LGBTQ writing by Alaskans and speaking to the Alaska experience might have seemed beyond imagining. But in *Building Fires in the Snow,* Lucian Childs and Martha Amore have built a collection both extraordinary and ordinary. Extraordinary for its breadth and quality of the poetry and prose. Ordinary in the aesthetic that pervades the collection, people living their lives in emotionally honest and complex ways. There's something for every reader in *Building Fires in the Snow,* a book to keep near at hand and to digest slowly and enjoy.

> Frank Soos, professor Emeritus of English at University of Alaska Fairbanks

The first story of this fine anthology, "Luke," is as local and Alaskan as a story can be. Here's what it feels like to be a fisherman, and what it feels like to miss another man. *Geology,* another story, is a beautiful meditation on a woman's desire and obligation, remorse and momentum and long love, against a backdrop of longer time. These are subtle, artful reflections that will place you, for a moment, in Alaska and deeper wildernesses as well. Essential reading if you want to know Alaska.

> David Vann, winner of 2010 *Prix Medicis Etranger* and author of *Legend of a Suicide, Goat Mountain,* and *Caribou Island*

A compelling anthology dwells in possibility. And this first effort to yoke together voices—of those that may or may not be Alaskan, LGBTQ, or even writers—offer solidarity of a kind. A possibility for this book may be that the voices that are not included in this collection—the voices, for instance, of Alaska's many indigenous LGBTQ poets, storytellers, and thinkers raised in the context of our identities as Native people marginalized and made invisible in our homelands—may find the courage in times to come to have their word similarly collected and championed.

> Joan Naviyuk Kane, winner of the 2009 Whiting Award, the 2014 American Book Award, and author of *Hyperboreal* and *The Cormorant Hunter's Wife*

Richly diverse and honest, there's much to like in this rewarding collection of poems and stories of lived experience.

> Ronald Spatz, editor, *Alaska Quarterly Review*

The Alaska writing cliché of the rugged white hetero male battling the wilderness is dead, and as it turns out its corpse makes a fine hummus, and good fertilizer, for what comes next. What comes next, I think, is *Building Fires in the Snow*, a book that, like nature itself, prizes diversity, and is full of stories of the urban and the rural, the domestic and the wild, the human—in its many flavors—and the animal, and all of it told on the vast, varied and glorious stage that is Alaska. This is just the kind of vision we need to start a new conversation about wilderness, what it means to be human, and how we can lead authentic lives in an increasingly inauthentic world.

David Gessner, author of *All the Wild That Remains: Edward Abbey, Wallace Stegner and the American West*

Like Alaska itself, *Building Fires in the Snow* defies easy pigeonholing. Whatever you might expect, this collection of LGBTQ short fiction and poetry will surprise, which is reason enough to add it to your library. Eclectic, original, and thought-provoking, it makes a unique and important contribution to Alaska's literary landscape.

Deb Vanasse, author of *Cold Spell* and *Wealth Woman*

The poetry and fiction of *Building Fires in the Snow* stakes a queer claim, not necessarily to the untamable terrain of Alaska itself, but certainly to its unfolding story. These writers bear witness to long winters, frozen country, hard hearts, a rugged history, deep passion, quiet moments, a past brought to light, and a future not allowed to be exclusionary. *Building Fires in the Snow* is a beautiful, diverse, and much-needed map of uncharted territory: LGBTQ life in our wildest of states.

Bryan Borland, author of *DIG* & founding editor of *Assaracus: A Journal of Gay Poetry*

BUILDING
FIRES
IN THE
SNOW

BUILDING
FIRES
IN THE
SNOW

martha amore
lucian childs
editors

University of Alaska Press Fairbanks

a collection of alaska LGBTQ
short fiction and poetry

University of Alaska Press
P.O. Box 756240
Fairbanks, AK 99775-6240

Cover and interior design by UA Press

Cover art © Indra Arriaga. *Duque y el Anturio*
Oil and Organics on Linen (in color)
24" x 18" *www.artbyindra.com*

Indra Arriaga is a Mexican artist, writer, and researcher. She actively exhibits and collaborates on art projects internationally and throughout the U.S. In addition to her work in the visual arts, Arriaga is a research analyst working on social, cultural and economic sectors statewide and internationally. Her freelance writing work includes critiques of film and other cultural aspects and events.

Library of Congress Cataloging-in-Publication Data

Names: Amore, Martha, editor. | Childs, Lucian, editor.
Title: Building fires in the snow : a collection of Alaska LGBTQ short
  fiction and poetry / edited by Martha Amore, Lucian Childs.
Description: Fairbanks, Alaska : University of Alaska Press, 2016. |
  Description based on print version record and CIP data provided by
  publisher; resource not viewed.
Identifiers: LCCN 2016019881 (print) | LCCN 2016006533 (ebook) | ISBN
  9781602233027 () | ISBN 9781602233010 (paperback)
Subjects: LCSH: Sexual minorities' writings, American. | Sexual
  minorities--Alaska--Literary collections. | American literature--Alaska. |
  Alaska--Literary collections. | BISAC: LITERARY CRITICISM / General. |
  SOCIAL SCIENCE / Gay Studies.
Classification: LCC PS508.S49 (print) | LCC PS508.S49 B85 2016 (ebook) | DDC
  811/.6058092066--dc23
LC record available at https://lccn.loc.gov/2016019881

Winter Country

We resist each other with words, or wordlessly
avert our eyes when tenderness
is too much to bear the wanting
heart to be only muscle. As if
this were a question of strength,
the answer of your eyes, and language,
one wing flying into itself, some bird we drive up
that feigns to draw us away from its nest.

Better the argument of axe and wood,
the rush of the stove, your face
barbarous in firelight. Always
the same stranger struggling from
your clothes, your eyes no longer
fists but hands. So many nights of gauge
and grapple, this hesitance to go
beyond our bodies. Outside the wind
bearing what it can't contain, erasure,
the rain shifting to snow. Better the white

at the windows, the space we enter
between words, this winter
country we've come to, settling
for the closeness we can.

—*Jerah Chadwick*

Table of Contents

Introduction

Modern Alaska life exists in the tension between what we call the Great Land—majestic beauty and vast wilderness teeming with wildlife where people still live off the land—and the everyday goings-on of its mostly urban people: trips to the supermarket, dinners with friends, and children's play dates. Lesbian, Gay, Bisexual, Transgendered, Queer, and Questioning Alaskans are just as affected by this dichotomy as our heterosexual neighbors. As harried as we all frequently are, we live surrounded by wilderness, which exerts a mighty influence on our lives. We dipnet for Kenai River reds late on a sun-filled summer night; we eat moose burgers and wild blueberry cobbler after a long hike; we argue with a lover out on the deck, Denali's enormous, calming presence looming in the distance.

What marks the particular concerns of Alaska LGBTQ fiction writers and poets—and which ties them to earlier generations of gay writers—is the quest for an authentic identity. For gay writers of the 1970s, '80s, and '90s, this quest often came in the form of the first-person, coming-out story, gay literature's spin on the coming-of-age tale. As Edmund White noted in his introduction to *The Faber Book of Gay Short Fiction,* "Since no one is brought up to be gay, the moment he recognizes the difference he must account for it . . . . Every gay man has polished his story through repetition, and much of gay fiction is a version of this first tale."

Queer identity, and the burgeoning gay culture it engendered, was inextricably tied then to the fast-paced urban centers, like New York and San Francisco, where LGBTQ people congregated. Gay literature of that era followed that trend, chronicling the travails of queer urban people as they sought the freedoms so long denied them.

However, another literary trend had begun in the '70s: Political and theory-based writing by women flourished. There were lesbian feminists, such as Audre Lorde and Adrienne Rich, critiquing the dominant white male heteronormative paradigm, and also eco-feminists, such as Mary Daly and Susan Griffin, who paralleled women and nature, arguing that the exploitation of the earth by Western patriarchal society was inherently connected to the repression and exploitation of women.

Likewise, among some gay men of the '70s, there took root a "back to nature" philosophy. Harry Hay and his followers, the Radical Fairies, popularized this theory, seeking to rid themselves of internalized homophobia and to transform gay consciousness through a spirituality grounded in hedonistic environmentalism. Gay rural journals and anthologies circulated, as writers began to venture outside the traditional queer space: the urban center. The gay and lesbian literary communities, though distinct then from one another, both contained elements of protest against heterosexist repression and the exploitation of the earth.

The stories and poems in this book span this radical ecoqueer tradition with the more mainstream identity concerns of earlier gay fiction. As such, the works in the collection are mostly urban: there are gay bars, garden parties, and roller derby. But the characters and poetic voices here are just as likely to be found hiking the back-country, or biking along the inlet in one of Anchorage's immense urban parks.

And, while many of those earlier gay narratives are expressed through the coming-out theme, the stories and poems here reflect a more varied, less polemical, understanding of what it means to be queer. People still fall in lust or love, but they do so less as sexual identity warriors, than as frequently befuddled individuals confronted by a multiplicity of concerns: childrearing, aging, putting food on the table or a roof over one's head. As such, LGBTQ literature is in a time of transition, and writers are more free than before to express any facet of the human condition.

Other LGBTQ anthologies have offered a historical literary perspective on the struggles of the community, such as Manguel and Stephenson's *In Another Part of the Forest* and Kleinberg's *The Other Persuasion*. Still others have highlighted particular gay communities, such as Ruff's *Go the Way Your Blood Beats*, which focuses on queer African American lives, or Williams's *G.R.I.T.S.*, where queer womyn's voices from the American South take center stage. *Building Fires in the Snow* is the first regional collection in which wilderness is the lens through which gay, primarily urban, identity is perceived.

Rugged nature has long been thought to be the domain of white heterosexual men who pit themselves against it, and each other, in order to prove their (hetero) manhood. The stories and poems in *Building Fires in the Snow* tell a different narrative—not of conquering, but of finding one's true identity through intimacy with nature.

The men in Jerah Chadwick's poems are not conquerors, nor are they proving their masculinity by living in rural Alaska. Rather, they struggle to find themselves by stoking a potbellied stove or packing provisions through the snow, by grappling with themselves and the body of a beloved.

A similar dynamic flows through Teeka Ballas's "Carrots, Peas: *in D Minor*," in which the narrator watches her lover cook ptarmigan while musing on their lifestyle of hunting, fishing, and harvesting vegetables. Sandy Gillespie's "The Trees Tell the Story" depicts friends converging to log the woods around their home, not to dominate the landscape, but to build a lovers' cabin. In "Mountain Man," Gabrielle Barnett writes of a "fading southern queen" who, in true Radical Fairy fashion, strives to keep the dream of homesteading alive. In the anthology's concluding novella, "Going Too Far," Mei Mei Evans depicts the wilderness, not as harsh and menacing, but rather as a sort of Shangri-la, where women are free to be independent and where the young protagonist can discover herself.

In the collection's stories and poems, the characters look to the Alaska wilderness for inspiration, comfort, and even models of harmonious action. In Martha Amore's "Geology," a woman struggling with her sexuality finds solace in her deep understanding of the long Alaska winter. Laura Carpenter's protagonist escapes the responsibilities of motherhood by speeding through the forest on her skis while recalling her former self: the unencumbered young athlete who got all the girls. Even as urban a character as Lucian Childs's protagonist in "The Go-Between" finds meaning in the invasion of wild arctic plants in a friend's city garden.

Alaska LGBTQ lives exist in the context of communities of shared interests and values, which are for some shaped by nature. In Elizabeth Bradfield's "Remodeling," a lesbian couple braves the opprobrium of their neighbors for the openness the spruce-shaded light brings through a new window. In Leslie Kimiko Ward's "Nest," two roommates, one gay, one straight, come to an accommodation through the trials of Northern domestic life. Dawnell Smith's "What Would Derby Do?" tracks a troubled relationship marked by one partner "walking the lower slopes of the Chugach Range alone."

History, too, is foundational in the building of community. And while most of the work in this anthology is set in the current day, a few, like Mei Mei Evans's "Going Too Far" and Lucian Childs's "The Go-Between," chart the anything-goes oil boom of the 1970s when Alaska's population exploded.

Even though the population of the state is small (736,732 in a recent estimate), Alaska communities are highly diverse. One neighborhood in Anchorage, as recently reported on CNN, was cited as the most ethnically diverse census tract in America. We editors wished to reflect this diversity in the collection and sought to publish writers from the state's many ethnic groups. In this we were only partially successful, as just a quarter of our writers identify as people of color/biracial, none of them of Alaska Native heritage. Similarly, while over a hundred languages are spoken in the state, including Spanish, Samoan, Yupik, Filipino, and Hmong, we only received a single bilingual submission, the poems of Indra Arriaga. Her work celebrates different shades of meaning in both English and Spanish.

Despite these limitations, the stories and poems in this collection traverse ethnicities, ages, genders, and sexual identities. While most of the works feature out and proud gay lives, for example Lucian Childs's "Black Spruce" and the poetry of Amy Groshek, a few, such as Alyse Knorr's "Fact-Checking," Morgan Grey's "Breakers," and Rosemary McGuire's tragic "Luke," revolve around an important Red State theme: closeted secrecy.

In Alaska, the reasons for such secrecy can be very real. Though there are recently won employment and housing protections in Anchorage for LGBTQ people, elsewhere in the state there are no such provisions. Indeed, several potential contributors declined to be included in the anthology due to fear of being out in such a public capacity.

Alaska is a huge state with a wide range of ecologies and terrain. Here too our goal was to include contributors who could reflect this diversity. However, fully half of the state's population lives in Anchorage, and the bulk of our writers live and have set their works there as well. For instance, Kate Partridge's "Earthquake Park" and Egan Millard's "Mondegreen," both of which explore the complexities of life in the urban context. There are a few works, though, drawn from other areas of Alaska, such as Teresa Sundmark's "Trespass" or the poetry of Vivian Faith Prescott and Amber Flora Thomas.

Most of the authors in this collection reside in state, though some have moved, as we Alaskans say, Outside. Zack Rogow, while not a resident, regularly travels here in his capacity as professor of creative writing at the University of Alaska Anchorage. The effect Alaska has on a person cannot be easily shaken. These writers continue to draw inspiration from their former home and, in turn, inspire writers in Alaska.

While we celebrate the voices of several emerging authors and poets, many of our fiction authors have been widely published: Mei Mei Evans, for example, whose novel *Oil and Water* was shortlisted for the PEN/Bellwether Prize, or Teresa Sundmark, who was recently nominated for a Pushcart Prize. Likewise, the anthology includes notable poets who have enjoyed wider recognition, such as Elizabeth Bradfield, Vivian Faith Prescott, Amber Flora Thomas, Susanna Mishler, Alyse Knorr, and the former state writer laureate, Jerah Chadwick.

We have also included authors who work in the spoken word, such as slam poets M.C. MoHagani Magnetek and Shelby Wilson. While spoken word is not often found in conventional literary anthologies, it is an important component of Alaskan culture. Whether it be *Arctic Entries,* the storytelling event that regularly plays to sold-out audiences in Anchorage, or a similar Pride week event, the unique and vibrant voices of our spoken word artists help stitch together the patchwork quilt of modern Alaskan life.

While some gay anthologies only include work written by queer authors or work that strictly adheres to queer themes regardless of authorial identity, *Building Fires in the Snow* maintains a blended philosophy. Though nearly all of the works within the collection are by LGBTQ-identified authors, we have included powerful pieces by a couple of ally writers. We believe that a skilled heterosexual writer can speak eloquently about gay lives, the most memorable recent example being Annie Proulx, whose "Brokeback Mountain" has become canonical. Likewise, not all of the pieces explicitly address gay themes, but written as they are by gay authors and read in the context of the surrounding material, the works resonate powerfully from a gay perspective.

Some readers might expect an anthology such as this to include the genre of nonfiction. Indeed, while our state is blessed with an abundance of award-winning nonfiction writers, Alaska fiction and poetry are not as well known. This volume serves as a corrective of sorts, showcasing some of the state's best practitioners of the imaginative literary arts. For we believe that fiction and poetry, freed as they are from a strict adherence to fact, allow readers to experience emotional truths directly.

The title of the collection, *Building Fires in the Snow*, speaks to the relationship we have with the land and each other. While the image of snow reflects the cold tone that many of these pieces contain, "fire" connotes both survival and passion. Moreover, the word "building" speaks to the community and love we create together. The title comes out of our unique Alaska lifestyle, where even in the cities we are free to build fires. From recreational camping to subsistence living, from urban bonfire parties to the all-too-common wilderness emergencies, sparking fires is an integral part of being Alaskan. In building fires, we keep warm; we enjoy ourselves; we survive; connected to each other and to the Great Land.

It is important to note that all the anthology's stories and poems were written before the historic Supreme Court decision declaring marriage equality to be a fundamental constitutional right and the more recent Anchorage municipal ordinance making it illegal to discriminate in employment and housing on the grounds of gender identity or sexual orientation.

Despite these gains, LGBTQ Alaskans exist within a larger community that does not always welcome them. Several of our stories and poems speak directly to the issue of discrimination and harassment, such as M.C. MoHagani Magnetek's "Shhh-Be-Quiet," Teresa Sundmark's "Worse Disasters," and Shelby Wilson's "Misread Signs." This collection, then, comes at a moment of great progress, but when there is still much work to be done.

In fact, as of this writing, a group of conservative activists are attempting to qualify a ballot measure that, if passed, would repeal the recently enacted municipal gay rights ordinance. In proposing this measure, these activists offer the most antiquated of stereotypes regarding LGTBQ people. We hope the voices in this anthology will help break down these stereotypes, allowing readers to better know their LGBTQ neighbors, so that discrimination in Anchorage will continue to be a thing of the past.

Moreover, we hope this first attempt to bring together the stories of LGBTQ Alaskans will serve as an inspiration to writers we were unable to identify or who chose not to be published in this book. We look forward to future collections that feature a wider range of languages, locations and voices, in particular those of Alaska Native people.

Within the strong currents of diverse cultures and social change, Alaska's rugged wilderness provides a unique backdrop and catalyst in the quest to live the authentic life. A life that honors the struggles and traditions of the past. A life that must be fought for anew, shared and celebrated, or, in pain and distrust, kept secret and endured alone. Unrelenting life—taking risks, carving out new understanding—showy, brave, and unruly. Life that persists, big and wild as the Great Land itself, the state of Alaska.

Martha Amore
Lucian Childs
Anchorage, Alaska
May 1, 2016

Martha Amore is a fiction writer and teaches at the University of Alaska Anchorage and Alaska Pacific University. She lives in Anchorage, Alaska, with her husband and three daughters. Her work has appeared in a number of journals and has been anthologized in Weathered Edge: Three Alaskan Novellas.

Lucian Childs is a short story writer who divides his time between Anchorage, Alaska, and Toronto, Ontario, where he lives with his husband. His short fiction has appeared in numerous literary journals, both in Canada and the United States.

ROSEMARY MCGUIRE

Rosemary McGuire has been working as a commercial fisherman for fourteen years, on boats from San Diego to Norton Sound. She has also worked in Antarctica and in field camps across Alaska. She has traveled most of Alaska's river systems by canoe. Her collection of short stories *The Creatures at the Absolute Bottom of the Sea* was published by the University of Alaska Press in 2015.

Luke

The night they brought Luke's body back to town, Pete drove out Orca to buy a net. He saw the *Arcturus* come into view, a black dot in the golden haze of an April night. It passed Seduction Point, heading for town, taking the shortcut because the tide was high. Its lights were so bright it was difficult to see.

He slowed to watch it coming in. Ahead, a pickup ground to a halt. The girl in the front seat was crying. As he pulled alongside, they stared at each other. A green-eyed girl in a T-shirt lettered, "Fuck me. I'm Mexican." He didn't know her, but he knew her face from the Reluctant Fisherman.

"You knew Luke, didn't you?" she said.

"Kind of," Pete said. "A while ago. We went to high school together, anyhow."

"Did you hear about what happened?" she said.

"I heard."

"What was it? I mean, what did you hear?"

"Just that the skipper found him in his bunk."

She rolled the window up, her face crumpling. "I don't know why he died," she said.

Pete shifted up. Out Orca, the cannery loft was deserted. He dug through old gear until he found the right net and pulled it out onto a tarp. The smell of brine and creosote and winter rain rose up around him. A truck rolled in outside. He heard the rattle of the chain hoist, a pallet jack. But no one came in.

Sweat poured down his face as he worked. He was thinking of Luke, the summer they first met, skateboarding outside the library, his nimble body folding in a jump as if he could take flight at last.

2

The rumble and grind as he fell to earth. His shout of exultation. Pete's answering yell.

He shook the net. Let it fall at last, the last fathom out of the bag. He'd flaked all the way through without seeing it.

Two nights later, after the wake, the guys started drinking on the shore. They lit a pallet fire before the weather turned. Rain drove against the flames, hissed, and rose up again as steam, leaving the coals half-blackened with water. The same green-eyed girl with too-heavy eyeliner stood over the embers, crying.

Pete left the harbor on a falling tide. It was blowing when he dropped the hook behind Grass Island. The outgoing tide hissed over hard, gray sand. Above him, a line of boats marched up the slough, facing the current. A gillnetter he didn't know had taken Luke's set. He watched it as his anchor line came taut, waited to see if his boat would drag, until another gust of rain drove him inside.

Inside, the boat jerked at its line. Water splattered in the window leak. He set the drag alarm and turned down the radio. Listened to the flat, monotonous chatter of the fleet.

"Getting pretty shitty out."

"Yep."

"This is the Miss Becky for Trident, we're in Pedall. Give us a holler if you need anything. We got ice and fuel." He flicked it off.

Next morning, he made a low water set inside the bar for nothing. They killed 'em in Softuk, farther east, but the tide was down, and it seemed too shitty out to run that far. He set out by the can in a nasty wind chop and got the line in the wheel on the first try.

"Goddammit. Oh. Goddammit." he shouted at the sea. "Fuck you, fuck you."

Last summer, near the end of May, he'd anchored for a while on the outside beach, the night before the opener began. Luke pulled up on his way east. They side-tied their boats, listened to the slow thump, thump-thump as they rocked together in the swell. The water smooth as silk, a pure, unbreakable blue.

They watched a whale go by on the horizon, its slow progression of breaths. Pete dug through the locker looking for food. "Don'cha eat, Luke?"

"Look on your own boat."

"There's nothing there." He found a half-empty jug of salsa and spilled some out on the hatch covers. "Here." He scooped it into his mouth with a taco shell. "Tastes kinda like chips."

"Kinda." Luke swept up the salsa with quick sweeps of his wrist. He ate like he did everything, like there could never be enough. There'd never been a time he wasn't there and wouldn't be. Just Luke.

The whale, submerged, left bubbles on the surface where it had been.

The fall he and Luke were both nineteen, they took Luke's old skiff out the bar, out Strawberry Entrance into the Gulf. It was a beautiful day. The breakers hissed quietly on the bar. The break was a long one, but they ran straight past the last taint of land and home, until they knew by the long glide of the swell that they were in the Pacific. Luke killed the motor just to listen.

They rocked slowly. A flock of birds passed.

"Murrelets," Luke said. He always knew.

The clouds overhead formed torn white lines. The distant line of white along the beach and all the other blues spilled into each other, the blue of sky and sea and the far-off mountains.

"When we buy our boats," Luke began, because they were both saving to buy into the gillnet fleet, and knew that that was what they'd always do; in class they'd picked out names for their boats. "*Sam an' Ella*," Luke's was named, because of how it would sound over the radio. "When we buy our boats . . ."

But suddenly it was too much to bear, the silence and the enormous sea.

"Let's get out of here." Luke pulled the cord, looking for the familiar rowdy clatter that drowned out thought, preventing panic, preventing doubt.

Nothing happened.

"Fuck." He tried again. "It should be warm." He choked it. Checked the gas. And they were out.

He looked quickly at the bottom of the skiff; saw the gear they'd dropped in for fishing, the Pepsi cans. The slap of brown water in the bilge. No old red dented can of extra fuel. He opened his mouth. Pete'd been carrying the fuel. Pete saw in his mind where he'd set the can while adjusting his load, saw it still sitting on the shore. Looked at Luke, the fear building in their eyes. Between them the knowledge they'd gone too far.

Luke looked back at the shore, too far away. Wondered aloud what it felt like to drown.

"We ain't gonna find out," Pete said, to shut him up, but the words were spoken. Pete's own voice felt hollow.

"Think they'll miss us?"

"No."

They weren't expected until night. Pete's parents had gone to Anchorage. He was staying with Luke, and Luke's dad didn't always come home. They looked at the shore. They were drifting out. At the horizon, where the weather would come from, if it came. Again at the floor of the skiff, and at each other.

Pete shifted very slowly in his seat. "I left it," he said. "It's my fault."

"Don't worry about it," Luke said. "It don't matter." He scrabbled in the gear at his feet. Toed out a busted Styrofoam cup. "We might's well bail. Got something we could put over to slow our drift?"

Later, they sat shoulder to shoulder on the bottom boards. Not talking much, only looking at the sea.

"How long do you think it takes?" Pete said.

"I don't know."

"Where do you think we go?"

"I don't think we go anywhere at all."

"Oh," Pete said.

It could've all ended differently. But late in the afternoon, someone just happened to go past, a gillnetter early for the opener. He saw them and realized what was wrong.

"That was thinking," he said, nodding at the sea anchor they'd rigged from a bundle of gear tied together with line. Holding the gunwale, he dragged them in over the side.

"We'da been all right," Pete said, half-joking, giddy with relief.

That night, they walked to Luke's father's lodge in the dark. Got in just before dawn. Luke's dad wasn't there. The two of them went straight up to Luke's bed and slept there together, holding on to each other, without even thinking about it. Two boyish bodies molded in the night, in deep sleep. Only Pete woke up crying in the night, unable to say what he had dreamt. And felt Luke's hand clutch in his hair, holding his head to comfort him. Luke's stale breath whispering, you're all right. And Luke's hard, live kiss under the blanket. Then two of them, young bodies touching vehemently in the night.

Something they'd never done before, and never would again. Something that Pete now could not stop thinking of.

They woke the next morning, crawled separately out of bed. A distance between them they couldn't break through. When Pete said he'd walk back to town alone, Luke looked relieved. Maybe he was afraid, as Pete was, that they would never be like other men. That this was something more than they could handle. But they never were as close after that night.

Luke started drinking harder that summer. Pete saw less of him. He thought he might've dated other men. But he would never know that, not for sure.

That fall after Luke died, a girl came up to see Pete. Rose. He took her to the boat when she got in. It was raining as they went down the dock. She wrapped her wet hair in her sweatshirt, leaned over, and kissed him. He felt her round, pale breasts and springy thighs. But it wasn't as good. It was never as good again. It had none of the clarity of that night with Luke. None of the urgency.

Afterward, she lay back, looking at the photo on the wall.

"Who's that?" she said.

"That's Luke. He died last spring."

"Oh," she said. "I'm sorry. Accident?" She rolled over, rubbing his stomach. He thought she meant to comfort him.

"I don't think. But I don't know. It could've been. I guess I'll never know. The autopsy said overdose."

"I see," she said again. "I'm sorry."

But she fell asleep, her back to him, the covers pulled tight around her unformed shoulders. He lay there thinking about what might've been. Rolled over, face into the pillow. Saw Luke so clearly. The slow contraction of his eyes, his hurried smile. The thoughts running, contradicting, in his mind. But he was gone.

"I miss you," Pete thought, but didn't say aloud. "I just miss you, Luke."

It was true and would be, and life went on. And it was too late to know how much it mattered, the things they'd never talked about and never would. Already, Luke's face was fading in his mind. He didn't want that, didn't want to be growing old while Luke himself would always be young. Didn't want to lose even this hurt. But it happened that way.

ELIZABETH
BRADFIELD

Elizabeth Bradfield   is the author of the poetry collections *Interpretive Work*, *Approaching Ice*, and *Once Removed*. An instructor in the low-residency MFA program at University of Alaska Anchorage, contributing editor for Alaska Quarterly Review, and editor-in-chief of Broadsided Press, she lives on Cape Cod and works a naturalist.

Eight Years

We pulled snowshoes from the back and crossed the five-lane
by the sports bar between two bad curves,
headed to the bog. It was midday,

sky low, traffic a light drone. We cinched
straps, stomped teeth into the trailhead,
took snapshots of ourselves and set off

for the muffle of woods and the snow we hoped
now would carry us, and mostly didn't, but still
seemed somehow better as we followed

tracks, reconstructed pounce and dodge, waiting
for the place to raise voice. And when it didn't
we turned toward home, stopped listening, and I

started mugging for you, showing off, and I thought
as I ran along the trail, snow slapping up the backs
of my thighs,
     maybe we have found it, the thing
where neither is better or cares or clocks the length.
The thing that makes us beautiful.
        And when I turned
to shout back, what escaped was

Moose. Dewlap swinging, shoulder hump

rocking in gait, heading out of the trees
the way I'd come, toward you.

> Somewhere, there's a tally sheet that reckons up
> how often we say we're happy and mean it,
> and we, in the messy and reasonable panic
> of our lives, just lost our chance to earn a point.

The moose ran out from the trees and I ran back
to you and we stared and backed away together,
frightened by the huge answer of its body.

Legacy
—for Vitus Bering

They've closed again the gap that you first sailed,
Russian-sponsored Dane, so cousins on the Diomedes

are in post–Cold War touch. But you made the map

that made the border, sighting lands just guessed at
between Kamchatka and America's west coast. And we
        write history from what's put down *officially*, maps

and logbooks made and kept by the survivors
of your death, of your loss of ambition from years

line-toeing across the forehead of Siberia. Finally you set sail for

glory—or not *for* but *from* whatever pushes us beyond
our birth-spots. What pushes us away? I, too, have left
        for some spot unknown by those who claim me, for

place unhooked from kin and story. I've fled
the watched life of any hometown where if

you kick a dog, infect a girl, break a window

the girl turns out to be your mother's landlord's
cousin, the dog a beat cop's mutt, and shards
      cut your sister's foot: Each chafed-at thing's a window

in your glass-house world. So the age-old lust for places
we pretend are free of consequence. It's the same

now as it was with Oedipus, poor stiff, running to escape his fate

and running smack dab into it, an awful
scene, a nightmare warning we need to keep
      repeating because, of course, fate

never seems immediate. For weeks Bering's crew feasted
on the delicious bulk of sea cows (now extinct).

They played cards, anted up with otter pelts that *promyshlenniki* later

stripped from the shores. Foxes bit the men's toes
at night. The land ate them as they ate the land,
      calling it need, worrying about it later.

Roughnecks and Rakes One and All, the Poet Speaks to Her Subjects, Polar Explorers

I won't write you that voice,
piggy, crass
forged by salt &
cold & isolation.
Filed to edge
by time-wrung,
absence-wrought rasping
or, if not those,
by what made you endure.

I know we're
bad luck on boats,
women, worse
on ice, too humid
for this hoar.
And you hate my pen
tracking through
your stories. But

I write you,
and that's what love you get,
meted out, doled like rum.
Through line and vowel, my
voice chooses
yours, forced
by yours.

I'd like to say
local deviations
make this
true enough
triangulation
for polar work,

that despite my distance
and the tendency of light
over ice toward mirage,
some shape comes through
that both of us
can recognize.

Correcting the Landscape

Even though the wrecked jeep
belonged to Pat, it felt like stealing to go through
chain link into the scrap yard, jack up
each corner and switch out his new tires
with our bald ones. It was twelve below.
The snow squeaked underfoot

like Styrofoam. We were trying to make it in a place
where everything we thought we needed
—sheetrock, tomatoes, polypro—
had to be shipped in from Outside.

There was a raven calling, watery cluck
echoing the lot. There was us cursing
the lug nuts, then another sound,
out of place, high and keen

and you and I startle like any goddamn bird.

I see your head tilt, ear
to sky, and while Anne is jumping
blood back into her toes and Pat is wrestling
with the left rear, there is within this scene another:
A peregrine calls and we both look up, catch each other doing it,

then laugh. Because it's not likely a falcon here,
February in central Alaska. The call sounds again,
and a few pigeons startle, birds that arrived with
the wires and poles. And that's why we hear it,

set on some timer to cry away
those pushy opportunists
at the foothills of the Chugach,
throats cold in the day's short light.

Creation Myth: Periosteum and Self

Hormonally imbalanced females of all deer species
have been known to grow antlers.
This is what I choose. Periosteum rampant on my brow
and testosterone to activate it at the pedicle.
    "Luxury organs," so called because they aren't
    necessary for survival.
I choose the possibility buried in the furrow
which has ceased to disappear between my eyes
in sleep, in skin my lover has touched her lips to.
    Females produce young each year. Males produce antlers.
Forget the in-vitro, expensive catheter of sperm
slipped past the cervix, the long implications
of progeny. I am more suited to other sciences, other growth.
    Researchers have snipped bits of periosteum
    from pedicles, grafted them onto other parts
    of a buck's body, and grown antlers.
I'll graft it to my clavicle. My cheekbone.
Ankle. Coccyx. Breast. At last visible,
the antler will grow. Fork and tine. Push and splay.
    Researchers have tricked deer into growing and casting
    as many as four sets of antlers in one calendar year.

It won't wait for what's appropriate, but starts
in the subway, in the john, talking to a friend about her sorrows,
interviewing for a job. My smooth desk, my notebook,
my special pen with particular ink, my Bach playing
through the wall of another room—not the location
of the prepared field, but what the light says, when
the light says now.
>   *Deer literally rob their body skeletons to grow*
>   *antlers they'll abandon a few months later.*

It could care less about the inconvenience forking
from my knee, the difficulty of dressing, embracing, or
piloting a car. It doesn't care
>   *Essentially bucks and bulls are slaves to their antlers.*
if I'm supposed to be paying bills or taking the dog
for her evening walk. There is no sense to it, no logic, just thrust.

It does its work. It does its splendid, difficult, ridiculous work and then,
making room for its next, more varied rising,

gorgeous and done, it falls away.

Remodeling
—for Lisa

We want a hole in the north wall, a hole
then a window, for light, for the green spruce
just beyond the vinyl siding. We've managed
to forget the night last spring

when Emilio, Michael, and Pierce, whose baseballs
we return, who we lecture on the sensitivity
of tomato plants to hockey pucks, who ring our doorbell
selling chocolate and wrapping paper

      . . . we've almost forgotten the night last spring
when the boys climbed the shed roof
and saw this:
      my shirt up around my neck,
your hand on my breast, my body beneath
yours, moving.

When I opened my eyes and said shit, you
buried your face in the couch, as if
they might assume your short hair meant man,
as if that might be better. And instead of cursing

them, instead of throwing open the window
and telling them off, I pulled the blinds and hid.

And for months we skulked to the mailbox,
walked the dog in distant parks, imagined
the stories rumoring and how they'd sound
when they reached the parents:

They were doing it in the back yard, under spotlights,
charging admission. We didn't admit

to each other that we waited for the spraypaint,
the busted taillights. Worse, we were ready
to understand . . . But now

we want a window in the north wall.
We want the spruce-shade. We want
to announce how much we love
the sky, how its light finds us, too,
even here.

Concerning the Proper Term
for a Whale Exhaling

Poof my mother sighs
as against the clearcut banks near Hoonah
another humpback exhales, its breath
white and backlit by sun.
                                Don't
say that, says my father, disapproving
of such casual terminology or uneasy
with the tinge of pink tulle, the flounce
poof attaches to the thing we're watching, beast
of hunt, of epic migrations.
                                But I'm the naturalist,
suggesting course and speed for approach. They
are novices, and the word is mine,
brought here from the captains I sailed for
and the glittering Cape Cod town
where we docked each night
after a day of watching whales.

Poof,
Todd or Lumby would gutter,
turning the helm, my cue to pick up
the microphone. Coming from those smoke-roughed cynics
who call the whales dumps, rank the tank-topped talent
on the bow, and say each time they set a breaching calf
in line with the setting sun, *What do you think of that? Now that's
what I call pretty*, then sit back,
light a cigarette—coming from them,
I loved the word.

          And even more
because the dock we returned to each night
teemed with summer crowds, men lifting
their hands to other men, the town
flooded with poufs free to flutter, to cry, as they can't
in Newark or Pittsburgh or Macon, to let
their love rise into the clear, warm air,
to linger and glow
for a brief time visible.

We All Want to See a Mammal

We all want to see a mammal.
Squirrels & snowshoe hares don't count.
Voles don't count. Something, preferably,
that could do us harm. There's a long list:
bear, moose, wolf, wolverine. Even porcupine
would do. The quills. The yellowed
teeth & long claws.

        Beautiful here: Peaks, avens,
meltwater running its braided course. But we want
to see a mammal. Our day our lives incomplete
without a mammal. The gaze of something
unafraid, that we're afraid of, meeting ours
before it runs off.

        Linnaeus was called
indecent when he named them. Plenty
of other commonalities (hair, live young,
a proclivity to plot). But no. Mammal.
Maman. Breasted & nippled
& warm, warm, warm.

August, McCarthy, Alaska

I do love you a little more
tenderly the first few days
after leaving home.
                    The river here,
sweetheart, is lined with beauty,
those pink flowers that grow first
in spring's flood-swept banks.
                        I'm half
here, half back with you. This
and this and this you'd love.
The cottonwoods. The peaks.
                    Fall
is breathing on the land's neck.
Another cycle that should give
comfort, and does, but only
                    in fact. Not
in metaphoric reach. I'll be home
soon. Not soon, but I'll be home. I'll work
to reconcile what I remember of us
                        with what
we are. The river is the river, despite
its new channel, which made the bridge
both pointless and ruined. Because we need it
it gets rebuilt every year.

MARTHA
AMORE

Martha Amore teaches writing at Alaska Pacific University and the University of Alaska Anchorage. She achieved her Masters of Fine Arts from UAA, and she has published stories in a number of journals and magazines. Her first novella came out in 2013 in the anthology *Weathered Edge: Three Alaskan Novellas.* In 2015, she won a Rasmuson Individual Artist Award to complete her collection of short stories. She lives in Anchorage with her husband, three daughters, two cats, and one big dog.

Geology

Geyserites. Black opal. Shale storm. Layers of rock covering the hot liquid core of the planet are more real to her than the ever-shifting human landscape. Once she had broken a bone. No, once a bone had been broken for her. Her stepfather in a storm and drunk, breaking her arm so that the white bone flashed for just a moment in the earth's long flow of time. Bright white before blood and darkness overcame her.

"My sense of time is all messed up," Kris says soon after we meet.

We are two women at a party full of bearded men, a sprawling Alaska affair with two bonfires, three kegs, and an edgy pack of dogs vying for salmon skin and dominance. My husband left hours ago, and now the cold of freeze-up has driven us into a cavernous garage. The cement floor is slick with beer, and the place smells of yeast and motor oil. A too-loud boy band has her coming in close, yelling her words. I like how she leans into me, her lips occasionally grazing my ear.

"Normal people think in terms of hours, days, weeks. I think in terms of millions of years." A sly smile spreads from her full lips to her dark lashes. Fine lines, three of them, stretch from the corners of her eyes, which, blue or green, I can't decide. "Lisa," she says, "do you know how old the earth is?"

I squint across the crowded room as though the answer were written on the far wall. The only number that comes to mind is eleven thousand, which is not the age of our planet but the number of wolves in Alaska. I match her smile. "Older than me?"

"What are you, thirty?"

"And then some."

"The planet is a bit older than that." As she speaks, she puts a hand to my hip. "Six billion years. Can you get your mind around that?"

"No."

Her hand stays on me.

Was it the broken arm that saved her life? Finally, a visible wound. Her mother had no choice but to take action and leave her stepfather. No, I think she saved herself. The form of escape she chose, not drugs or self-loathing, but college. Geology.

The first day her professor cast away the syllabus and hefted a cracked-in-half stone. A private universe of bright sherbet lacework lay hidden within the thick gray husk, and at the very center, a hollow the size of a child's fist.

"This is a geode," her professor said, walking up and down the aisle with the cracked stone in his palms. He pointed to the blue crystal ring, "Quartz," and to the spread of pink, "Dolomite." Then, he smoothed his finger along the purple streaks of crystal and said, "Amethyst."

When he returned to the podium, she followed, taking the seat before him. "And this?" she asked, indicating the empty core.

Her professor smiled. "Trapped air, perhaps? Or maybe the remains of a small animal burrow?" He looked at her and blinked, his shaggy, gray eyebrows matching both the great mane on his head and the hair sprouting from his nostrils. "Imagine with me, miss. Millions of years ago, some minute amount of life found its way into this rock, perhaps a bacteria or just a mere trickle of water? And time pressed on and on and on, species of dinosaurs emerging and dying out, the shifting of continents, the birth of countless animal species, including our own. And through it all, there is this rock." He paused, regarded her over the tops of his bifocals, and for the first time in her life, she felt seen by somebody.

"In Iceland," he said, "they say the rocks are alive, that in fact, they have souls."

Years later, when she had completed her graduate thesis, he gifted her the geode, wrapped in red ribbon with a card reading, *A souvenir from the Miocene.*

The musicians take a break. The bearded men stagger from the garage to the bonfires outside, but we remain huddled close, our voices dropping low. A charm is strung around her neck. I reach out for it, a small purple crystal, and my fingers rest against her warm skin. Up close, I see that the crystal is not a solid color, but many different shades, ranging from clear to lavender to nearly black.

"Beautiful," I say.

"Amethyst."

We smile at one another. She takes a drink of beer and licks the foam from her lips. I wonder what it would be like to kiss her? What harm is there, I think, in a kiss?

We startle to the noise of the garage door. It opens, revealing the dark night outside. Wood smoke overpowers the scent of motor oil, and with the rush of cold she shifts her body against mine. I make out black figures around a blazing fire, but their voices carry away into the night. My eyes adjust, and in the moonlight there are the jagged white tips of the Chugach Range. How small we are at the base of such mountains.

Then comes the sound of the garage door closing. Everything disappears. There is just the two of us, and we are private people. I understand that when she holds her arm to me, a broken wing, it is an offering of compromised privacy. I smooth my hand over the calcified ridge. Some wounds heal. Her skin a pale scar under my fingertips, I want to tell her that if she had been my child, I would have protected her.

But what I say is, "My husband and I have two kids, a boy and a girl."

She nods once, then twice more. "I figured."

In the silence that follows, she opens the side door and peers out to the black night. "You got married young, didn't you?"

"I guess."

"That's good," she says, turning back to me. "Love is a good thing."

"It is." I'm thinking about my children. I try to focus solely on my feelings for him, my husband alone, but what comes to mind is how the kids look when they laugh, Jay still missing his two front teeth, Stella's bright eyes through her tangle of curls, and I know I can't separate him from them. "Love *is* a good thing." After a moment, I add, "I'm sorry."

"Why?"

"I just am."

She searches for her coat in the pile of down and wool and fleece, mine falls to the floor. I don't allow myself to think. One arm and then the next through the coat sleeves. When she walks out the door, so do I.

Stark autumn cold hits us, goes right to the marrow.

"It's always like this before the snow comes," I tell her as we walk to her car. "Freeze-up in Alaska is cruel."

Under our feet, the brown chaff of birch leaves. This year a big Chinook stripped trees to bones in a matter of hours, and then the cold stomped down on the yellow leaves, quickly grinding them to mash on the frozen ground.

"Not the beautiful season you're used to Outside, huh?" I say.

"Outside?"

"What we Alaskans call everywhere else."

She smiles, shakes her head.

"This is the Far North," I say. "Winter drops down hard on us. Like a hoof."

"When do you think it'll snow?"

"Soon, I hope. It's better when it does. Warmer. Brighter."

"I don't know if I'll ever get used to it here."

"It takes three winters." I remember I said those same words to my husband when I met him all those years ago. My father had just died of cancer, and it was my first year at UAF. I remember the lost feeling I'd carried within me, like a small skiff in big waves. So long ago, it's as though it happened to someone else, like I'm remembering someone else's life. Was that college freshman really me? Now a pulse of guilt beats through me. "If you make it three winters, you stay," I say. "You're Alaskan."

"Like you?"

"I was born here. I had no choice."

She stands back on her heels and regards me. "What's your deal?"

"What do you mean?"

She smiles, patient, and I see the scientist in her. White lab coat hunching over a microscope.

"I don't know that I have a deal."

The scientist waits.

I blow on my fingers.

"I can always tell," she says.

"Tell what?"

"About women. It's like identifying a mineral. You don't go by the color, you go by the fracture."

"What fracture? What are you talking about?"

"I'm talking about you."

I stare back at her. "What do you mean?"

"Suffering. That's what I mean."

I pull my coat tight around my neck. "But everybody suffers."

She nods, smiles at her data. "And?"

"And so what?"

In graduate school, she was mentored by her professor, favored above all the other students. When they talked about rocks, it was as though the two of them were in love with the same woman. But where there might have been jealousy, there was only passion. He sent her daily emails, and when they stopped to chat in the university's long echoing hallways, minutes ticked into hours. They were lost in events that occurred two billion years ago.

Once, late at night, she stopped by the lab to collect a forgotten scarf. Her professor was standing at the rows of rock specimens, his hands on the counter, and she could tell by his caved-in expression that he was not looking outward, but inward to a different time.

She meant to leave quickly, to not disturb him, but he turned and said, "My wife had a strange habit. Whenever faculty would come for dinner, she would polish the baseboards and banisters, all the wood in the whole house. Always, that was that day she chose. I hated the smell of Murphy's Oil, and it would last throughout the dinner, overpowering whatever good smells were coming from the kitchen." He laid a hand on the counter, tapped a finger. "I see now that she did it simply for something to do. She was nervous having the university crowd over. She never felt worthy of the conversation." He laughed. "Rocks. Always about rocks."

Kris knew that his wife had been dead many years. "I'm sorry."

"And yet the parties were always her idea. I never would have thought of feeding people. She took care of me in that way, you know."

"You must have loved her a lot."

He smiled, turned back to the dusty rows. "I still do. Be careful with your tenses, my dear."

"I should go," she says, a glance to her car.

I take her hand in mine. It's cold as concrete. Another memory sparks, though this one is close to the moment, no question it is my life. "You know, you remind me of a woman I loved. A long time ago."

"Did she love you back?"

"No."

She smiles, tries to suppress it.

"Okay, so I was fourteen. She was my math teacher. She never knew."

Now she's laughing, and soon I am, too.

"I'm sure she did," Kris says. After a moment, she sobers and asks in a quiet voice, "Are you sorry the way things turned out?"

I look down at the frost on my thick rubber boots. I'm thinking about my children, how I sometimes wake in the night just to watch them sleep. "No."

The features of her face are complex to me, a terrain of great depth and meaning. I want to remember her exactly as she is: eyes not blue but green in the moonlight, cheekbones sprinkled with last summer's freckles, a wide mouth with full, chapped lips. I tell myself that what I feel is an impulse, that's all.

But when she takes a step toward her car, a wild ticking starts up in me. Not an impulse but an instinct, like the instinct to keep warm.

Her hands are back in her pockets. "I should go." She draws in a breath, and when she releases it into the cold still night, the steam remains a cloud just above her head. "There is no institution that I respect more than marriage. Marriage and family," she says. "I've never experienced it, family I mean, but I've seen how it can be . . . in other people's lives. There's nothing more fundamental."

"That's true."

"And I'm not an asshole."

"Neither am I."

The cold presses in on us, heaving up from the leafy chaff under our feet and also dropping down from the stark bones of trees overhead. I reach for her, a hug goodbye, but there is the ticking within me now, too strong a pull, and I won't let go.

Her kiss is surprising. She is searching me with a particular purpose in mind, anticipating my reaction to her every movement. She is well trained. She kisses me deeply, pressing the small of my back, her hands so precise, a scientist's hands. I am discovered.

Her professor decided to take a trip to the Canadian Shield. He invited three students, but cared only that she went. On the plane, they drank vodka tonics and discussed different qualities of granite and gneiss, giddy with anticipation of setting foot on Precambrian rock. He told her that there was amethyst between the Proterozoic and Archean layers, and she told him that she would like nothing more than to touch her fingers to it, even just for a moment. His eyes flashed under their shaggy brows, and he laid his age-freckled hand lightly over hers.

"Amethyst. My dear wife's birthstone."

She fell quiet.

He patted her knuckles and produced a baby blue handkerchief from between several pencils in his shirtfront pocket, wiped each wet eye and then his cracked lips. "And what can you tell me about amethyst?"

She was used to these drills. "Silicon dioxide," she said. "Six-sided prism ending in six-sided pyramid. Conchoidal fracture. Insoluble."

"Very good. But did you know that medieval soldiers wore it round their necks during battle?" He carefully folded the blue handkerchief and stowed it back between his pencils. "They believed the crystal would keep them safe in the cold world of war. Such was their faith in silicon dioxide."

And she understood that he was telling her something about love.

In her bed, our bodies shine white with moonlight. All I think about is right now. This moment. Her skin is unbearably soft over the workings of hard muscle and bone, and her small breasts press against mine. Deep in her hair, the scent of chlorine. She wears nothing but the charm strung around her neck on a loop of leather. Amethyst. And I wonder which is more beautiful? The crystal or its home at the hollow of the base of her throat?

She is more naked with her necklace than I am with nothing at all.

At the Canadian Shield, her professor, donned in a white Panama hat, kid leather gloves, and brand new walking shoes, pulled his blue kerchief up over his mouth and nose. She told him he looked like a dapper terrorist, a description he rather liked. Soon the dust of the quartz pit stirred, and she had to hold her sleeve over her mouth.

They descended through the millennia, the layers bold and easy to read.

"Caldera," her professor sang out, pulling his kerchief from his face. "The Earth's most private and ancient recesses heaved up by volcanic explosion." He gave a grand stamp of his shellacked walking stick. After a moment, he added, "We're tourists, but I'm sorry to say that we are not, in fact, time travelers. We can read the drama that took place here, but that is all. We missed the action by billions of years."

The other students grew restless, dust-choked and hungry. They shouldered their packs and climbed back to the present day. She and her professor stayed in the mine, no longer talking or taking samples or photographs, but simply remaining.

I displace the crystal and press my thumb in the hollow of her throat. A perfect fit. I look at the bedside clock and laugh. "I've known you for exactly eleven hours and thirty-six minutes."

"It doesn't matter how long."

Her words travel through my right hand. "True," I say. "It's just the beginning. The start."

Silence.

"What's wrong?"

She lifts my wrist and taps the gold band around my ring finger.

I fall back into her arms until morning. It's still dark, and now I am crying. She refuses to negotiate. Frozen stiff, she's become a fountain statue, a piece of garden art. I continue to lie against her only because I don't know what else to do. I think, *I'll never say another word to you. Not even goodbye.* That will be her punishment.

I cast my gaze around her bedroom. The quarters of a bachelor: rented white walls, furnishings straight out of a box store display, a navy blue bath towel slung across the bathroom door. There is nothing in the room that shows a private side of her, or any side at all. But then my eyes take in the crusted lump on her dresser. In the moonlight, the crystalline shades of color and intricacy are undecipherable, and her souvenir from the Miocene looks like nothing more than a chunk of concrete. My urge to hurt her falls away.

"In Iceland," I say, "they believe rocks have souls."

She stirs. She presses her face against mine, and I can feel that she's smiling.

I want to say something more to her, a compliment maybe, words of how beautiful she looks in the icy flood of moonlight. Or perhaps I want to tell her that I love my family and that she's torn my life apart. But I know that what she wants me to say is the one thing I can't: *You've had no effect on me at all.*

My thoughts turn to leaving as the sky goes light. I peer out the window and study the empty yard. The grass is green with just a trace of frost. I crack the window by an inch, and the air feels wet and cool against my skin. Then I see the dark, low clouds moving in.

"I know a little something about time, too. I can predict the future."

She looks at me with the solemnity of a child.

"Snow is coming."

"How do you know?"

I point to the gray mass plowing toward us.

"And it'll be warmer when it snows?"

I kiss her, and she kisses me back in that way of hers, and though I know that she won't last three years in Alaska or even three months, I release her and smile. Then I take her hand and hold it to the stream of air coming through the window.

SUSANNA J. MISHLER

Susanna J. Mishler was awarded first place in the Poetry Open of the University of Alaska/*Anchorage Daily News* Statewide Writing Contest in 2001, and the winning poem was published on LitSite Alaska. Since then, her work has appeared in *Alaska Quarterly Review, Hotel Amerika, The Iowa Review, The Kenyon Review Online, Michigan Quarterly Review, RATTLE*, and elsewhere. In 2004 she received an MFA in Poetry from the University of Arizona in Tucson, where she also served as an editor for *Sonora Review*. She teaches workshops at the 49 Alaska Writing Center. Her collection of poems, titled *Termination Dust*, is available from Boreal Books/ Red Hen Press.

Anniversary at the Evening Cafe

Cups of coffee steamed in our hands. The courtyard
purpled under vines. On her index finger,
suddenly, an emerald mayfly—wings veined,
  abdomen swooped up.

Mayflies live one day and expire. They flicked through
my dreams last night. Under an olive tree, once,
Archimedes dreamed of the space an object
  fills as divorced from

thing itself. Or, said in a different way: new
means of quantifying what isn't there. We know
the exact dimensions of absence. Tesla
  witnessed his dying

mother rise, heard singing and *saw angelic
figures* cloudborne, *marvelous beauty . . . floated . . .
vanished.* He detested the enigmatic
  nature of visions—

everything's explainable, he believed, if
we can ask the right kinds of questions. Like, what
occupies the space in my cup when coffee's
  gone? How can creatures

like the mayfly live without mouths? Once, I thought
the size and shadow of her loneliness matched
mine: a space in each of us domed, bottomless,
        open like a bell.

Two bells without tongues, waiting. Evening thickens.
We expect the mayfly to spring and vanish,
but it stays. My hand upon hers—a boat on
        water—we're strangers.

Poem That Begins in Address to Nikola Tesla and Ends Up Offshore

You might like it if I said here
"He was married to Elektra,"—which
lends nobility to the lack
of wife or lover—"it was selfless
celibacy; work trumped women."
But the fussy woodstove takes my
eyes from the page, its fan blades
spin as if underwater, the motor
slowly choked of charge.
Snow sits deep on the cooling
cabin. Ice on open channels
skims up the Arm, then gathers
back toward the Inlet. The floes
are daily evidence of how
the Arm unweaves itself:
Turnagain. Cakes of ice
bump shoulders, murmur like a crowd
at fairgrounds, their eyes ready
for the world to be different
from the place they imagined it was.
A crowd looked on as you
lit wireless lamps, made metal discs revolve
at considerable distance
from a spinning field like moons looping
round a planet. It wasn't for anyone
in particular to see when you grasped
the live terminal and tentacles of light
streamed from your spine. Yet something
like a curl of hair, or a woman's earring,

you found too distressing to touch.
Twilight grows between thin branches,
pools above the Arm like smoke.
We crank the radio for cheering
voices, snap on lights, set water to boil,
each of us quiet, roving
privately. I drop a fist of
pasta in the pot, and listen
to the news: another hunter
stranded, cut adrift by shifting
ice. The fracture shot between
an uncle and nephew stalking seals
in Hudson Bay. I pour two mugs of
wine and rest one at her elbow,
wondering what the hunters did when
one had no way back—the moment
they became aware. I crack
the stove door, turn the flue for air
on coals. The uncle might have
thrown some dry meat or an extra sleeping bag
across the rift. They may have
yelled encouragement, instructions.
There came a time when the only thing
to do was watch
each other's features fade in hooded parkas,
see how small his shadow looks on the floe,
and how, at such a distance,
he could be anyone.

Hemispheres

His half is smaller,
his yellow wing
darker on its leading edge.

Her wing splays large,
also yellow,
a small triangular tear

in its trailing rim.
Both wings veined
like a river delta,

both misted with
black ovals as if someone
flicked ink on them

as they flapped by.
Their brown is the brown
of an overripe banana—

camouflage for fall leaves.
His antenna fans,
eyebrow-like,

hers a smooth, penciled arch.
Say the letter
"p" into your palm and that

whisper is how their body
feels, perched
on your hand.

Their fleeced head, thorax,
abdomen fuse
them together:

male on left, female on right.
Two sovereign hemispheres
operate a moth body.

This never happens
to us, our hormones
make other

mistakes. Even if it could,
we're crosswired:
female brain would flex

male thigh, male brain
would extend female bicep.
The man with mincing

walk, the woman with
cocky shoulders would then
somehow negotiate

to walk themselves
as a single person,
to the store, at first, for oranges

that they take home,
peel at the kitchen table
and feed to each other,

sticky juice
dripping
down their chin.

Tired, I Lie Down in the Parking Garage

Last night I dreamed you set our truck on fire
in a parking space next to the elevator. It burned a blue
alcohol flame and you opened the passenger door
as if I would drive us somewhere before it
exploded. Today I float on stolen time,
not awake and not asleep though it's nice
and quiet here in the chasm
between a crew cab pickup and a meat
delivery van with the window rolled down.
You drove us out of town once with no window,
past the lake with fat swans kicking
air with black feet, heads
dabbling underwater. Haze—we wondered
was it smoke or dust—made the road
converge on itself early, as if the Earth was curled
into a tighter ball.
Driver's window stuck open, we drove
out the delta anyway, wearing parkas
in late October, past the last highway sign as more
silt—yes, silt blown from riverbeds—filled the air,
the car, the spaces between our teeth. The mountains
vanished in a fog of their own sediment, so thick
your shape blurred next to me. When I can't love you
I want to make this a romantic moment,
when we crossed the main channel, grit
hailing in on us until we bent double
to hide from the window's stinging gape.

You managed to turn back
over silt dunes and bridges, our tracks erased, the next thing
unforeseeable as if we had never
passed that way. The last highway sign read,
"Travel Beyond This Point Not Recommended," to which
someone added, "FOR PUSSIES".
Protected by the passenger's window, we yodeled
with Hank Williams tunes, substituting
the word, "pussy," every chance we got.

Eve of the Apocalypse

Last month the city barred ravens from citizenship. The birds
agitated, strutting on dumpsters with picket signs: "Garbage
Collectors $60k/yr., Ravens $0" and,
"SILENT NEVERMORE!"
The issue divided families. Skeptical fathers found
red paint and black chicken feathers on their pillows
after commenting that, next, nuthatches will demand
Medicaid. The ravens have skipped town—
people say the moon owes corvids a favor
for liberating her from a giant. But who believes in giants?
Birdfeeders are deserted in a show of avian independence.
One jogger reported puncture wounds from a startled
flock of waxwings. Church membership, insomnia,
and canned good sales are up.
Now's when the story of a young raven's rise from dumpsters
to famous wealth,—and the ensuing big-budget film—
could win a conciliatory victory for ravens,
yet make townspeople feel secure and big-hearted.
Contrary to expectations, our garbage is not tidier.
It's been three weeks, five days, and ten hours.
We wake to the same darkness, we drive the same routes to work, drink
at the same bars. Everyone talks about ravens now
that they're gone—as if
we wonder how they got to leave. Or we wish
that we resembled our own shadows more.

LUCIAN
CHILDS

Lucian Childs is a recipient of a 2013 Rasmuson Foundation Individual Artist Award. He has been awarded residencies at Byrdcliffe Arts Colony and at Artscape Gibraltar Point and was a Peter Taylor Fellow at the 2015 *Kenyon Review* Writers Workshop. He is the winner of the 2013 *Prism Review* Short Story Prize. His stories have appeared in a number of literary journals, including *Grain*, *Sanskrit*, *The Puritan*, *Jelly Bucket*, *Quiddity*, *Rougarou*, and *Cirque*.

The Go-Between

1.

It is hard to believe that I was so wild then. But in Anchorage in 1981, that's what was done: dirty bookstores, all-night bars, downers, poppers, coke, sex. Was I going to say no to that? Throw a wet blanket on the zeitgeist just because it made me uncomfortable?

Besides, that's how I met Jacques—that summer, stripped to his shorts, doing pirouettes on the dance floor at the Village Disco—sweat spinning off his muscular body like a lawn sprinkler. (I'd probably wedged myself into the standard uniform: 501s and a white T-shirt.) Jacques tore through the dance floor that night like he tore through men. They loved to hear him talk dirty in French-Canadian while he fucked.

I was one of them. For that night and for a while after, he was my sexy Quebecker and I his blond *bon ami.* We banged around downtown Anchorage like *Astérix* and *Obélix*—hitting the 5th Avenue bars, drinking martinis (a habit Jacques acquired at his home in Montreal from his *père*), doing lines of coke off the counter with shirtless bartenders.

It was the post-pipeline boom, money and men flowing like the oil, back and forth from Anchorage to the North Slope. Guys came off three weeks of twelve-hour days, seven days a week, to party and get their rocks off.

As for myself, I was just out of college, determined in this place of reinvention and mystery to shake up my boring self. I adopted the motto of the moment: so many men, so little time. Still, I panicked when Jacques no longer wished to bed his blond, mustachioed little buddy and moved to the next in line, Stephen Traynor. I doubled my efforts to ingratiate myself with them and their friends, a hard-partying bunch who, like Jacques, never seemed to work. Drug dealing was the rumor, though if that were true for Jacques, he sheltered me from it. I ran into those friends of theirs everywhere— at the Raven, at the Jade Room. I'd chat them up at the health clinic when we were being treated for clap. I even played with some in dirty bookstore stalls and bragged to Jacques about it after. I thought it was a way in.

This was my last-ditch attempt at fabulousness, the monumental failure at which Jacques was mercifully amused. He valued me for being stalwart, as ballast for his ever-shifting Ship of Fools. It was he, in fact, who suggested I renounce *la débauche* and take up my studies in engineering, his father's profession and one he knew I held in high regard.

Also, the plague was among us, which put that crazy time in closed parenthesis.

2.

A few weeks ago, I was invited to a midsummer garden party. The host is a refugee from those Glory Hole days as well. He accompanies me now to the opera and the symphony, which is about as crazy as we ever get. His garden retains a touch of wildness, though: fireweed, cow parsnip, and devil's club. Plants of the forest or the side of the road.

At the garden party I filled my plate and went out to the deck to search for a place to sit. Though it was almost eight o'clock in the evening, the sun was high and cast shimmery circles through the leaves of an ash tree onto the white tablecloths. There was that particular smell of an arctic summer: under the profusion of new green, the moldy-leafed decay of years past. I took a seat at a table among some fellows I know and, to my surprise, who should be across from me but Stephen Traynor. I hadn't seen or heard from him since the mid-80s. I recognized him instantly, though. His complexion was like rose alabaster—no doubt from his old habit, a rigorous application of facial cream—and he was handsome still, deep-set eyes and a dimpled chin. His face had become jowly, though, and his belly overhung his belt. (I've fared better since I retain my slavish devotion to the gym.) Back in the day, we were forced into an accommodation because of our mutual friendship with Jacques, but, try as I might, we never became friends. In fact, his catty remarks about my stodginess, though cloaked in humor, had often seemed excessively barbed. We had all shared many cheerful moments, nonetheless, and through several helpings of prime rib, he and I joked and reminisced.

The party was festive and it was after midnight by the time I drove Stephen to his budget hotel in mid-Anchorage. The Chugach Mountains, the green wall emblazoned with patches of snow that borders the back of the city, were ruddy with alpenglow. For old times' sake, we stopped along the way at the Kodiak, formerly our old haunt, the Village Disco. Though the place had greatly changed, in tenor it remained the same. It was the middle of the week, and there was only a smattering of regulars, but if I squinted, the scene before me was from almost thirty years ago. There was José, the three-hundred-pound drag queen, seated at his spot at the corner; Sugar Bear, down in his cups on his night off from bartending at the Jade Room; and a couple of twinks on the dance floor grinding in time with the music.

I thought Stephen and I might walk down Memory Lane a bit more. But his usually jolly face grew hard, his eyes squinty and mean. He showed little interest in talking further about old times, or in my subsequent accomplishments, but seemed principally motivated to grill me about Jacques. Had I seen him? When had we last spoken? How could he be reached?

Jacques had been Stephen's first great love, and he had breathed in the Quebecker the way a drowning man gasps for air. Except for its urgency, I would have attributed the inquiry that night to a middle-aged man's nostalgia for lost love. On our second drink, the urgency was in part explained when he filled in details of a story which I knew only in broad strokes.

In 1983, Jacques started up an import business—high-end furniture and accessories for the newly minted rich in their big homes on the hillside. He had tired of partying and threw himself into the enterprise. He was determined not to take advantage of his family's fortune and connections in doing this. He didn't want to provide his father with even the slightest consolation.

As it happened, Stephen became an entrepreneur himself. With money inherited from his grandfather, he participated in the general real estate frenzy overheating the Anchorage economy. Over the next two years, he became one of the city's condo kings, riding the wave of oil.

He and Jacques moved in together in Stephen's own large house on the hillside. The view from their deck was spectacular: Denali, Foraker, and Hunter (the huge mountains visible in the distance to the north), the Alaska Range trailing eastward down the Inlet, sugar-frosted and spiky. They hosted fabulous parties, like a couple of Jay Gatsbys. In the summer light that ran without interruption from dusk straight into dawn, bearded men draped off deck rails, played in a foamy hot tub, popped pills from a fishbowl on the kitchen's Carrara countertop.

All this I knew mostly from hearsay. What I had not heard was the account of their affair's abrupt end. One day, Stephen said, then paused for effect. One day, he said, Jacques disappeared, not to be heard from since.

3.

I tried to put all this together as I made my way up the hillside to my house, a sprawling affair not far from the one that had formerly been Stephen's. After the real estate crash of the mid-80s, people left Anchorage by the thousands. So in that, Jacques' disappearance wasn't extraordinary. But the urgency of Stephen's inquiry and the dramatic manner in which he delivered his news, led me to believe there was something he was hiding.

All this dredging up of the past unleashed a torrent and memories of Jacques flooded my thoughts. I recalled the weekend he and I traveled to Montreal. (This was his way of softening the blow for having recently thrown me over for Stephen.) He promised to introduce me to his *père*, a force in provincial politics and a noted engineer. I was soon entering the program at the University of Alaska and Jacques thought I might benefit from a confab with his father. The meeting never took place; they'd taken up their spat again by the time we arrived. The old man wanted Jacques to leave off wasting time in our frontier town and return to his studies in Montreal. Jacques refused, and not in a nice way. Though my French is creaky, I believe what Jacques yelled into the phone means "leave the country" but is usually translated "fuck-off."

Our hotel reservations extended through a long weekend, so Jacques decided we'd make the best of it and tour the city. When he stood me up for the second time at the Musée des Beaux-Arts, I realized I'd had enough. All the missed appointments throughout our friendship, the late entrances, the feeble apologies (or none at all) and me at a restaurant with ice cubes melted in my glass. No amount of Gaulish *charme* could make up for that. I rebooked my flight, and though Jacques protested in that passionate Quebecker way of his, I don't think he minded. I had the feeling he'd rather smoke dope and hang with his high school pals, his *copains*.

I remember the lights on the St. Lawrence the last night, like undulating neon, below the bulk of Mont-Royal and, from the plane, the city twinkling through the clouds.

Back in Anchorage, over the following year my friendship with Jacques and Stephen lingered, grew tepid, invitations to their parties far between. At last, it fizzled. University was demanding. I lectured myself: eliminate unnecessary distractions! I lost touch. I could no longer stave off the inevitable: we were simply not a good fit.

4.

At my friend's garden party, I had exchanged contact info with Stephen and I emailed the next day, saying how glad I was to have run into him. That those heady days of our youth, though fraught, were nevertheless grand, and I was happy our visit had allowed me the occasion to remember them.

His reply, though somewhat chilly, was impeccably polite. He added this unusual postscript which delivered the *aha* I had been seeking. Back in 1983, Stephen had taken loans on his properties to jumpstart Jacques' import business. Jacques was out of his depth, and immediately the concern began to sour. Bills unpaid to manufacturers, customs fees stranding inventory in Seattle on the docks. No inventory, no business.

As a result, when the Anchorage boom went bust and Stephen was unable to make his loan payments, all his properties perished in the equation. He recouped not one *centime*, a setback from which it had taken him decades to recover.

He started from scratch in San Francisco: an assortment of jobs (clothing salesman, timeshare purveyor, assistant to a real estate developer). Finally, with the easy money available in the early aughts, he began developing properties on his own.

Although unstated, his urgency to find Jacques now became clear. It's 2009, and while we Alaskans suck happily at the pap of Big Oil, the rest of the world teeters at the abyss, in the throes of the Great Recession. Stephen needed money.

After one boomtown disaster, you could hardly find fault with his desperation at the prospect of another. I sent him a short condolatory reply, then deleted his email, as I did not expect or wish to hear from him again.

5.

Thoughts of Jacques continued to nag me. Everywhere there were reminders: my French housekeeper, an Atom Egoyan DVD from Netflix, the Stanley Cup on television at the gym. My lack of spontaneity has been replaced by a thoroughness in my personal and professional lives, and I could not let Jacques rest.

One night—I'd had a bit too much Burgundy—I Googled him. Jacques Turcot. Three pages of hits. His companies out of Montreal and Vancouver: Jacques Turcot, LTD.; Turcot Frères Import-Export; Turcot Asia, a subsidiary out of Vietnam. (It seemed *le père* Turcot had taken the black sheep back into the fold.) And surprisingly, a Monsieur J. Turcot, *candidat, Bloc Québécois, District électorale fédérale La Pointe-de-l'Île, Montréal.* There was a campaign website, a LinkedIn page, but no personal contacts. Just official phone and email.

There were pictures, though—one of him chummy at a Montreal Fashion Week party with Jean Paul Gaultier; another at *Le Festival des Films du Monde* on the red carpet with Céline Dion draped from one arm; another of him looking dashing, cooing to a baby at a political event.

6.

At work the next morning, I thought to call Stephen at his hotel to relay these findings, but decided the better for it. Obsessed with Jacques as he now seemed to be, doubtless Stephen knew all this already and was preoccupied making inquiries of Jacques' old friends.

Besides, I had to prepare for a trip to Seattle. The engineering firm of which I am a partner was in merger talks with a large international company. The countercyclical nature of our economy makes Alaska one of the few places where investing is profitable. Now, like me, Anchorage is grown up, responsible. Most of the bars and bookstores downtown from the boom days have been demolished, replaced by an upscale shopping mall and a palace for the performing arts.

Beginning my career, I dreamed of engineering structures like these, but my talents have led me elsewhere. I am an excellent negotiator, a tactician, and an amply capable project administrator. My creativity lies in my personal life: I possess a large set of friends, all interesting in their own way—engineers and contractors, mostly—women and men both, gay and straight. My family in Texas adores me, and we visit every second year. Though single, I do not lack for boyfriends, men who, at our age, consider reliability a desirable asset.

7.

I was staying at the W Hotel in downtown Seattle. After a long day of negotiations, I was tired and ready for bed. I switched off my cell and was about to slip between the hotel's impossibly silky sheets when the landline rang. The receptionist at the front desk was apologetic, professional. Even so, I was about to be short with her when she said there appeared to be a matter of some urgency. A Jacques Turcot was on the house phone. Would I take the call?

My breath hitched. I thought for a moment it might be a joke. After Jacques proved his bona fides, we agreed to meet in the cocktail lounge downstairs. In the elevator as I descended, each floor my heart beat louder.

We settled into leather chairs in a dimly lit corner. He was thinner than I remembered, with a white streak down the front of his thick black coiffure, which gave him a decidedly patrician air.

Jacques explained his assistants had located me via the Internet. Two of them sat near us on a sectional, a boy and a girl in their twenties, baluster-thin, their oriental faces washed in the glow of their iPhones. Scheduling problems, Jacques said. He told me he frequently traveled on business to Seattle and considered our meeting fated when he found that particular weekend I would be there as well. Precisely how that was determined, he would not say. My office would not have given out the information.

The waitress delivered our drinks—martinis, for lost times, Jacques said to me and winked. I felt cowed and a little turned on.

He brought himself to the point. His people had made him aware his bad behavior toward Stephen Traynor was becoming the cause of a certain difficulty. Apart from that, he had shame, and because they once had loved, he would like to set things right. It had become messy, though; Stephen had made some little threats. For this, Jacques blamed himself. He wished to meet with Stephen, but evidently a complicated reencounter must not be. They had hired lawyers, of course, private detectives, but to take the scent from the hound, Jacques still felt the matter needed the personal touch. He understood at present Stephen was in Anchorage trying to sniff him out. He paused, then said sweetly that he knew he could count on me to do him *une petite gentillesse*.

8.

By mid-week, the merger negotiations were bogged down over our company's evaluation—something for the number crunchers to re-solve—so I headed back to Anchorage to attend to the favor Jacques had asked of me.

I was to pick up the money he owed Stephen (plus interest) at a Vietnamese restaurant on Spenard Road, an area that still retains a whiff of its original rough and tumble. There are bars on either side of the street where at night hookers roam like wildlife in its natural habitat.

On the day of the meeting, an assistant called to reschedule. That appointment also was broken. Finally, the time was set for Monday night, and though it contradicted Jacques' wishes that I alone handle the transfer of funds, that morning on a whim I called Stephen. He was livid—jealous, I suppose that I had been selected for the duty—but excited for the money; excited, too, I think, at the prospect of any possible communication with Jacques. Whether for retribution or reconciliation, I couldn't tell.

Because of the meeting, I cut short my dinner engagement at the home of a man who, I admit, really interests me. He's that rare bird, an artist who doesn't at all mind my fastidiousness. We ended the evening at his front door with a lingering kiss and made plans for the coming weekend. I then collected Stephen at his hotel, and as we drove the short distance to our assignation, we chatted amiably.

The restaurant was closed, but a bald, sallow-faced individual answered the door. We followed him through a corridor to a back office. He sat behind a desk and presented me with a sheet of paper, which Stephen snatched away. The man shrugged, drew the corners of his mouth down, then handed Stephen a pen.

Bursts of air from flared nostrils accompanied Stephen's reading of the document.

The sallow-faced man took a manila envelope from a desk drawer, thumbed one corner, and after several minutes said, He sign, or no?

Whatever, Stephen said. With the pen, he quickly scrawled his name and slid the sheet of paper back across the desktop.

Wiggling his head slightly, the man looked at me, looked at Stephen, then handed him the manila envelope.

Out of it spilled onto the desk a glossy photo of the three of us at the Raven, young and trim, looking like lumberjacks in our tight jeans and plaid flannel shirts. Jacques stood smiling between Stephen and me, his arms flung over both of our shoulders.

Stephen flicked the photo away, which revealed a smaller envelope. This contained a cashier's check and a short note. He rolled his eyes and thrust the note in my face. It read:

Cher, désolé. So sorry. Forgive me.

As I drove Stephen back to his hotel, he didn't say a word. It seemed clear he nursed his disappointment: no *billet-doux,* no Jacques. A tiger cannot change his stripes. What did Stephen expect?

In the rearview mirror, Cook Inlet's waters glimmered in the sun. Though late for a weeknight, traffic was heavy, others bound for appointments, too keyed up by the long day's light to go home. I attempted some pleasantry. Stephen's face soured. He turned away. It was as if, uninteresting as he had always seemed to find me, I wasn't even there.

This stung, certainly. Angered me. But I reminded myself, I had my life. It didn't matter, this old story.

Black Spruce

Something about our new condo puts me off. Maybe it's this furniture. When Wilco accepted the deal at British Petroleum, I told him: let's ditch that hodge-podge we've cobbled together in Houston and get new stuff.

Before escrow closed on this place, I ordered these new pieces, pared-down classics of modern design like I'd studied in art school. As I edge toward decrepitude, I crave the pristine line. It's not about order but the lack of any sort of compromise.

Still, with the final piece, delivered just two weeks ago, Corbu's famous lounger, I find its swoop isn't as attractive as in the Bauhaus photographs, and the molded plywood Eames chairs appear smaller than they had in the Design Within Reach catalog, while Wilco's leather armchair seems overscaled.

To really spoil the broth, in our one concession to the past, Wilco insisted I dust off some canvasses I'd painted in my twenties. A ghastly lot. To prod me on, he said. They hang reproachfully on one wall.

"Honey," I say, "I want to rearrange the furniture."

"David, again? I've just gotten used to the way you did it yesterday."

Wilco slurps his coffee in his tall wingback. I can't see him, only a hand and forearm that pounce now and then on the armrest. By disposition and because he used to lift weights every day, that forearm is solid, like the rest of him. I can almost see the seams of the chair pull apart under his weight, which is absurd, of course, given how tautly the Italians have stretched the white leather.

The armchair faces a set of glass doors that give out onto a deck, which in turn looks onto the jagged mountains at the easternmost edge of the town, a bright green wall in the early morning summer light.

"Complacency," I say, "is the enemy of the good."

"I thought it was perfection."

"That, too."

Wilco never holds out for long against my wishes. It's his essential Scandinavian/Minnesotan go-along-to-get-along thing. *Whatever*, as my students used to say. Or as Wilco's jolly father, a man with a nonetheless healthy sense of limits, might growl, just let me be to eat my lutefisk.

Boy, Wilco really puts his foot down this time: he insists the placement of his beloved wingback be left untouched by my interior desecrations.

"Fine," I say. "We'll make it the centerpiece—just like you, darling—the thing around which everything revolves."

"You have to joke about everything."

"*J'accuse!*" I say. "Really? And so early in the morning."

"Everyone's got to have a hobby. Mine's golf, yours is hilarity, apparently."

"Now who's being funny?" I get off the red Ligne Roset couch and walk to the front of the living room to contemplate my first move. "Difference is," I say, "I can practice my hobby all year. You can golf, what, two months in this godforsaken place?"

Snow on the ground all the way through April. Last February, Wilco took a promotion that required a transfer up here to the middle of nowhere (a.k.a. Anchorage, Alaska). I'd followed, dutifully, of course. *Wither thou goest . . .*

I tried then, as I do now, to look on the bright side. Wilco's new salary is greater than our former incomes combined. He's much too consumed by his new job to be interested in taking back on our, to me, onerous role as a civically minded gay couple always out and about for some cause. And I'm no longer required to work. I only had a couple years left to retirement anyway, and trying to cram a love of art down the throats of privileged youth had lost its allure.

What remained was a workmanlike quality, a sense of accomplishment that I gave up.

In recompense, the plan was for me to return to painting, to pick up my glorious career where I'd left off. But since unpacking the brushes, I haven't so much as picked one up. I find the habit of art has atrophied. Forty years is a long time. One backslides. One becomes someone else.

Now I mostly rearrange furniture. Also, like my mother, I watch daytime TV. I've become personal friends with any number of fictional characters on the soaps. Especial favs: Wyatt Spencer, and, even though he's a devious shit, Victor Adam Newman Jr., who's *très* gay and has the cutest set of boyfriends he abuses. I try not to yell at the bitch, but really, sometimes it's not possible.

"Five months," Wilco says, returning to the subject of golf. "A guy at the club told me you can play up here five months."

"Four, I think. Unless you want to tee up with icicles."

"At least it gets me out of the house."

"I walk to the mailbox every day."

"Except you drove the half block last winter."

"It was minus twenty degrees!"

"Only for a couple weeks. Otherwise, the temp was around zero."

"Are you listening to yourself?" Wilco's attempts to prove himself right are so infantile. "We could have stayed in Houston where it's warm, but no. Wilco has this thing for Alaska."

I say this too pointedly. My humor has always bordered on the acid. Plus, though I've soured on this move, I've promised myself not to harp on it. What's done is done.

"That's okay, hon." I slip into my old West Texas accent to soften the effect and speak to the back of Wilco's big chair. "You sit there and look purdy while Momma fixes up the house. Admire your precious Great Land out that big ole winder."

I move the Corbu lounger a foot to the left halfheartedly, pick up one of the molded plywood chairs and set it back down. I sigh theatrically. I collapse on the couch, bury my face between the cushions, and breathe in that new leather smell.

Immediately, I think of my father's Cadillacs he bought every third year. He was a pious, self-important man who discouraged frivolity or release through the senses. Those cars were for his personal use or for important family occasions. When he allowed us to ride in them, we had to sit, hands folded, quietly in the back. We couldn't eat or drink or chew bubblegum or our mother smoke her menthols or wear her fabulous Shalimar cologne. So that new car smell lasted longer than was natural. It always made me sad when I realized it was gone.

"I thought you were getting the place ready for *Architectural Digest*."

"I was thinking of my father."

"You know how that upsets you."

"It's my form of self-flagellation. In this, he and I are not so far apart." I finger the corner of the book he's been studying on local hiking trails. These hold no interest to me, but there's a chapter in the back on arctic ecology I find intriguing. "Are your mountains pretty today, honey?"

"I'm doing a crossword puzzle."

"Mind-rotting piffle."

"It beats rummaging through your past and making yourself unhappy. You have to know things to fill out crosswords."

"You have to know *everything* to make yourself unhappy about your past."

Out the glass doors, shadows of fluffy summer clouds smudge the mountains. A sliver of lake sparkles in the gap between the houses on the opposite side of the road. A group of ravens persecutes a bald eagle in a midair ballet. Who would think we'd live in such a place? Wildlife out our window nearly every day! We might as well be camping out. I loved Houston. The only thing *sauvage* there was traffic and the lack of zoning regulations.

"Come on," I say, resigned to the prospect of a little physical exertion. He's bound to bring up the subject eventually. "We don't get nice days like this often. How about a walk in your precious mountains?"

"Promise not to complain?"

I reach the book on hiking trails around the corner of the chair and drop it. "Pick something easy, please."

The thunder's repeated retort is muffled by the distance. From what I understand, there's almost never lightning in Anchorage—too cool, too close to the water—but the big towers to the north loom and spark over flatlands wedged between rows of mountains.

"Don't you love global warming?" I fan my face with my Astros baseball cap. "I'd be miserable in Alaska without it."

"When all that carbon gets released from the tundra, there'll be water way up here."

We're on a promontory off the trail, high above the only road between Anchorage and the communities to the south, on the Kenai Peninsula.

"Look on the bright side," I say. "We could both get jobs as gondoliers."

Voices of hikers on the trail grow louder. A man in his early twenties bounds through the gap in the trees to join us on the rock. A woman, also young, follows a minute behind him.

"Wow, look at that," the young man says. "Awesome."

After some initial chit-chat, I nail them. If nothing else, my years as a teacher trained my powers of observation with young people. And though I'm a *cheechako*, a tenderfoot in Alaska, this Sean from Ohio exhibits that soft, doe-eyed idealism I've been warned about, of people new to this place who make a religion out of the beneficence of nature. Already this summer, one of them has died not far from here, in sight of the road below, people speeding along the black line to their comfortable houses.

His girlfriend, Samantha, seems to practice a sharp-eyed idealism. Hers is a no-nonsense orientation, driven no doubt by a tedious need to be precise. With the two of them, Wilco and I find ourselves huffing up the trail, at her exhortation.

Immediately, I'm out of breath.

"We'll put you up front," Samantha says. "A group can only go as fast as its slowest member."

"I used to be so fit," I say.

"Sucks to be old."

"Gee, thanks, Wilco. I needed to be reminded of that."

"How old are you, anyway?" the young man asks me.

"Sixty-two, sixty-three."

"That old, it's hard to keep track," Wilco says.

He steps on the back of my boots and I stumble. I'm starting to feel irked by his niggling. He's ingratiating, over-eager around young people. I've given up pretending to have much in common with them, but Wilco hasn't relinquished the attachment to his youth.

"Compared to them," I bring him back down to earth, "even you're practically ancient. He's forty-six, by the way."

"Wow!" Sean said. "Same age as my dad."

"The cranky Luddite."

"Sam likes to use big words. She thinks I don't know what they mean. I got a 740 on my verbals, you know." Sean's deep voice assails us from behind. "Actually, my dad is kind of a drag. He thinks iPads mean the end of civilization. Wouldn't let me play computer games until I was fifteen. Made me take up reading. Sort of stunted my growth, I think."

"Me," I say, "I prefer videos about ginkgoes. Wilco here is interested in unusual stories about bugs."

"Cool. I dig the Nature Channel." Judging by his earnest reply, the boy hasn't picked up the concept of irony from his Harry Potter books. "Samantha's an artist. She prefers ambiguity."

"Knowing things gets in the way," she says.

Ambiguity: I may have misjudged the girl. "Sounds like something you'd put on your tombstone," I say while gasping for breath. "Which art form?"

"I'm studying painting at Antioch. That's where we met."

Roots washboard the path and slow our pace. Wheezing, bent over, I stand to one side, too overcome to express my interest. "You all go on ahead," I say. "I'll catch up in a bit."

"It's hot," the young man says. "I think I'm pretty much going to leave my shit here, pick it up on the way back." Sean strips off his long-sleeved shirt and ties it around his waist. He pulls a small bag from his pack and slings it over his shoulder, then tosses the pack out of sight in a clump of fiddleheads.

My eyes trace the tight arcs of the young man's chest, then down the vein that protrudes from his bicep. There are photos that tell me I was once this delectable, but I'd been too wrapped up with school and my puny art career to take much advantage of it. At the sight of this boy, absolutely at the height of his beauty, fidgeting with the bag's straps, practically chomping at the bit to get started up the trail, desire mingles with regret.

"There's another overlook a couple of minutes ahead," Wilco says. My man has done his homework about the trail; I'll give him that. "We can rest there."

"Right on." The young man retrieves his pack from the clump of ferns and dangles it from a shoulder.

I sigh and we move on.

"This is what you wanted," Wilco says.

"I've told you before, feel free to correct me when I'm so clearly mistaken."

"Come on," Wilco says, ignoring the pointedness of my remark. "Just a couple more feet, honey-bunch."

Honey-bunch gets me every time. I straighten, wedge my hands into my pockets, and plod up the path with a renewed vigor that proves all too momentary. The hill quickly bests me. I feel weary in body, but in spirit also. This jaunty little outing of ours can't belie the fact that I feel old, as well as adrift in retirement. Worse, isolated in that house, I'm beginning to look for advice on what to do about this from my soap opera friends. In my situation, how would Suzi or Kendall plot their next move? Whatever it was, it'd be bold. It'd be beautiful.

The *pièce de résistance* to this little pity party: my boot slides into the deep socket of a tree root. I hear a pop and find myself face forward on the ground, blood streaking from my nose and a stabbing pain at my ankle.

"Whoa, dude! You okay?" The young man hurries over and lifts me by the armpits to a standing position. Gently, as if I were a decorative porcelain egg.

"Ai yai!" I put weight on my damaged foot.

Sean hands his pack to his girlfriend and crouches. "Jump on."

As he waits for me to mount, the muscles of his back glisten with sweat. I wrap my arms around his shoulders, and with my good foot hop on. He smells of skunk and cooked cabbage. As we pass Wilco, I lean my face against the ropy muscle at the young man's neck and flutter my eyelids seductively.

Samantha coils a spongy Ace bandage around my foot with a gravitas that makes me think of mummies, she the Egyptian priestess wrapping me, having first placed my organs in a jar. My foot is blue and swollen. When she finishes, I elevate it on my pack and lean back on my elbows to take in the view.

Sitting on the rock a little distance from the young woman, solid as a fireplug, Wilco pulls on his shades to shield him from the sunlight reflected off the inlet.

Samantha returns the First Aid kit to her pack, then slides out a sketchpad and a clear plastic box of pencils. She traces on a page the line of mountains opposite us, patches of snow clinging to their sides like wayward jigsaw puzzle pieces. Below, the watercourse at low tide veins the mud flats.

The young man plops down beside me and motions to the mountains with his chin. "Friggin' gorgeous, man. Bet you don't get tired of that." He takes out of his bag an Altoids tin held closed by a rubber band. "You all get high?"

As an art student, I smoked up regularly with my fellows on the roof outside our third floor studio. Our laughter echoed off the building where the Philistines studied business administration.

Sean pulls a small pipe from the tin. "Dude, this is some major shit, so go easy. Scored it from a guy playing frisbee golf in a park in downtown Anchorage. I walked right up to him and asked."

Stubble stipples the young man's square jaw. His eyes are sunk into deep sockets under overhanging brows. His straight nose, the axis of a perfect bilateral symmetry, is bounded by high cheekbones. It's the stereotypical beauties I crave. That's why I like the soaps. There are no plain people.

"Sean changed his major from art history to business," Samantha says, looking first at the mountains and then at her pad. "Now he thinks he's a man of action."

Sean flicks the lighter and holds it over the pipe bowl. "Doing stuff is where it's happening. Nobody gives a shit about art history, Samantha."

I hadn't pegged him for a Philistine, but people are often less than they seem. I could take his remark as a rebuke, except that it was so obviously aimed at the young woman. Besides, I've long ago become resigned to my own insignificance. The world belongs to people like this young man and Wilco, entrepreneurs and engineers, makers of the tangible, the useful.

Samantha draws a large X across the sketch of the mountains, tears the sheet from the pad, balls it up, and throws it in a clump of alders.

"Hey, Sam. That's not cool."

"Biodegradability," she says. "Nobody had to invent that. It just is."

"Dude," Sean says as he stands. "I think this is where I'm supposed to go pee." He whistles some song unknown to me as he disappears into the bushes.

I take a long toke and then pass the pipe to Samantha. After a puff, she taps Wilco on the shoulder and hands him the pipe. Another round of smoke and I feel like a head without a body.

"You two are together, right?" Samantha asks, suddenly stoner serious.

I readjust my foot on the pack and laugh.

"I didn't want to assume," she says.

"On account of the difference in our age?"

"I thought it might be impolite."

I'm impressed. One doesn't often find a sense of propriety among the young.

"Fifteen years, now," I say, "since we first met. It used to feel like only yesterday."

Wilco turns and gives me one of his eat-shit looks that are not to be taken seriously. Still, I know to tread lightly.

"And you," I say, "how long have you guys been together?"

Samantha strikes a straight line across the middle of the page: the water's edge under the mountains. "I don't think we are together, not really. I'm not sure I want that anymore."

"And him?"

"It's like the Magic 8 Ball app on my iPhone: reply hazy, try again."

"So much of life is that way."

Samantha nods. In her altered state, she seems to think this profound, whereas I was only repeating what Pamela "Pam" Douglas said last week on *One Life to Live*.

She rips the sheet from the pad and tucks it in the back. She looks at me with a singular concentration and draws with a pencil across a fresh sheet a curve that twins the outline of my head. I still myself and assume a three-quarter profile pose, that of a wise Socrates in the presence of his adoring Alcibiades. Wrong gender, I know, but a pleasant image nonetheless.

She sketches quickly, glancing back and forth from my face to the pad cradled in her lap.

"You have the touch," I say, glancing at her progress. "The facility of line, I used to tell my students."

"Your students?"

"Forty years an art teacher."

She works hard to draw the shape of my shoulders. She holds the pencil like she might break it.

"You might loosen the line a bit. It's all about breath, really. Precision in art does not result in merit." I look back to the inlet and resume my pose.

"I bet you were a good teacher."

"That wasn't the plan, you know. I studied painting at university as well. After I got out, I rented this sweet house in the country and painted every day. I wasn't without recognition: some awards, grants. I never could get paid though. It was my father's idea to double-major in education. Something to fall back on."

She shades the shadowed side of my face. I hear the pencil scrape across the rough paper. "I'm down with that," she says.

I risk over-sharing, like you sometimes can when you're stoned and with people you're never going to see again. "Thing is, I gave up painting, but I never stopped thinking about myself as a painter. The teacher stuff was supposed to be temporary."

"I wonder," Wilco says, "if we shouldn't get you back home and ice up that foot." He uses his business voice, plainly displeased by my *Kumbaya* moment with this stranger.

Just then there's a rustling in the bushes, and the young man strides back onto the overlook.

"Dude, just saw this hella big moose. So close. Way cool."

Wilco peers over his shades. "Careful, moppet, those things'll stomp you to death."

Sean sits between Samantha and Wilco, reaches across the girl's lap for the pipe and takes another puff. He hands the pipe to Wilco. "You know that's the name of a band, don't you? Wilco. Never heard anybody else use it."

"My family's from Minnesota," Wilco says. "Totally white bread.

Men had names like Algernon and Horatio back in the day. Dad's name is Theodore. I guess they'd gotten around to the W's by the time I was born."

I roll onto one elbow to look at the sketch. An old man stares up from the pad: bald, jowly, wrinkled about the eyes. I don't like it, but a picture can't lie. This one captures none of the sexy *joie de vivre* I use to mask the truth. Old is old, it says.

"You know," Sean says, drawing a line with his finger down the length of the inlet. "All this beauty, plus practically getting stomped on, makes me think."

"Uh oh," the young woman says. "He's been reading *Zen and the Art of Motorcycle Maintenance*."

"Hilarious, Samantha. Dude seems cool." Sean turns to me. "If you don't mind. I mean, I don't know a lot of old people. Just my Gramps and I couldn't ask him this. So, uh, are you, like, stoked for death, or what?"

I rise onto both hands and give him my best incredulous look.

"Sean, don't be clueless," Samantha says. "That's a little too personal, don't you think."

We're quiet for some time, magpies flitting in the cottonwoods, testing their raucous calls. Believe me, there's been enough death in my life to make it more than just a concept. "It still feels like," I say, trying to offer something reassuring, "what happens to other people."

"Dude, seriously. A bear could come through here right now and turn us all into lunch meat," Sean says.

"Not likely." Wilco crosses his legs and pulls down his cap. The sun is getting lower. More time has passed than I thought.

"I don't know," I say. "Maybe death's a good thing. There's only so much a person can take."

"What is this?" Wilco says. "Truth or Dare? I'm officially tabling this discussion."

"I'm seventeen years older than him. He doesn't like to think about me dying."

"Come on, David," Wilco says. "Where's my funny guy?"

"You know, my father was strict with me too," I tell the young man. When I'm stoned, I become trapped by my thoughts. I can't turn the ship around so easily, not even for Wilco. "I didn't have a TV until after I went to college. He was a religious man, vice-chancellor at Texas Tech. With him, it was all about personal betterment and service.

"Wilco's dad's a champ, though. We go back there each Christmas, and his father takes me ice fishing. Nobody else will go with him, and I don't mind. We drink whisky from a flask and look out the porthole window at nothing. Only catch a few puny fish. I never did anything remotely intimate like that with my father. Wilco doesn't know how lucky he is. He's got the complacency of the well-adjusted."

"I'm right here, you know," Wilco says.

"He's never had to give anything up."

Wilco hauls himself onto the balls of his feet, fingertips tented on the rock like a sprinter at the starting line. I know I'm in for it. "I told you, you could say no. We could stay in Houston."

I turn to Sean. "He'd have blamed me for ruining our finances and our future happiness."

"Dude, I got no idea what you're talking about."

"You hated that job," Wilco says.

"I had something to do every day."

Sean fidgets with the pipe. "Maybe you guys should take another hit."

Wilco stands. It's time to go. I want to linger, this patch of rock apart from the world and we, like gods immune to complications of our own, hovering over it.

Below, between the mountain and the road, a shadow bisects the remnant of a pond, a bog of electric green grass. Increasing in height outward from its center, a troop of stick figures marches ten or so yards, the dense encircling forest halting its progress.

Black Spruce. I read about them in the back of that hiking book. The spruce, they seem so fragile—scraggly, gray, seemingly half dead—but they carve a place for themselves where little else can, with sedges at the damp edge of a bog.

It's probably the marijuana or a case of too much sunlight, but something about how sad and brave they look makes me feel giddy. "Come to the house, Samantha," I say. "For dinner. Are you vegan?" She seems as though she might be vegan.

"We're thinking of walking to Rabbit Lake," Sean says.

"Long way back in there," Wilco says.

"Land of the midnight sun," Samantha says. "We can walk all night."

"Tomorrow, then," I say. "This has been so much fun. I feel already like we're friends. We're all about making new friends. Right, Wilco? Real friends, I mean, not soap opera ones. And you should see our place. It looks right over the water to the mountains. Wildlife outside our window practically every day. It's almost as good as camping out, plus you have all your stuff. You should see what Wilco has done with it. Everything right out of the box. The furniture has that new leather smell. You know, the smell of beginnings, of no impediments."

I can tell our moment is over and that I'm sort of freaking Samantha out, but I'm a stoner on a roll. "Come to the house," I say, "before you leave Alaska. Just for a beer, even, out on the deck. I can't tell you how good that place makes me feel. It's perfect."

AMBER
FLORA
THOMAS

Amber Flora Thomas is the recipient of several major poetry awards, including the Dylan Thomas American Poet Prize, Richard Peterson Prize, and Ann Stanford Prize. Her published work includes: *Eye of Water: Poems* (University of Pittsburgh Press, 2005), which won the Cave Canem Poetry Prize, and *The Rabbits Could Sing: Poems* (University of Alaska Press, 2012). Most recently, her poetry has appeared in *ZYZZYVA, Callaloo, Orion Magazine, Alaska Quarterly Review, Saranac Review,* and *Crab Orchard Review,* as well as *Angles of Ascent: A Norton Anthology of Contemporary African American Poetry* and numerous other journals and anthologies. She received her MFA from Washington University in St. Louis in 1998. Currently, she is an Assistant Professor of Creative Writing at the East Carolina University. She was born and raised in northern California.

Marlboros at Dusk

Light clouded, a nighthawk cuts
across the last threads, as though what can be seen clearly—
your foot cupped in my hands, the growing veins
of tree limbs darkening above us—contains its own crude

light. Silence changes us without our turning
to know it happens in the other's eyes: love,
a rich sadness we can afford the longing for.
Your look retreats in a haze of smoke.

I lift the arch of your pale foot to my lips.
Desire does sustain its hold. We are invented
by what we let pass through us.

Aubade

I know my leaving in the breakfast table mess.
Bowl spills into bowl: milk and bran, bread crust
crumbled. You push me back into bed.

More "honey" and "baby."
Breath you tell my ear circles inside me,
curls its damp wind and runs the circuit
of my limbs. I interrogate the air,

smell Murphy's oil soap, dog kibble.
No rose. No patchouli swelter. And your mouth—
sesame, olive. The nudge of your tongue
behind my top teeth.

To entirely finish is water entering water.
Which is the cup I take away?

More turning me. Less your arms reaching
around my back. You ask my ear
where I have been and my body answers,
all over kingdom come.

A Woman's Jewelry

The woman in line at the coffee shop
wears a shark-tooth earring. Its jagged leaf
hooks back and forth on an inch of chain,
sharpness aimed away from her chopped
hair and acne-scarred face. It's the right

place to touch her. I reach for its pendulum
dangling there, ask after its petrified origins.
It's a tangible beginning: her leaning her ear
toward me. In this jeweled splurge, I sense
the beginning I've found with every lover.

The black-beaded choker dangling threads
of malachite over the stammer of raised veins.
The loose-fitting ring when the setting turns
and a small amethyst eye gazes from her palm.
She tells a lie and her hand reaches for the lapis

bracelet, which she twists until the clasp is there,
fingernail snapping the release. Her tongue
drawing its barbell ring along my thigh,
hot bead flicking its own course at the light.
The intricate battle of the bent ear-wire catching

on my sweater, its stainless steel holds her head
to my chest, though we've finished kissing.
Her moonstone brooch clear and cloudy,
at once a way in or a way out.

Hotel Reverie

My lover keeps the room: the faded comforter
tangled between her legs, a barely creased Bible
open on her pillow, clothes she drapes on a chair.

I straighten a picture over the bed: tumbling spore
of dandelion, a red barn in the background.
I can find no single history the maid's stark finish

won't erode. Frayed edges fringe the bath towels.
An incidental landscape of stains falls across
the bleached cushions of the couch.

Some other lover may have looked up, untangled herself
from the brushed polyester bedding to belong
to the instance getting away. So comes my first desire:

to carve initials in a wood bench, mark name and thought
in a bathroom stall: *I was here* and I buried in the middle of her
—the heart of me. She left me wordless. *I was here*

at the window, counting on that one, ominous blackbird
who follows. *I was here* surveying the room with her eyes
and I saw my incompleteness. I saw she had settled into me

like a bone caught in swallowing. *I was here* and light
broke a crack and cut down the middle of me.

Lake Shore Deer

You break the jaw from the crushed skull, collecting
more remnants for the mantel, souvenirs you'll lose
the meaning for. In the bony cavity, teeth rattle

the *clack, clack* of abandoned purpose.
I lift the yellow bone to my nose. Breath and cry
remembered. The well-worn molars ridged in black.

A heron heaves off its post. An eclipse of wings
like a blue bow over the lake. I don't forget
the whole task of prayer and longing. I hold

the deer's unclean break of mouth and a gray feather.
I hold your fingers, which I steal to my mouth
to keep from talking, to keep the want from invading the purpose.

I deliver you quiet and shaking. You say, "I'll kiss you
because no one's looking." I summon that mouth of grazing molars,
mud in the crevice, beetle fleshing the bone back to dust.

In the jaw, our inadequate chewing. It seems we've acquired the beast
when we put it in our pocket, because we take it with us.

Come in from the Sky

A cathedral waited in my mind
as I leaned over her mouth.
The shelves around us spilled
casebooks, encyclopedias, dictionaries.
I repeated the doctrine: a man should not
lay down with his neighbor's wife.
Her dildo's curved beak glistened
as it left my body.

The curfew on my flood
of shame was punctuated by her moan.
I heard a chorus in her throat, the bird's ribs
snapping against her palate. She might have
spoken if not for my kiss, the fat sound
rolling around in my mouth like a jaw-
breaker: affirmed, allowed.

Had praise been the clitoris's silky crown,
and not a bud of oak or elm.
Had the hymns been practiced by shaky
woman tongues we put each into each,
I would have sheltered here.

In the Georgia O'Keeffe Museum

A swollen hive opens its fluttering eye.
My gaze slides over ten unnamed cities.
So many people not to think of,
so many countries of thought
where I cannot take refuge.

Stopped at the viewing line,
I lean toward gold-framed petals
and wade into red cannas.

I burn your letters again,
unsettled your vases, my face
and mouth full of your weather.

I am exalted by the pianist ruffling
the same notes in the lobby. Across the room,
heels snap the floor into applause.

I'm undoing your sashes again,
lowering your skirt. Into the rushes, up against
the veins and dew, I press my mouth;
horses canter into the red wake.

Era of a Happy Heart

It was a marriage of August and dirty dishes.
A moth settled for three days on the wall behind the bed.

I brought my eyes into the room of her eyes.
I came away with black brown heather muslin dust.

I said, "Now I'm going to undress you"
and washed against a creature of air.

The ceiling spoke a trick of wood knots, changing
scripture of the slope. I wondered about a life spent alone.

For hours a violin played down the hall. I said, "Look,
a hundred black birds rising in unison."

The mind of sadness was unified flight,
the aerodynamics of the flock in a neighboring field.

The dogs in the valley tore the silence open
for a passing fox. Her breath fasted on dream.

I came away with black brown heather muslin dust.
Shadows stole knowledge of her in their disposal of the day.

Here

I call your body *home* and listen
for all the rooms I'll occupy,
the brag of my heels on marble,
a curtain's steady notes,
tonguing the wall.

Quiet afternoons
when the postman passes
at three, sorting the day's news.

The prayer I bend into you
finds a thief with her hand
in the silverware drawer.

The light divvying up
dust motes where red silk poppies
anchor a web by the door.

I fall into the greedy
snapping of breath in the well
which is your kiss.

And later, silence is a trophy
in every room, owning the days
with its crumpled sheets and
many, many questions.

ALYSE
KNORR

Alyse Knorr is the author of *Copper Mother* (Switchback Books, forthcoming), *Annotated Glass* (Furniture Press Books, 2013), and *Alternates* (dancing girl press, 2014). Her work has appeared or is forthcoming in *Denver Quarterly, Hayden's Ferry Review, ZYZZYVA, Columbia Poetry Journal, The Greensboro Review,* and *The Southern Poetry Anthology* (Texas Review Press, 2012), among others. She received her MFA from George Mason University. She serves as a founding co-editor of Gazing Grain Press and teaches at the University of Alaska Anchorage.

Fact-Checking

"You're a long sad book about love," she said. Or I said, about myself. We were smoking inside Darwin's—back when you still could smoke inside—and eating the free popcorn and drinking the cheap beer. After the Rainier bottle-cap puzzles ran out, we'd turned to a game called Which Book Are You. She was a bestseller I lost on the bus. She was a work in translation. She was the one I kept starting over.

She picked up my wrist and held it. She was always doing that—tugging at me, staking her claims. But she had none, at least technically. I was dating a man at the time—a truly Good Guy. And she had set us up.

"Let's try and see the Titbook," she said next. "I'll ask the waitress."

"No," I said, "It's taking advantage."

"Don't you want to see what another woman's breasts look like?" she asked. This was a test or a flirtation or both.

"I have to work early," I said. "I'll call you for lunch." And so there were no tits that night.

The truth is, I'd loved her since we were fifteen and met on the ski team. She was always warm, no matter what the temperature. She could sit beside me on the bus and heat me like a furnace.

My job at the paper was to check the facts and edit the copy. In practice, this meant correcting commas for eight hours a day. I didn't mind cleaning up after others. I didn't mind having no byline. It felt comforting to make a decision and immediately take action on it, even about something as small as a comma.

The fact-changing began as a one-time affair. I still remember the headline: "MOOSE OVER-RUNNING KINCAID PARK." I'd gone back and forth on whether to add the word "are": "Moose *are* over-running Kincaid Park." I didn't want to insert a clunky "to be" verb, but as it was, it sounded like only one moose was over-running the whole park.

And that's when I got the idea. The article's lead read, "A female moose protecting her calf charged a skier Monday at Kincaid Park on the Roller Coaster trail." And just as easily as I would correct a comma, I changed "calf" to "calves." Just like that, the moose had twins. In that moment, reality changed entirely, and I was the one who had changed it.

In fact, the closest I ever came to dying, I had thought of her. We were on a team-building trip whitewater rafting near Hope. Six of us in the boat plus the red-bearded guide in the back shouting out paddle commands. She was right behind me, and she was seventeen like me. Seventeen meant I had never once thought of death.

We hurtled over an eddy and crashed down bow-first. Water rushed into my corner of the raft, and the front lip caved into the river, and then I couldn't breathe—sucked out of the raft and helmet smacked against rock, and my very next thought was, *Did she see it happen?* I was hoping to make her worry, to wring her hands and watch me drift downstream, struggling to turn onto my back like the guide had instructed: *Let the current take you; don't struggle.*

I looked upstream for the raft and saw a yellow speck. Cold river trickled under my fingers, and I imagined the way water flowed over her skin in the shower, her fingers running through her soapy hair. She actually dyed her hair purple later, in college down in Seattle, and gained weight, then lost it again—plus much more—on an all-saltine cracker diet she adopted for various roles in various plays put on by the theatre troupe.

Through the window of the sandwich shop, we watched a line of tourists shuffle around the block clutching cartoon maps and water bottles.

"You know I skipped bingo for you," she said. She worked at an assisted living facility called Anchorage Manor. Her job was to plan the activities—crafts, spelling bees, and movie nights where they served mocktails. Those living with assistance were never allowed alcohol.

"Listen," I said. "Do you think the Titbook's real?"

Specific rumors about the Titbook varied depending on whom you asked. According to some, only women were allowed access to it—and only if they agreed to a Polaroid of their own breasts first. Like a sisterhood of tits. Others had it that the exchange was "a shot for a shot." And still others claimed that there was no Titbook at all, or that the bartenders only showed the book to those they thought would be too drunk to remember it.

"Why don't you do a story on it and find out?" she said. "Isn't that the whole point of the paper? To uncover the truth?"

"Yeah, right," I said. "I'd never do that."

"What are you so afraid of?" she asked, and her eyes locked on mine and made their point known.

For years we'd been doing this dance—testing each other, slowly building a case. About 60 percent of the time, I was sure she wanted me. But that wasn't enough to tell her. There was too much at stake. It was too great a gamble.

A week or two after the moose, in an article about the Salmon Derby in Seward, I changed the weight of the prize salmon from 51.4 pounds to 51.9. I knew the winning fisherman wouldn't call in to report an error half a pound in his favor. This was the art—getting away with it, of course, but more importantly, ensuring that the fact change did not disrupt anything essential to the story's meaning. That, I decided, would be unethical, and I am a very ethical person.

So I never gave misinformation or invented quotes. It was the small details I altered, and in this way it felt like leaving my mark. Like an artist's signature—like finding the artist's hand in a painting's tiny brushstrokes. I started to love seeing copies of the paper around town in a way I never had before. A thrill went through me every time, knowing at least one of my secrets always lay inside.

One year I flew down to surprise her when she was a Shark in the chorus of West Side Story, and I was shocked at how thin she was. All golden eyes hungry and hollowed out in her skull. She didn't even have a speaking part. All I wanted was to hold her shaky bones in my hands and feed her directly from my mouth, and I wanted to put her fingers into my mouth, too, and that's when I first realized that, like her, all I am is hunger and need.

Sometimes she'd call me from the Manor after she put the Assisted to bed. We'd do crosswords over the phone together or watch *Bewitched* and fight over which Dick we liked better. I'd cross out commas and listen to all the things she had to say.

"It's depressing around here," she might mutter.

"Isn't it your job to keep them happy?" I'd ask.

"There's only so much you can do," she'd say, "to make them remember who they are."

That afternoon, I made my biggest fact change yet. The story was about a brown bear who'd been shot in Girdwood after breaking into a house. He had smelled a pizza cooling on someone's kitchen counter and had smashed in a window to get it. The homeowner had shot him three times with a shotgun.

My first thought was: What a stupid reason to die. For pizza, of all things. But then I felt embarrassed for the bear, and then I felt sorry for him. He was either so hungry he had to barge into someone's home, or so brave he didn't care. One was pitiable and one was admirable, and as I sat at my desk, oscillating between these two feelings, I realized that I couldn't tell the difference, and that the difference didn't matter.

I was *The Great Gatsby*, and she was *The Sound and the Fury*. I was *100 Years of Solitude*, and she was *Gone with the Wind*.

I was surprised when she came back North after college. I thought she'd move to New York and star in off-off, then off, then Broadway productions. Singing and acting and dancing were all she'd ever cared about. Once I'd asked her how she could be so completely—so believably—someone else, and she shrugged and said, "That's why it's called *acting*." And I knew then that she would ruin me all the way through.

The only thing that could be done to restore the bear's dignity was to retell this one part of the story—how many shots it had taken to bring him down. In one quick moment I blacked out the "three" and changed it to "six." Then I stood up quickly and carried the page down the hall to the copy chief for final proofing.

The whole walk back to my desk, my hands shook and I was hot with fear and relief. I reached for the phone as soon as I sat down.

"It's me," I said. "Do you have a movie night tonight?"

"Yeah, *A League of Their Own*," she said. "But I can skip."

"Okay. Let's do Darwin's at nine."

"I've always loved what a wild woman you are," she said.

By ten we were silly drunk and by eleven she had cried once, put her hand on my knee once, and interrupted me in the middle of a story to hug me because I was so funny and she loved me so much and she was so, so glad we're friends.

As the night went on, tourists smelling like hotels and buses started crowding the small bar, knocking over beers with their elbows and pointing at locals indiscriminately.

"Let's get out of here," she said, taking my hand, and we walked down Sixth to the Inlet.

The ravens had all changed into their summer whites and were cawing so loud I could barely hear her when she said, "Tell me a secret."

"What kind?" I asked. "You know all of mine."

"If I knew all your secrets," she said, "I wouldn't still hang around you."

I thought of the bear dying with the taste of hot bread in his mouth. I thought of the way her chin tucked to her chest when she glided down a hill. I thought of myself, in the ladies room after her play, holding my head in my hands and breathing.

"Tell yours first," I said, and the gulls cawed at the thumbprint moon, and we both felt lonely.

"I don't think I've ever been really loved," she said. "Except by you."

"What?" I asked. A hole tore open in my stomach. "You know?" And she did.

"No," she said. "Tell me."

"Well, it's true."

She was sitting beside me in the cool air pumping out heat like a radiator. Across the bay, Susitna slept in the purple light, waiting in the water for her love to come back to life.

"Yes," she said. "It is." And that's when she put her hand on top of mine, and my chest tightened and released all at once. In that moment I felt like she'd opened some kind of backdoor in my life I didn't know was there. I was seventeen again—seventeen still—and I would never, ever die. She kissed my hand, and I couldn't believe it. She looked in my eyes, and I couldn't believe it. She leaned in, and my heart was drowning itself.

We talked for hours, long after the sun finished setting. Making plans, telling our stories. Laughing about how long it had taken. I felt like I was at the first act of my own wedding. She held my hand, and she traced my lifeline. She found herself in all my futures.

Once, on the trail, her boot had unclipped from her ski and, frozen, wouldn't snap back in again. I stopped and walked through the pines the rest of the way with her, our poles and skis propped across our shoulders. We were still half a mile out when two huge, snow-covered dogs came sprinting down the path toward us. Their harnesses jingled, and their tongues lolled, giddy.

"Hey!" she said. "Just where do you think you're going?"

The dogs stopped immediately, looked at one another for a moment, then turned around and ran back the way they'd come.

"Everything is urgent when you're in love," she'd said.

She took it all back the next morning, of course. I had run all the way home and barely slept. At six I got out of bed, put on my best shirt, and cooked a big breakfast of waffles and eggs. Made a smoothie and drank it too fast, imagining and imagining what could possibly happen next. I had never been happier.

I was washing the dishes when she called. My heart hummed like an engine.

"Hello?"

"Hi, it's me. Listen, we need to talk about what I said last night."

"Okay?"

"I wasn't feeling well, and I had taken a lot of cough syrup and Tylenol PM. I don't remember what I told you, exactly, but whatever it was, I didn't mean it."

The way she said it—the complete honesty in her lie—felt like a new silver fish just pulled from a foreign river—glittering, cold, and alive. Like these were the first words ever spoken in time. They were so pure and beautiful in their devastation that I didn't even try to fight it. "Are you sure?" was all I asked.

"Yes, it's true."

If the Titbook is real, then it is full now of breasts that might be dead, might be biowaste, might be full of milk. This is why I am afraid of it. The permanence of a photo is not what's troubling, but the impermanence of flesh. All those women and their lives— their possible, delicate lives.

I stopped changing facts after the bear, but years later, I woke in the night thinking, Of course I'm not the only one. Perhaps the home- owner changed the facts. Perhaps the State Trooper who salvaged the skull and pelt did. Perhaps enough facts have been changed, or could be changed, to alter the bear's fate entirely. Perhaps he is on this very day eating a king salmon on the bank of a cool fast stream.

After I hung up the phone, this is what I did. I sat completely still and listened to the stillness. I listened to her words in my head and to the clock's second hand and to the trucks rattling down the highway and to a dog standing on top of his doghouse barking. The answer, it finally dawned on me, was to take action and go someplace else.

But there was nothing to do, nowhere to go to survive that stillborn love. So I finished the dishes and left in my good shirt and walked under the brilliant, manic sun to the office. I let myself in with my keycard and took the elevator up to the paper and crawled under the copy table to shake like the addict I was. If this was an earthquake then I would hold on, surrounded by whatever I called facts.

Anchorage Epithalamium

Love punched my brains out like
Artie in the post office parking lot—
"A big Samoan hit me and now it feels
like there's computers in my eye."
Everything big and distorted with
the 19-hour days and the 19-hour nights,
mountains balding into summer now
as tourist traffic materializes onto streets
we first learned empty and white. All
I want: to explore the wilderness of Costco
with you in the Dimond District,
buy a new set of Tupperware with red
lids and smooth sides. To be tamed
with you and tell you every night
which are satellites, planes, and stars.

Moose are over-running the park and this makes me think of love

In autumn, everyone weds—the moose find one another
to mate and calve, tolerating gasps and photos until
an "incident" occurs. Too many dogs off leash.

Too many runners distracted by iPods. Too many reasons
not to trust, not to say about the beautiful thing: *That is beautiful.*
Like the frosty October morning when the man, whose face

bones were crushed last year by a charging bull, reaches for
his handgun at the sight of a cow with twins. Haven't we all been
crushed? Haven't we all closed our eyes once? To love—

just to speak of it—requires a courage that only love itself provides.
In this line, the cow and her twins slip back into the trees.
In this one, I hold your hand and we marry in the trees.

The trees marry the moose. The moose marry the runners.
But weren't we the runners all along? Running toward each other—
toward the call we heard before we even recognized it.

an epithalamium for Larissa and Brian

The Object Towards Which the Action of the Sea Is Directed

is the Aleut word for Alaska, a passive voice
construction that would mean docked points,
were this a sentence in one of my freshmen essays
about a belief they hold or a problem they see
in the world around them. *One problem is passive
voice,* I say. *Cultivate your own unique voice,* I say.
One girl writes of her reign as a native beauty
pageant queen. Another, of the smell of whale
blubber frying in a city so far north, haloes of ice
arc above the sky. Slowly, Ovid's Io turns to Isis
turns to Raven and takes off. Their textbooks lie
open on the desks. The days are growing colder.

The Sleeping Lady

Susitna slumbers high above Anchorage,
dreaming of her beloved, who took a javelin
to the gut the day before their wedding.
And you, biking home from work tonight,
are 20 minutes late. If you die, who will
cover me in snow and trees? Who will keep
me sleeping, with you not there to weight
the room?
        At the Crow Creek Gold Mine,
I found three flakes of gold, you, four, all seven
included in our plastic baggie practice packets.
We walked a trail of rusted shovels to a cold
river, singing "sluicebox, sluicebox" because
we liked the sound. We returned to a wedding
reception with a DJ and cake.
        If I could marry
you, I would marry you in a river full of gold.
Inside one ghost cabin, a tiny balance scale
weighed a nugget and two pennies. On the wall,
a black and white photo of someone's mother.
Your face mirrored the glass and the music
kept playing. Trail maps, table of lanterns,
bear pelt bed and foggy moonshine bottles.
And we wed and wed and wed.

Conservation & Rehabilitation

Because we want to take pictures of bears and moose
without actually coming near them—though
already I have called to you, unloading groceries
from the car, when a cow and her calf clopped down
our street, taller than I thought, and faster, too—because
we want to look like *real Alaskans* to those East Coast
city slickers, those smog-breathers, those subway-riders,
our friends back home, we drive down the only highway
to the Center where, every five minutes for the duration
of our visit, we hear the eerie shrieks of the elk, calling
for one another in urgent lust, which at first I decide is
the angry scream of a small girl throwing a tantrum
in five-minute intervals but which Wikipedia
informs me is "one of the most distinctive sounds
in nature, akin to the howl of the gray wolf." And later,
when we learn from a colorful sign that females are attracted
to the elk that bugle the loudest and most often, I sympathize
more with the elk and with the caribou, too, locking
their antlers into one another because everyone in this Center
is in love, including me, because when I stare at you staring
at a muddy bison sleeping pressed flush against the wire
of her fence, and when I see your mouth move, and then
later, before I put my mouth on you, when I ask what you talked
with the bison about, you say *We understood each other,* which
I take to mean:
      Bison: *There is nowhere for me to be safe*
      Woman I love: *I have been your kind*
      [an elk shrieks]

Love, let's be the black bears that refuse our sirloin
steaks, turning our noses up to the Lead Naturalist,
or the intern—whoever is feeding us that day—waiting
patiently for a handful of frozen berries flung into
our yard. Let's be those bears who come when called,
eat our fill of this land, then pad back together into
the thick brush, trying to be as wild as we still can.

TERESA
SUNDMARK

Teresa Sundmark lives in Homer, Alaska. She has an MFA in Creative Writing from UAA. Her poetry and fiction have been featured in *Cirque: A Literary Journal for the North Pacific Rim*, and her essays have been syndicated through *High Country News*. In 2011, she was the winner of the Nicole Blizzard Short Story Contest. Teresa works in a public library and teaches for the Kachemak Bay Branch of the Kenai Peninsula College. She blogs about writing, small-town life, and various other subjects at loftyminded.com.

Worse Disasters

The first time we saw Lola in her pink housedress and rubber boots, shuffling across the road to show us the small rental house she owned, we had lost our faith in landlords.

It was 1972. A year earlier, when Leah and I were nineteen years old, we'd left Colorado and hitchhiked up the Al-Can together. It wasn't unusual for adventurous, single girls to head for Alaska, but everyone assumed we'd each embarked on the journey in order to find a man. What we really wanted was just to get on with living our lives far away from our families.

My family and Leah's family attended the same church. There's no way we could stay in the same small Colorado town and not get found out, so we hatched the plan to head to Alaska. Everyone thought it was unsavory for two church-going girls to embark on such a journey, but since everyone knew about the high ratio of men to women in Alaska, they didn't put up too much of a fight about our going.

Our year away from home had been eye opening. Anyone new to seven-month-long winters and never-ending summer days could say the same thing, but I doubt that most people experienced the same renting trouble that Leah and I experienced once we landed in Anchorage.

Our first landlord was Bob and he was great ninety-eight percent of the time. But the things about us that didn't seem to bother him when he was sober, he felt free to comment on during the two percent of the time when he was drunk.

One summer night, he had some friends over for poker, and when we walked toward the mother-in-law cottage we rented in his backyard, he yelled out his screened window, "Hey girls, come on in. An hour or two with us and you might decide you like dick after all."

He acted genuinely surprised and disappointed when we moved out at the end of the month.

Our next landlord was Regina, and besides being crazy, she raised our rent after we wouldn't do LSD with her and her boyfriend on Christmas Eve. Our time living in her little conglomeration of log cabins was short-lived.

We were hopeful that our most recent landlords, Mr. and Mrs. Pitman, would mind their own business and leave us alone. And we were careful around them. We even lied to them, telling them that we were just two single girls waiting for our boyfriends to get home from Vietnam. We'd had a decent six-month run of renting from them until one Saturday in mid-August when Mr. Pitman revealed his true nature.

"Mrs. Pitman would be heartbroken if she knew about the two of you," he said after a Bloody Mary fueled morning of mowing the grass around the duplex. "She doesn't think your way of life is natural." He wiped his brow with his arm. "Hell, I don't think it's natural either, especially for a couple of nice-looking women like yourselves."

Then he looked us over. When his gaze stopped on Leah's chest, I knew it was time to start poring over the classified ads again.

We bought the *Anchorage Times* every day, but none of the advertised rentals seemed like a good fit. The landlords either lived too close by—a problem with people in our situation—or the price was too high. We'd almost resigned ourselves to staying in creepy Mr. Pitman's duplex when we came across an index card pinned to a bulletin board in the Laundromat.

The card was hung vertically, and an intricate, pencil-drawn tree took up three-quarters of the space. Above the tree it said, *Small house for rent. Wooded neighborhood. Fenced yard.* No price was listed, so we called the number from a payphone. We made arrangements to go see the place.

We had trouble finding it because the streets weren't clearly marked and the directions I'd taken from Lola Miller weren't exactly easy to follow: *First turn left off of Northern Lights onto Haddock Street, then follow that road until you see the house with the jeep. Then turn left and go around a bend. Then when you get to a place where the spruce trees have been cut and a trailer is on the side of the road, go about another half mile. When you see the house with the ducks in the yard, you'll know you're on the right track. Take your next right and then you're there.* Finally, after driving around in the rain and looking for a house with ducks in the yard, we found what we thought was the right place to turn.

"I want it," Leah said, before we'd even gotten out of the car.

"This might not even be it," I said. But I looked at the door and knew it was the right place. A tree, in the same design as the one on the index card, was carved into the front door.

I wanted it, too.

The house was green and small—tiny, actually—but it looked well put together. The unassuming front of the house faced the street, and a newish-looking wooden fence enclosed the backyard. A chimney jutting out of the roof suggested a woodstove—something we both wanted—and the raspberry patch in the vacant lot next door was dripping with overripe berries. Lola Miller said she would meet us there at five o'clock, but we were ten minutes late since we'd had trouble finding the place.

"What if we lost our chance?" I asked, but right after I'd spoken the words, we saw a small, dark-haired woman step out of the house across the street and begin to head toward us. She looked up just long enough to give us a cursory wave, and then she walked the rest of the way with her eyes on the ground. Even with the rain coming down hard, her steps were small, and her movements slow.

When she finally arrived next to our truck, keys to the house in hand, she was nearly out of breath.

"I'm sorry we're late," Leah said. "We got a little turned around."

"It's fine," Lola Miller said, looking up at us again finally.

Her skin was so pale it was nearly translucent, and her brown eyes were set back far into her face. Her lips were bright red with lipstick, applied recently, as though lipstick alone was all that was required as far as appearance was concerned.

"Mrs. Miller," I said, since I was the one who had spoken to her on the phone, "I'm Annie, and this is my friend Leah."

"Please call me Lola," she said.

"Lola, is this the house? Because it looks like it would cost more to rent than what you quoted us on the phone," I said.

"Yes, this is it," she said. "I suppose I could get more for it. I don't know though, I'm new to all of this. Do you want to have a look around?"

Lola struggled to get the key in the lock with her shaky hands. Watching her was not confidence inspiring.

Inside the house, there were men's boots and jackets in the arctic entry. In the living room there were *Life* magazines on the coffee table and a sweater folded over the back of the sofa.

"When will the house be vacant?" I asked Lola Miller.

"It's been vacant for almost a year," she said, without offering any explanation for the personal items strewn about the house.

Behind Lola's back, Leah gave me a look. It was a look she reserved for the times when words couldn't be exchanged. She'd given me that look on our way up to Alaska, when a man in a station wagon picked us up and instead of talking like a normal person, he sang all of his conversation with us. "Where are you going, young women of grace?" he'd asked us, in operatic form. It went on like that for two hours through Canada.

And now, at this house that seemed perfect in so many ways, we could tell that something was wrong. Really wrong. Maybe Ms. Lola was crazy.

"I'll tell you what. I'll give you the first month for free if you can clear the stuff out of here. There's not too much because my son only lived here for a month. He still wasn't entirely moved out of our house across the street when he died."

Leah and I exchanged looks again.

"Oh Lola, I'm so sorry," Leah said. She was so good in these kinds of situations. She always knew what to say, unlike me who wanted to slink out the door unnoticed when things got uncomfortable. "What was your son's name?"

"Darren," Lola said. "He couldn't cope well with things."

She didn't offer more information. Instead she continued showing us through the house. It didn't take long since there were only five rooms including the arctic entry—a kitchen, living room, bathroom and bedroom. The stovepipe we'd seen was attached to a woodstove that had clearly never been used.

"We put in the woodstove for backup, in case the electricity ever went out, but we never had a reason to use it," she said by way of explanation.

Lola then took us into the backyard. It was completely overgrown, like nobody had touched it all summer.

"How are you girls with yard work?" Lola asked.

"Good. Really good. I don't mind shoveling snow, either," Leah said.

This time, I was the one giving Leah the look. Potentially renting this house from Lola Miller made me nervous. Lola made me nervous. I'd only been around her for a few minutes, but I could sense that she needed more from us than rent money, and I wasn't sure if we were the ones to help her.

"How do you feel about dogs?" Lola asked. "Because this backyard was designed with a dog in mind."

That was when Lola Miller started crying.

Right there, in that moment, I saw the biggest difference between Leah and myself. While I started backing toward the door, Leah went right to Lola. She put her arms around her shoulders and led her toward the sofa. She sat her down and then went into the bathroom and returned with a box of tissue.

"I gave myself a year," Lola said, between sobs. "But maybe it's too soon."

"It's okay," Leah said to her in her most soothing voice. "If you're not ready to rent the place out, we'll understand."

"Do you like the house, though? Do you think you'd like living here? It only has one bedroom, you know."

"Well, Mrs. Miller—I mean Lola, we only need one bedroom. And I think we'd love living here. It might even be good for you to see people living over here."

Lola stopped crying and looked up, first at Leah and then at me. I wanted to exchange a look with Leah, but for the first time, Lola Miller was looking up at us for a sustained amount of time.

Leah and I had agreed that this time around we'd work hard to hide our relationship with each other from any potential landlord— it seemed like the most prudent thing to do if we found a place we really wanted—but now Leah had blurted out that we only needed one bedroom.

"You might be ready to rent the house out, but maybe not to people like us," Leah finally said to break the uncomfortable silence and to aid Lola Miller in her state of bewilderment. "You wouldn't be the first."

That was just like Leah to give people the first out, to give them the words they might not know that they were looking for.

Lola Miller straightened her hunched shoulders. She grabbed another tissue and blew her nose.

"Let me tell you girls something," she said in a voice stronger than I thought possible out of someone who just moments before seemed so meek. "A week from tomorrow is September 4, and do you remember what happened last year on September 4?"

"We were just moving here in September last year," I said carefully, because I felt like giving the wrong answer would not be okay in this situation.

"I remember," said Leah. "We'd just arrived in Anchorage, and it was all anyone could talk about."

I remembered the headlines now.

"My husband and my son were on that airplane. It crashed right into the side of a mountain in the middle of the day." Lola stood up and walked toward the front door.

At the doorway she turned back to look at us.

"Every day for the past year I've played the last conversation I had with my son over and over in my head. 'You don't need to be so afraid of flying,' I told him. 'You just pull yourself together and get right on that airplane and it will be over before you know it,' I told him."

She leaned her head against the doorframe. "He had trouble coping, you see, with everything. He couldn't go to the store by himself. As a boy he'd get sick just going to school. He was thirty-two years old and moving into this house right across the street from his parents was his single biggest accomplishment. Getting on that airplane was his second biggest one."

"I'm sorry if I've upset you," Leah said. "And I'm so sorry for your loss. I can't even imagine what this year has been like for you."

"I'm not upset with you," Lola said in her steadiest voice yet. She lifted her head from the doorframe, and ran her fingers through her hair. "I know I must seem a mess, but every day for a year now I've wondered about that moment of impact. Every day I've wondered if either of them even had time for a final thought before the plane crashed into the side of that mountain. Every day I've wished I hadn't pushed my son toward every single thing he was afraid of." She paused for a second and then said in almost a whisper, "That, my dear girls, is a lot to cope with."

Lola Miller opened the front door of the little green house that a few years down the line we'd eventually buy from her and stepped down onto the lawn. She walked a few paces toward her own home before she turned back.

"After the year I've been through, I think there are worse disasters than two women sharing a bed, and I'd be a fool to let something like that bother me. A damn fool."

Then Lola continued across the street. She walked twice as fast as when she walked over. She no longer kept her eyes on the ground.

Trespass

David's first reaction when he saw the snapshot of his daughter was to clench his jaws and mutter a prayer. It didn't matter that she looked good or that her smile was more at ease than David had seen in a long time. In the photo she wore a backpack on the top of some mountain with her long hair pulled back in a purple bandana. The view behind her looked like it could be in Colorado, or maybe Utah.

It wasn't unusual for him to get a postcard; she sent one whenever her nursing job landed her in a new location. But it had been a long time since Rebecca had written a letter. And after seeing the photo, the first he'd seen of her in nearly three years, he knew this was the one he'd been expecting, dreading for the past few months. Without reading it, he tucked it back in the envelope postmarked this time from New Mexico, and stuffed it into the pocket of his flannel shirt. He turned his four-wheeler away from the mailbox and headed toward the primitive trail he'd worn into the sage and scrub-grass covered hill behind his house.

Rebecca called every May, even though he'd stopped answering a long time ago, and her message was always the same. "Daddy, I think about you this time of year," as though he hadn't moved on from the accident that had happened over twenty-five years ago. She was only a toddler when her mother died, and David couldn't understand her nostalgia for a time before her memory was fully formed. But he didn't understand much of anything about his daughter and had long ago decided to give his relationship with her over to God. Praying for her was much easier than talking to her.

"Lord, have mercy on Rebecca," David said between breaths as the four-wheeler started its climb up the slope. "Help her find her way back to You."

David was anxious to get to the spot where he had been spending his afternoons lately when Vivian wanted him out of the house—to the place on the top of the hill where he could settle in for a while under the shade of an old stand of juniper trees and look across the valley to the sandstone cliffs on the other side. From there he could look down on his town, see it from a different perspective.

David had only glanced at the picture of his daughter, but her image stayed with him as he struggled to navigate the ATV over the rocky terrain. She looked so much like her mother. They had identical dimples on their right cheeks and the same slight gap between their two front teeth; big enough to make their smiles memorable, but not so wide as to render them unattractive. And it didn't slip past David that Rebecca was older in this photo than Ivajean had ever been. He stopped part way to wipe the sweat from his forehead and take a drink of the iced-tea from the thermos Vivian had packed for him, but the heaviness of the letter against his chest persisted.

He restarted the four-wheeler and lurched forward, still awkward with the clutch even after several months of practice. "Heavenly Father, help me get to the top of this hill," he whispered. He had spent the summer trying to make himself an outdoorsman, but he suspected it might be too late for him. He'd always felt most comfortable indoors with a stack of books and a cool glass of water nearby, not exposed on a hillside in the heat of the day.

He wished he could turn around and drive back to town—find some solace in his old church office. But he wasn't a pastor anymore. He didn't have any sermons to write or any parishioners to counsel and the new minister had moved in and made changes David couldn't understand. Was it really necessary to use a slide show from a computer to keep a congregation's attention? What was the matter with good, old-fashioned preaching? Vivian warned him about getting worked up, but he didn't like the way things were changing, didn't like that nothing with his daughter or with his church were as he'd imagined they'd be. But David knew things weren't meant to be easy. He knew that with everything, there was a price to pay.

When he was young and fresh out of Bible school, David thought he was prepared to lead a quiet life, serving his congregation and setting an example of pious living. But seeing Ivajean in the second row of the choir on his first Sunday at the Billings First Assembly sent him in a direction that strayed from his best intentions. She was too beautiful to be a minister's wife. He should have passed her over, should have paid closer attention to the girl standing beside her with the glasses and the straight brown hair, but his eyes stopped on Ivajean, her black hair, her red lips against pale skin.

He claimed it was Ivajean's love for God that captured him, and it's true he noticed the way she closed her eyes as she sang, true that she looked enraptured. But what he knew, and was ashamed to admit, was that seeing her in such a state made him imagine being on the receiving end of her attention, and that notion, once in his head, wasn't something he could shake. They were married two months later and after their honeymoon in Helena, David suspected that he'd taken more than he was meant to have.

He thought the heat between them would die down, but the passion persisted, grew even, and carried over into places it shouldn't have, like his church office, and behind the pulpit, and on the red-carpeted floor in front of the altar. One Thursday afternoon, she brought him his lunch from the parsonage, like she did every day, but this time her hair was still damp from her bath and the lavender scented powder she would often sprinkle on before bedtime caught his attention. Her crossed legs, smooth and unencumbered by stockings, beckoned to him from across his desk as he ate his sandwich. He tried to tell her about the sermon he was preparing for next Sunday's service, and she pretended to listen for a moment, but then she raised her index finger to her mouth. "Shush, why don't you take a break for a few minutes, let me minister to you for a while." She pulled the curtains closed and made her way to him.

David knew that married couples would have sexual relations, and he thought he knew what that would entail, but Ivajean had a way of surprising him at every turn. That first time he let it go too far, she went to him, guided his hands up her legs to reveal that she wore nothing beneath her skirt, and before he realized what was happening, they were sprawled on the flat hard surface of his desk, doing things he knew should only happen in the marriage bed. And when they finished, and Ivajean walked toward the door with his empty brown lunch bag in her hands, David told her that what they'd done could never happen again.

But Ivajean continued to bring him his lunch several times a week, even after their daughter was born. And on the days she didn't, David would find himself agitated with guilt and distracted by longing. Her afternoon visits only stopped when she drove away from his office that warm afternoon in May and never returned.

Getting remarried after Ivajean died was the right thing to do. David would never have been able to raise a child on his own, or keep up with the demands of his church without Vivian. She was always ready with a snack or a cool drink if a church member stopped by, and she could pull together a hot dish on short notice if there was a death or a new baby in the congregation. And it didn't take long for him to see that Vivian was a better homemaker than Ivajean had been. She knew how to discipline Rebecca and how to time supper just right so it was ready for him when he came home from the office. Vivian seemed to delight in housekeeping, whereas Ivajean, who had been known to let Rebecca run wild while she spend hours flipping through magazines, showed little interest in domestic chores.

With Vivian, David could concentrate on the plans God had in store for him. He didn't have to worry about church members knocking on his office door at inopportune times, or spend hours praying for forgiveness. He could put his energy into compelling sermons and community outreach. In fact, he noticed that his congregation began to grow shortly after Ivajean's death. He wondered if the vibrancy of his church meant that God had not forsaken him. Ivajean was gone, and that was his cross to bear for the way he'd allowed her to distract him from his church, but maybe he was still a part of God's plan.

David finally reached the top of the mesa where the trail flattened out. His breathing returned to normal with the difficult portion of the ride behind him and his destination only a few hundred feet away. He kept a folding chair there and always brought along the tuna fish sandwich that Vivian packed for him. Sometimes he would hike around, looking for arrowheads or deer antlers, but mostly he just sat and talked with God. He felt powerful up there where he could look down on the town and pray for God's protection over the schools and the churches and the business district. And he knew he was making a difference. Just a couple of months ago, the school board passed a resolution stating it wouldn't allow evolution to be taught without the mention of Creationism. He had hoped his prayers for Rebecca would be so potent, but as far as he could tell, nothing with her had changed.

He may not have noticed it on his own, but Vivian, always more observant, began to see signs when Rebecca was in high school. For one, she never seemed interested in babies. While the other teenaged girls relished every opportunity to help out in the church nursery, Rebecca kept her distance. And she didn't care about the normal girl things, like fashion, or boys. At first David was angry with Vivian for suggesting such a thing about his daughter, but he began to think she might be right when Rebecca, shortly after her eighteenth birthday, left town with a woman five years her senior.

The letter in his breast pocket, the one he had been dreading, was long, and David knew what it would say. She'd given him some warning of what was to come when she mentioned her friend Molly in the last three postcards. They were traveling together, she'd written, and looking for a more permanent place to settle down. It was her way of telling him, without telling him, and now he wished that would have been enough.

God could change Rebecca. David believed it without a doubt. But so far, his prayers had gone unanswered. As he parked his four-wheeler in its usual spot beside the trees, he wondered why God would care more about his concerns for the school board than the situation with his daughter. He sat in his folding chair, relieved to be still for a moment after his journey up the hill. "What more can I do, Lord?" he asked out loud, leaning back in the chair to let the early afternoon breeze drift over him.

If it hadn't been for the breeze, David probably wouldn't have noticed the fire. But as it was, a small southerly gust caused the fire to crackle, which in turn caught David's attention. On closer inspection, he could see the most subtle drift of smoke arising from the charcoaled log that sat in the fire pit.

In the spring, when the mornings were still damp and cool, David sometimes built a small fire and drank his coffee while he waited for the day to warm. But his last fire was several months ago. He put his hand next to the coals to see if his eyes were tricking him. He felt heat. He got up to look around for more evidence of the trespassers—food wrappers or footprints, perhaps. At first glance, nothing seemed out of the ordinary, but when he was about to return to his chair, he noticed a brown-and-black checkered blanket folded in the shade of the oldest juniper tree. It was camouflaged by shadows. He saw it only because of a small speck of red sticking out from between its folds. David walked over, stood above it, and with the point of his cowboy boot kicked open the blanket to reveal a small box of condoms.

He knelt down to inspect the package and was relieved to find it unopened. Clearly though, someone left the condoms with a plan of coming back. He tried not to, but he couldn't help imagining a young couple, intertwined and fumbling, shameless with just the thin, checkered blanket between their bodies and the soft earth. Maybe the girl was a dark-haired beauty with pale skin. Maybe the boy was tall and skinny—his back covered in acne like his own had been when he was first out of Bible school.

He thought of throwing the blanket and its contents into the fire or strewing the lovers' belongings around in an attempt to shame them upon their return. But instead, he found himself refolding the blanket, tucking the box back into the folds, taking great care to leave his discovery exactly as he'd found it.

Back in his chair, David bowed his head to pray. He meant to plead for their salvation, but the words he spoke were different than he intended. "Dear God, protect them."

Down the hillside and inside his home, Vivian worked hard to keep everything in order. She vacuumed the already clean carpets. She balanced the checkbook to account for each penny.

Below, in town, anonymous cars ferried people to and from their jobs. Indistinguishable children ran and yelled in the schoolyard.

As David reached for the letter in his pocket, he remembered the first time he held Rebecca—her rose petal lips suckling at the air, the tight grasp of her delicate fingers around his own. With the memory of that tiny, perfect child in his arms, David felt a swell of heat come over him, not from the fire, not from the sun. With the surge, which lasted for only the smallest of moments, came questions. Was it possible that God wasn't trying to punish him? Was Ivajean's death simply an accident without any kind of a lesson attached? Was Rebecca living her life exactly as God had intended?

Then David, afraid of the ideas that were multiplying in his mind, stopped himself. He tucked the letter back inside his pocket, bowed his head into that familiar pose, and asked God to forgive him, one more time, for his sins.

INDRA
ARRIAGA

Indra Arriaga is a Mexican artist, writer, and research analyst. She enjoys the great Alaska outdoors from the comfort of warm spaces, along with good food, strong drinks, and great company. A Libra, she is fascinated by noses and is a sucker for full lips.

Fragments

Fragments of light
In the sea.

Fluid pieces
Like blood spilled that runneth over
And taints and stains pieces of my skin.
And suddenly I feel creation, all over again.
I become the lifeless Adam,
Touched by you.

I am now back on my native island, surrounded by the sea and
green fields.
The only noises are the waves and the wind on the trees.
Everything moves really slowly and I am resting with my sister
who is pregnant
And as happy as ever.

So many questions keep racing in my head
And I don't know when I'll know the answers.
It's hard for me to understand that the months will pass and
You will be far away.
You have given me so much,
All of which I carry with me further on in my life.

Now I hear the distant thunder, I better move inside.
Within minutes it will start raining.

Fragments of me,
Divided by you.

Raindrops are fragments of sky,
Droplets of sea returned to me.

Pedazos

Pedazos de luz
En el mar.

Piezas fluidas
Como sangre derramada que se corre
Y tiñe y mancha trozos de mi piel.
Y de repente siento la creación, toda otra vez.
Soy el Adán sin vida,
Tocado por ti.

Ahora estoy en mi isla natal, rodeado del mar y
campos verdes.
Los ruidos sólo son las olas y el viento en los árboles.
Todo se mueve muy lentamente y yo estoy descansando con mi
hermana que está embarazada
Y más feliz que nunca.

Hay tantas preguntas acelerando por mi cabeza
Y no sé cuándo tendré las respuestas.
Es difícil para mí entender que pasarán los meses y
Tú estarás muy lejos.
Tú que me has dado tanto,
Todo lo cual lo llevo conmigo más allá en mi vida.

Ahora escucho los truenos en la distancia, es mejor que entre.
Dentro de unos minutos comenzara a llover.

Pedazos de mí,
Divididos por ti.

Las gotas de lluvia son Pedazos de cielo,
Gotas del mar que vuelven mí.

How different the world through shattered glass.

How different my heart from having loved you.

My mother cries,
At a distance she can see me in pieces,

A useless attempt to gather, and replace.
I sweep as she taught me,
I weep as I walk,
Her footsteps followed.
The light shattered.

The lamp fails,
Its nature distorted and destroyed by fragments of itself.
It's funny how you noticed the different colors of the lizard on the
postcard. The first thing I
noticed was how he laid on his back, dead—or maybe resting. Why
do you think I noticed only
that he was on his back and not the colors that you immediately
saw?

I see how much you miss home.

I don't know if it's better to be in a place that reminds you of what
you love the most . . . or is it a heavy load on your heart to be
reminded of it so often?

Now that I carefully study the belly of the lizard, I notice the blue
of his belly and how it travels to the other parts of his body and
dominates the other colors, but his feet are without color and
they're disfigured and it pains me.

The heatwave . . .
It is unbearable.

Que tan diferente es el mundo a través del vidrio roto.

Cuán diferente mi corazón por haberte amado.

Mi madre llora,
A una distancia ella me puede ver en pedazos,

Un intento inútil para recoger y reemplazar.
Barro como ella me enseñó,
Lloro mientras camino,
Sigo sus pasos.
La luz rota y estrellada.

La lámpara fracasa,
Su naturaleza es distorsionada y destruidas por los Pedazos de sí misma.

Es curioso cómo notaste los diferentes colores de la lagartija en la postal. La primera cosa que yo noté fue que estaba acostada sobre su espalda, muerta—o tal vez descansando. ¿Por qué crees que sólo noté que estaba sobre su espalda y no los colores que tú viste inmediatamente?

Veo lo mucho extrañas tu hogar.

¿No sé si es mejor estar en un lugar que le recuerda de lo que más quieres . . . o es una carga pesada en su corazón el recordarlo tan a menudo?

Ahora que estudio cuidadosamente el vientre de la lagartija, noto el azul de su vientre y cómo viaja a otras partes de su cuerpo y domina los otros colores, pero sus pies no tienen color y están desfigurados y eso me duele.

La ola de calor . . .
Es insoportable.

Right now I'm in a bathing establishment (only females).
The air is filled with high-pitched voices and laughter.
I have been fixing my bicycle all morning, and finally, I made it work.
I'm not a wiz with mechanics but my stubbornness brings out results.
I think of you often, I think of what I'll show you . . . someday, when
I'll be showing you around in my town.

How different the world through shattered glass.

How different my heart from having loved you.

The light shattered.

The lamp fails,
Its nature distorted and destroyed by fragments of itself.

I miss your voice.
Your laughter and clever comments on life and
Other causalities.

It's past midnight; I'm at school, still working; though my eyes start
to fail.
I have coffee at my side, pushing and helping me along.

I think of you in the most peculiar moments and I enjoy it, though I
wish you were closer to me. But things can change quickly.

Fragments of me,
Divided by you.
Raindrops are fragments of sky,
Droplets of sea returned to me.

Ahora estoy en una casa de baños (sólo mujeres).
El aire está lleno de risas y voces con tono altos.
He estado componiendo mi bicicleta toda la mañana, hasta que por fin hice que funcionara.
Yo no soy un genio con los cosas mecánicas pero mi terquedad da resultados.
Yo pienso en ti a menudo, pienso en lo que te voy a mostrar . . . algún día, cuando te mostrare los alrededores de mi ciudad.

Que tan diferente es el mundo a través del vidrio roto.

Cuán diferente mi corazón por haberte amado.

La luz rota y estrellada.

La lámpara fracasa,
Su naturaleza es distorsionada y destruidas por los Pedazos de sí misma.

Extraño tu voz.
Tu risas y chistosos comentarios sobre la vida y
Otras causalidades.

Ya es medianoche; Estoy en la escuela, sigo trabajando; aunque mis ojos comienzan a fallar.
Tengo café a mi lado, empujando y ayudándome.

Pienso en ti en los momentos más peculiares y lo disfruto, aunque deseo que estuvieras más cerca de mí. Las cosas pueden cambiar rápidamente.

Pedazos de mí,
Divididos por ti.
Las gotas de lluvia son Pedazos de cielo,
Gotas del mar que vuelven mí.

How different the world through shattered glass.

How different my heart from having loved you.

It's Sunday evening, the sky hangs heavy on the city and
I am alone.

I feel trapped! My life is small and narrow these days.
Autumn is heavy and in my private life I am torn.
I miss you. I miss a lot of things.

Life goes on around me, people around me are getting married and
having babies, and I don't want any of it. I want out . . .

I'm going to do whatever I want to. I wish so much that you were
here . . .
(I miss driving rented cars . . .)

How different my heart from having loved you.

A useless attempt to gather, and replace.
I sweep as she taught me,
I weep as I walk,
Her footsteps followed.
The light shattered.

Que tan diferente es el mundo a través del vidrio roto.

Cuán diferente mi corazón por haberte amado.

Es domingo por la noche, el cielo se cuelga pesado en la ciudad y estoy sola.

¡Me siento atrapada! Mi vida es pequeña y angosta estos días.
El otoño pesa y en mi vida privada me siento dividida.
Te extraño. Extraño muchas cosas.

La vida sigue a mí alrededor, la gente que me rodea se casado y tienen bebés y yo no quiero nada de eso. Quiero salir . . .

Voy a hacer todo lo yo quiera. Me gustaría tanto que estuvieras aquí . . .
(Echo de menos conducir choches alquilados . . .)

Cuán diferente mi corazón por haberte amado.

Un intento inútil para recoger y reemplazar.
Barro como ella me enseñó,
Lloro mientras camino,
Sigo sus pasos.
La luz rota y estrellada.

In the Bay

I wish you could see what I see
Grey shades layered
Like thick paint on a canvas
Sea.   Sky.   Grey.   Light.

A grey giant ship with blue letters
And red cargo
Is followed by an even bigger one,

Red and black . . . white letters that say HANJIN.
The fog is closing in
And in the middle of it
A small shimmering white boat
With sails against the wind.

En la Bahía

Deseo que pudieras ver lo que yo veo
Sombras grises en capas
Como la pintura espesa sobre lienzo
Mar.   Cielo.   Gris.   Luz.

Una nave gigante y gris con letras azules
Y carga roja
Es seguida por una aún más grande

Rojo y negro . . . letras blancas que dicen HANJIN.
La niebla se cierra
Y en medio de ella
Un pequeño bote blanco y brillante
Con velas contra el viento.

There was a time, she said

There was a time, she said
When cobbled streets were wet and
My footsteps to your door reflected more
Than my feet and the underneath of my red dress

Tak, Tak, Tak
There was a time, she said

When the smell of dirt was being freed by rain
And it made angry ants move animals, plants and
Made us to jump

Ay, Ay, Ay
There was a time, she said

When you foolishly collected clothes drying out in the dark of night
And I heard my name from your lips invoked
The ants grew angry at your feet
Oof, Oof, Oof
There was a time, she said

When the angry ants were no match for me,
Nor my hands, nor my feet
There was a time.
Hubo un tiempo, ella dijo

Hubo un tiempo, ella dijo

Hubo un tiempo, ella dijo
Cuando calles empedradas estaban mojadas y
Mis pasos a tu puerta reflejaban más
Que mis pies y la parte inferior de mi vestido rojo

Tak, Tak, Tak
Hubo un tiempo, ella dijo

Cuando el olor de la tierra fue liberado por la lluvia
E hizo que las hormigas enfadadas movieran animales, plantas y
Nos hicieron saltar

Ay, Ay, Ay
Hubo un tiempo, ella dijo

Cuando tontamente recogías la ropa a secándose en la oscura noche
Y oí mi nombre invocado por tus labios
Las hormigas se enfurecieron a tus pies

Oof, Oof, Oof
Hubo un tiempo, ella dijo

Cuando las hormigas bravas no fueron nada para mí,
Ni para mis manos, ni para mis pies
Hubo un tiempo.

19 Crescent

Queen: "How, from where we started, did we ever reach this Christmas?"
King: "Step by step."
—*The Lion in Winter*

After all the years, all the lovers, and a few significant relationships that broke my heart so it could open; after late nights spent greasing the wheels of corporate America and enduring the inadequacies of the public sector; after making a million mistakes, hurting and being hurt, I still sleep well at night.

I don't know if it's because my conscience is clear or if I've simply lost count of all the lovers that comprised the landscape of my life. Sleep comes no matter what, and all things lived, big and small, are folded into my body's history.

Illusions and disillusions, doing and undoing, creating and destroying, it all leads to the same place.

The 19 Crescent rattles the tracks and cradles my sleep. The journey is long from New York to New Orleans. The landscape is foreign to me. The South unravels. It is far wilder than the North. I recognize the state of entropy reflected in the rail-side chaos washing up to the tracks. I mourn the loss of passenger trains in Mexico. I remember the sleeper train from Laredo to Mexico City. The luxurious dining car with waiters carrying towering trays of porcelain dishes and wearing ill-fitted tuxedos, serving fine foods, whiskey, and wine. The towers of clanking dishes swaying foretold of dish implosions and a chaos that never came. I still blush remembering the gentle knock at my compartment door by a stranger briefly encountered in the bar asking to spend the night. The tracks cut across the Mexican desert.

19 Crescent

Reina: "¿Cómo, desde donde empezamos, es que llegamos a esta Navidad?"
Rey: "Paso a paso."
    —*El león en invierno*

Después de todos estos años, todos los amantes y unas relaciones significativas que me rompieron el corazón para que así pudiera abrir; después de las tardes noches dedicadas a engrasar las ruedas de la América corporativa y soportando las deficiencias del sector público; después de cometer un millón de errores, hiriendo y siendo herida, aún duermo bien por las noches.

No sé si es porque mi conciencia está limpia o si simplemente porque perdí la cuenta de todos los amantes que forman el paisaje de mi vida. El sueño viene sin importar qué y todas las cosas vividas, grandes y pequeñas, se pliegan a la historia de mi cuerpo.

Ilusiones y desilusiones, haciendo y deshaciendo, creando y destruyendo, todo conduce al mismo lugar.

La Media Luna 19 sacude las vías y acuna mi sueño. El viaje es largo desde Nueva York a Nueva Orleans. El paisaje es extraño para mí. El Sur se desenreda. Es mucho más salvaje que el Norte. Reconozco el estado de entropía que se refleja en el caos ferroviario que se arrincona al costado de las vías. Lamento la pérdida de los trenes de pasajeros en México. Recuerdo el tren con cabinas de Laredo a ciudad de México. El lujoso coche comedor con camareros que llevaban bandejas imponentes de vajillas de porcelana y vistiendo trajes que no les quedaban, y servían comidas, vino y whisky. Las torres de platos que sonaban y se balanceaban anunciando una implosión de trastes y caos que nunca llegó. Todavía me sonrojo recordando el suave toque

The value of the land lies in the placement of these tracks. Otherwise, the land is dry and cracked, and only cactus, snakes, and lizards have a chance to thrive. Defying the uninhabitable nature of the landscape, socially invisible people construct wooden dwellings. Scattered across the shores of the railroad, these wooden shacks squat on federal lands. In other areas, the squatters constitute the underbelly suburbs that hide the secrets of larger cities. Standing in the open-air cars of the train, we passed anthills of existence. Kids run alongside the train the moment the engine slows down. Their dissimulated smiles veiled desperation, a hopelessness trailing in the poisonous smoke, only to be left behind with the whining and elongated sounds of the screeching steel. I never knew how to feel or what to think, there wasn't time. Well-dressed passengers standing beside me waved imperiously and smiled at the hordes of half-naked and dusty children. Standing among the bourgeois in the open-air cars, I was just as guilty.

Cutting through the lower 48, the changes in the soil evoke imagery of a geographic crosscutting, with layers representing time. The soil has turned from mossy green to black, from black to red, from red to yellow, and now from yellow to white. Buried in metaphysical layers are the histories of the places, from the beginning of time to the present. In this part of the country, the calcified history of slavery and injustice sustains the tracks that carry us. Cold steel grows hot and sparks fly at high speeds. As we hug the curves following the contours of rivers, opposite trains pass at the same speed, somehow without colliding into us. The physics is truly poetic.

The unraveling of the South loosens my ties to Alaska. The more I lose, the more of myself I regain. Retracing my steps from the tropics, to the sandy deserts, to the creeping fog of San Francisco, north to the arctic desert, and to now, I am humbled by the realization that I am an orphan. My greatest consolation is that I am among a family of orphans like me. Friends become family. At home we say that one doesn't know what one is made of until one learns to love God in a foreign land. I am an atheist, but I think I understand. Love is the

a la puerta de mi compartimento de un extraño conocido brevemente en el bar que preguntando si podía pasar la noche. Las vías atraviesan el desierto Mexicano. El valor de la tierra se encuentra en la colocación de estas vías. De lo contrario, la tierra es seca y agrietada y sólo el nopal, las serpientes y lagartijas pueden sobrevivir y prosperar. Pero aún así y desafiando la naturaleza del inhabitable paisaje, la gente quien es invisible ante la sociedad, construye viviendas de madera. Dispersas a las orillas del ferrocarril, las chozas de madera se aferran a las tierras federales. En áreas más densas, esta gente forma los suburbios ocultos en los cuales se esconden los secretos de las ciudades más grandes. De pie en los vagones del tren y al aire libre, pasamos hormigueros de existencia. Niños corren junto con el tren justo en el momento que el motor se ralentiza. Sus sonrisas disimuladas esconden su desesperación, una desesperación que se arrastra por el humo venenoso del tren, y se queda atrás con los sonidos del acero chirriante que lloriquean y se alargan. Nunca supe cómo sentirme o qué pensar, no hubo tiempo. Pasajeros bien vestidos, hombro con hombro se paran de pie junto a mí y arrogancia saludan y sonríen al montón de niños semidesnudos y polvorientos. De pie entre los burgueses en los vagones al aire libre, yo soy igual de culpable.

Cortando a través de los 48 estados continentales, los cambios en el suelo evocan imágenes de un corte transversal geográfico, con capas que representa el tiempo. El suelo se ha convertido de verde oscuro a negro, de negro a rojo, de rojo a amarillo y de amarillo a blanco. Enterrados entre capas metafísicas están las historias de los lugares, desde el principio de los tiempos hasta el presente. En esta parte del país, la historia de la esclavitud y la injusticia calcificada sostiene las vías ferrocarrileras que nos transportan. El acero frío se calienta con las altas velocidades hasta que saltan chispas. Se braza el tren de las curvas siguiendo los contornos de los ríos, otros trenes vienen hacia nosotros y pasan rasándonos a la misma velocidad, de alguna manera no chocan contra nosotros. La física es verdaderamente poética.

El desenlace del sur afloja mis lazos con Alaska. Entre más pierdo, más recupero de mí misma. Recogiendo mis pasos, desde el trópico, a

beginning, the sustaining force and what we look forward to in the end—but along the way there is the responsibility to be outside one's self, no matter the heartache, we owe the world more than it will ever owe us. I have no right to complain.

The farther south we go, the more frequent the delays. A passenger complains that he has to be somewhere and will now be late. I think he should get off and push. It's curious that the temperature in the train drops whenever we're at a standstill. There are parts of the South that are rusty, the trains are rusty, and machinery is left to rot on the backside of lands along the tracks. There are old or badly damaged cars that sit in lots waiting to vanish with the ages. In contrast, the Meridian Mississippi Union Station stands proud and well loved amid manicured lawns like a red-brick gatekeeper. The South is a cross-section of American history that, like the geographic layers of a riverbed, has in its folds the remnant histories of the past. The industrial America piled on agricultural and Civil War America, with LNG cars rolling on top—manufacturing skeletons on top of displaced farming roots. The firm soil gives way to swamps, the trees are drier and the light is brighter.

Nestled into the southern wilderness are pockets of affluence. From tee to green, far in the distance small speckles of white fly toward flags dancing on skinny poles. In the lounge car a man sits alone playing solitaire. He seems frustrated, his opponent must be better than he. The lazy sun throbs through the curtain of trees like it does in the tropics.

The heartbeat of the earth is never felt as strongly as on the nights of zafra, the sugarcane harvest. As soon as the sun goes down and the moon is ready, we ignite the fields. The fire pulses, the cinders dance, the air becomes drunken and sweet. A heat so strong, it can melt glaciers.

A few years ago You and I went to the archaeological site at Tajín, about a five-hour drive from town. On the way back, I took a wrong turn at the lighthouse and we ended up lost for hours and hours. When we finally found our way, we were amid the biggest

los arenosos desiertos, de la niebla que se arrastra por San Francisco, hasta del norte al desierto ártico, y ahora me siento humillada al realizar soy un huérfano. Mi mayor consuelo es que pertenezco a una familia de huérfanos como yo. Amistades que se convierten en familia. En casa se dice que uno no sabe lo que es está que aprende a amar a Dios en una tierra ajena. Soy atea, pero creo que entiendo. El amor es el principio, la fuerza sustentadora y lo que esperamos al final—pero en el camino tenemos la responsabilidad permanecer fuera de uno mismo, sin importar la angustia, le debemos más al mundo, que el mundo a nosotros. No tengo derecho a quejarme.

Entre más profundo nuestro camino al sur, más frecuentes son los retrasos. Un pasajero se queja de que tiene que estar en un lugar y ya será tarde. Me harta. Es curioso que la temperatura en el tren baja cada vez que se para. Hay partes del sur que están oxidadas, los trenes están oxidados y hay maquinaria pudriéndose en la parte posterior de las tierras a lo largo de las vías. Hay coches viejos o dañado que siendo abandonados esperan a desaparecer con el tiempo. En contraste, la estación de tren, Meridian Mississippi Union Station se encuentra orgullosa y muy querida en medio de jardines, con la frente en alto, es un guardián de ladrillos rojo. El sur es una muestra representativa de la historia Americana que, como las capas geográficas del lecho de un río, tiene en sus pliegues los restos de la historia y el pasado. La América industrial se amontona sobre América agrícola y sobre la América de la Guerra Civil, con los vagones transportando LNG que ruedan sobre tapas de los esqueletos industriales y raíces agrícolas desplazadas. El suelo anteriormente firme cede a los pantanos, y a los árboles que son más secos, y a la luz que es más brillante.

Ubicado en el desierto del sur se encuentran nidos de opulencia. Desde el verde, y a lo lejos las pelotitas pequeñas y blancas parecen moscas volando hacia las banderas que bailan en postes flacos que señalan su meta. En el vagón de descanso está un hombre entretenido con su juego de baraja solitaria. Parece estar frustrado, seguro su contrincante es mejor que él. Y más allá, el sol perezoso vibra a través de la cortina de árboles como lo hace en el trópico.

El latido del corazón de la tierra nunca se siente igual de fuerte como en las noches de zafra, la cosecha de la caña. Tan pronto como cae el sol y la luna está lista, incendiamos el campo. El pulso del fuego, las cenizas que bailan, el aire que se emborracha con dulzura. Un calor tan fuerte para derretir glaciales.

Hace unos años Tu y yo fuimos a la zona arqueológica de Tajín, a cinco horas de la cuidad por coche. De regreso tomé un camino equivocado justo al llegar al faro y terminamos perdidas durante horas y horas. Cuando por fin encontramos el camino, nos hallamos en medio de la zafra más grande de la temporada. Había fuego por la carretera por muchas millas, a nuestras izquierda imponentes llamas de fuego, a nuestra derecha lo mismo. Manejaba rápidamente y perseverantemente hasta que el olor y calor que palpitaba en mi pecho y mi corazón se detuvo. Detuve el auto y me enfermé con una abrumadora emoción. Sudé frío en medio del fuego y en un instante confundí el dulce olor de la noche con el olor azul que tiene la nieve cuando está a punto de caer en Alaska. El fuego volvió mi ser al revés y mi piel se quemó junto con la caña de azúcar. Me sentí igual de desnuda que la caña tierna. Fue entonces que me di cuenta de la fuerza transformadora de la cosecha. No pude manejar más, así que Tu lo hiciste. La oscuridad crecía mientras nos alejábamos del fuego, y mi cabeza, que previamente se había ampliado y distanciado, regresó en su lugar.

Ahora estamos corriendo contra el atardecer a Nueva Orleans. Sospecho que vamos a perder. El sol se pone más rápidamente de lo que podemos viajar. Casi hemos llegado a la frontera con Louisiana. Alucino el olor del mar salado. No he vuelto a Nueva Orleans durante años. Esta vez no ay amigos a mi lado. El aire es caluroso y húmedo. Los amantes del pasado se destiñen, abriendo camino para los nuevos amantes. Duermo bien, sueño con mi madre, sueño con amigos y con mis perros. También sueño con la traviesa de pelo castaño que me deleito con su conversación, un platillo "de basura" que se acostumbra en Rochester, y con su tierna compañía.

EGAN MILLARD

Egan Millard's poetry has appeared in *Cirque, The Worcester Review, Used Furniture Review,* and elsewhere. Originally from New York, he lives in Anchorage, where he is an editor for *Alaska Dispatch News.* He is the host and founder of *The Siren,* a poetry and music show in Anchorage.

Mondegreen

Most of the city is asleep, or nearly so, since it's late on an October Sunday night. Downtown Anchorage is deserted, but crackling with the sound of ice pellets bouncing off pavement, windows, rooftops. Just the night before, hordes of people—boy-men, soldiers, bachelorette parties, and the last tourists of the year—flooded Fourth Avenue, their full, round faces gleaming with sweat after emerging from the Gaslight, the Avenue, the Pioneer or the new dance spot where Club Soraya used to be, which no one seemed to know the name of, if it had one at all.

Now there are no shouts, no clouds of breath or taxis double-parked. Cars navigate the slick streets cautiously, purposefully. The lights of Fourth Avenue still shine behind bar windows, but as the glass becomes clouded by ice and freezing fog, "OPEN" and "COORS LIGHT" look less like advertisements and more like disembodied thoughts floating in the night.

A figure pauses at the corner of Fifth and C, then turns east, holding the hood of his red sweatshirt low over his face. The wind is blowing directly at him now, and he walks diagonally, almost sideways, so the ice pellets won't blow down his shirt.

The clouds over the city are churning rolls of sea foam, glowing a dirty yellow as they absorb the lights of the city, as if lit faintly from within.

Mad Myrna's is dead, even for a Sunday. There are four people inside, and each is wondering why he's there. At this point, they're mostly waiting around to see if the sleet will let up.

Like the other downtown bars, Myrna's has had a rowdy Friday and Saturday, so its regular crowd is mostly at home recovering.

There's still a dusting of glitter and confetti on an unswept corner of the empty dance floor, and the marquee over the doorway to the cabaret room still reads, "CHARLOTTE'S HARLOTS—1 NITE ONLY $7."

The stocky bartender is unloading glasses from the dishwasher under the bar as he chats with the young bar-back, who's leaning against one of the pool tables. They're commiserating about someone named Brian. One of the old *Star Wars* movies is playing on the muted TV.

The two patrons are seated at opposite corners of the rectangular bar. In the corner by the cigarette machine, a bald middle-aged man peruses a copy of the *Press* while his bottle of Blue Moon goes warm. At the other corner, by the pool table, an old man in unconvincing drag is perched on a stool, sipping a Mai Tai and peering out over the room with the eyes of a vaguely annoyed cat.

"Yeah, I mean," the bartender sighs, "that's all he would've had to say. You know me—that would've been fine."

"Yeah, totally," nods the bar-back. "Just be real. Nobody has time for those—"

The door swings open. For a second or two, the sound of sleet crackling against the pavement outside carries into the bar, clear and crisp. The man in the red hoodie steps inside. The door shuts with a metallic *clunk*. He's a young man. The draft of cold, damp air washes over the bar. He removes the hood of his sweatshirt; a rosy blush lingers around his nose and cheeks. He's just a kid.

He shuffles over to the bar, rubbing his hands together. His eyes dart back and forth as he surveys the scene. He settles on a stool halfway down the bar, near the bald man, trying to appear as casual as possible. The bartender sets a glass up on the shelf and leans forward.

"ID, please?"

He digs an old snakeskin wallet out of his pocket, along with a crumpled piece of paper, which he quickly stuffs back inside. He takes out a Delaware driver's license and slides it across the bar. The bartender holds it up and studies it, his eyes flickering back and forth. Then he stares into the young man's eyes for a long moment. He sets the license down.

"What can I getcha, sweetheart?"

"Um . . ." He looks up at the rows of bottles. "I'm not sure yet."

"OK," the bartender laughs, turning away. "Well, when you—"

"Do you like Irish coffee?" the bald man asks, swiveling on his stool and setting down the paper. "You look cold. It'll warm you up."

"Yeah, I guess."

The bald man holds up two fingers. The bartender nods and walks down to the coffee maker at the other end.

"Thanks," the young man says.

"Sure." The bald man smiles and looks back down at the paper for a while, then folds it closed and pushes his glasses up to the top of his head.

"So," he says. "Delaware?"

The young man lets out an unexpected laugh, as if it had been a punch line, then quickly gathers himself. "Yeah. It's a long story."

"I've got time," the bald man says, his smile inching wider. "I'm Marty, by the way." He offers his hand as the bartender sets their drinks down.

"Oh, I'm James." He puts his hand in Marty's.

"God, you really are cold," Marty says. "You don't have a coat or anything?"

"No, I'm fine." James wraps his hands around the warm glass and stirs it with the little straw.

"I guess you haven't been here long, then."

"Just a week, actually."

"Ah, a *cheechako*!" Marty finishes off his Blue Moon and gives his Irish coffee a quick stir, then takes a sip. "So what brings a young man like you halfway around the world?"

James gazes up at the bottles again. Many of them bear the names of much warmer places: Malibu, Curaçao, Havana Club, Bombay Sapphire. Outside, a gust of wind whips a barrage of ice pellets against the window facing Fifth Avenue.

"I mean, it seems like everyone in this state has some kind of crazy story about how they got here," Marty continues. "Except me. I was born and raised in Juneau. Lived there for most of my life. But I come up here every year for the pediatrics convention. That's what I do—I'm a pediatrician."

"Oh, OK," James says. "Do you . . . have a partner or anything?"

"No. Not at the moment. Used to be married, though."

"Oh."

"And I have three kids. Two of them live with their mother in Juneau and one's in college in Oregon."

"Do you get to see the younger ones a lot?"

"I do. I'm very lucky. There've been times when I thought I wasn't. Really bad times. But God, I realize now I was lucky all along. For all of it."

The bar-back goes over to the stereo to play "Chandelier" for the third time. He hops up on the corner of the bar and sways lazily to the music, singing under his breath.

"So what's your story?" Marty asks James. "Visiting someone? Working?"

"I followed someone up here," James says, turning to face Marty. "A man." He raises his glass to his lips and sips.

"Ah." Marty smiles again, but looks a few years older this time. "And how's that working out?"

"It's not. It didn't." He takes a bigger sip. "I guess I knew it wouldn't. I shouldn't have expected . . ."

"He took you up here with him from Delaware? Or you came on your own?"

"I went with him. I wouldn't say he took me."

"That's a long way."

"Yeah." James drinks, then sits up straighter. "You ever been?"

"I have, actually."

"Oh, no way!"

"Rehoboth Beach. Beautiful."

"Yeah." James sighs. "I'm from Dover."

"Mmm. Air Force?"

"He is."

"Commissioned?"

James's voice softens. "He's . . . he's high up."

"Oh." Marty sets his drink down. "I see. Wow."

"Yeah. Wow."

The old drag queen sets down her empty glass and starts drumming her fingers along the side of it, her rings clinking against the glass, summoning the bartender back from the pool table.

"One more, Jolene?" he asks.

She nods sleepily.

"You driving tonight?"

Jolene shakes her head, her red wig hanging a bit askew. The bartender refills her glass, going lighter on the rum this time.

"So," James asks Marty. "What's Juneau like?"

"Smaller. Warmer. Prettier. More like Delaware."

"Mmm. Is there . . . much of a gay scene there?"

Marty chuckles. "If you know where to look. Which is harder than it used to be, at least for me. I don't have any of those apps that everybody uses now. When I was younger it used to be about certain places. Bars and cafés. And that's still true to some extent, I guess. There's the Triangle, which is kind of gay, but it's not an actual gay bar. So every time I'm in Anchorage I like to come in here."

"Is it always this quiet?"

"Oh God, no. You just came here on the wrong night. You come in here on a Saturday and you'll be fighting guys off you."

A low smile appears on James's face for a moment. He lifts his eyes to the muted TV, where Yoda is mouthing his last words. There are no captions, and James hasn't seen the movie in years, so he doesn't know what Yoda's saying. The only sound in the bar is Daft Punk's "Get Lucky" playing over the speakers. James is caught off guard by his own laughter.

"What?" Marty asks, laughing a little himself.

"Just this," James says, gesturing to the TV. "Sorry," he says.

"I guess I'm tired." Then he falls into laughter again. "So, you know, this part of the song, when it goes into the robot voice—I mean, I know he's saying 'we're up all night to get lucky' but I always hear it as 'we'll rob a Mexican monkey.'"

"Huh." Marty listens and grins.

"Right? You hear it?"

"Yeah, I do! You know, there's a word for that. One of my favorite words in the English language."

"A word for what?"

"For when you mishear song lyrics and your mind substitutes something else. It's called mondegreen."

"Mondegreen. Mmm."

The door opens—halfway at first, cautiously, then all the way. A man dressed in hunter's camo and a beige safari hat and a woman wearing what seem to be pajamas step inside and hover near the back wall. Water is dripping off the man's hat onto his shoulders. He leans over and whispers to her, dripping onto her as well. They stand in silence. After about a minute, she walks back out the door and he follows.

"Well, I'm sorry it didn't work out for you with him," Marty says. "Do you have any other connections here? Family or . . . a job or anything?"

A resigned smile. "I . . . no. You have to understand. I didn't . . . I wasn't expecting . . ." He laughs, shrugs, looks Marty in the eyes. "I had no other plans. He's got a big house on base here. Biggest bed I've ever seen. View of the mountains over there. I just wanted to live in his house. Sleep in his bed. Walk his fucking dog. Cook for him. Love him. But I guess he got scared. I still don't really know why. He won't answer my calls." James finishes his drink.

"I'm sorry, James."

"Yeah. I guess I just misunderstood. Or—I didn't want to understand."

Marty stretches, then reaches into his pocket for his billfold. He leaves a twenty on the bar. "Listen. I know this guy meant the world to you. And I know it feels like you'll never get over this. Believe me. I know. But you will. Your life belongs to you, not anyone else."

"I know. Thank you." The corners of James's mouth twitch a little. "It's just scary. Suddenly realizing where I am. That I made a mistake."

"Forget that. Things happened. They can't be undone. The idea of a mistake is only in your mind, after the fact. So don't look back. You're here. You're young. This place is . . . full of surprises. Go live your life."

James wipes his eyes with his napkin. "OK."

"Do you have a place to stay?"

"I'm at the Black Angus now. On Gambell."

"Oh, honey!" Jolene interjects from across the bar in a loud, raspy voice. She shakes her head disapprovingly.

"She's right," the bartender offers.

Marty pauses for a moment. "Look," he says, handing James a clean napkin, "I'm here for one more day. I have a nice, comfortable room at the Hilton. With two beds. This isn't a come-on or anything. But you're welcome to stay there, and maybe I can help you figure out something tomorrow. Up to you."

James glances around the room. The bartender is wiping down the other side of the bar as he talks to Jolene in a hushed voice. The bar-back is on his phone, continually scrolling down with his finger. Through the small window facing Fifth Avenue, the sleet seems to be letting up.

"Thank you," James says, flustered. "I mean, I just don't want to . . . intrude—"

"Oh, it's really no trouble. It would be nice to have some company. And again, just platonic—it's up to you."

"I think I'm OK. But thanks. Really."

Marty nods. "OK." He stands, pushes in his stool and puts on his jacket. "If you change your mind, I'm in room 1410. You can call me there too if you'd like." He extends his hand, and James shakes it. "Good luck to you, James."

"Thanks. You too."

Marty waves at the bartender and heads for the door.

On Fifth Avenue, the sleet has turned into a light freezing rain. The street has become hopelessly slick, and two police officers are trying to push a car out of an intersection without much success. A few men slip out of the Polar Bar for a cigarette. Somebody flashes the lights inside—last call. One puts his cigarette out on the sidewalk, tucks it behind his ear and heads back in. The rest stay, shrouded in a haze of smoke and ice and breath.

Across the street, a lone man in a red sweatshirt emerges from the alley between Myrna's and Mammoth Music. He pauses when he gets to the street and puts his hands in his pockets. He's listening. He looks east. The sky is much darker now, a dusty violet. It's quieter than before. He flips his red hood over his head. With careful steps, he begins to walk west.

Agni

There was no color
as far as we both could see—
nothing that was not white
or gray or brown
except for my eyes,
bloodshot and blue.

I hadn't seen you
in months. I'd lingered long
in another king's palace,
another man's motel room.
You would not touch me.
I still smelled of him.

The wind blew
and I trembled,
still your vassal,
still your vessel.

So I gathered logs
and built a pyre,
praying to the god of fire,
invoking the words
I'd read on the back
of a cigarette pack:
"IN HOC
SIGNO
VINCES"

Then I blazed and burned
and danced for you,
pure as the day I was born,
a golden-red sylph
glowing in the snow.

Your face, as you stood and watched,
was inscrutable as dogwood,
veiled like early spring.

Koimesis

This is the way things did happen.
I happened on a hill
between Sunday and Monday,
looked back at the mountainside
from which I'd come—
a hundred glinting houses,
a hundred circling camps,
a hundred flickering candles
in open windows. The road
draped the coast-crags
with pale diamonds
and a woman lay down
over it all,
lustrous and low. I tendered
my resignation
to any who would accept it.

Two moose
hovered on the hill.
I saw the cow and calf
and melted into the trees.
Seven ages passed.
A flock of cranes
mourned the loss of the day.
It occurred
to me,
we should all agree
we are nothing
and should remain so.

Vacation

Already the day is done.
Blue has become green.

New love sleeps
in my hotel bed.
Already
it is old.

Whether it stays remains
to be seen.

I don't have a second key.
A little snow tomorrow night
will not accumulate.

Try it a few times
just to make sure

[it locks behind you]

fire on the hillside
a staircase into the night
let me go

Proudly scattered on the beach,
shards of plates and bones,
remains
to be seen.

ZACK ROGOW

Zack Rogow is the author, editor, or translator of twenty books and plays. His eighth book of poems, *Talking with the Radio: poems inspired by jazz and popular music,* was published in 2015 by Kattywompus Press. He is also writing a series of plays about authors, incorporating their writing into the action. The most recent of these, *Colette: A One-Woman Show,* had its first staged reading at the Millennium Stage of the Kennedy Center in Washington, DC, in February 2015. He is the editor of an anthology of poetry of the United States, *The Face of Poetry,* from the University of California Press. Currently, he teaches in the low-residency MFA writing program at the University of Alaska Anchorage and serves as poetry editor of *Catamaran Literary Reader.*

The Voice of Art Nouveau

If we have to smother our candles
and let electricity in through the front door
If you herd us into cities
where we'll be shelved one
on top of the other
If our furniture will be assembled
like automobiles
and our streets will be forests of steel

Then let our lamp necks be twisted
into the stems of the flowers we won't see anymore
Let their glass shades be colored
like the wings of the most flagrant insects
Let the outsides of our buildings thrive with jungles of ornament
and the smashed tiles of old floors be crazy-quilted into a
serpentine wall
whose only purpose is to be beautiful
Let all right angles squares and rectangles be stretched bent melted
or warped
Let us have our revenge
          on the perfect straight line

M.C.
MOHAGANI
MAGNETEK

M.C. MoHagani Magnetek is a transgender African American anthropologist, writer, poet, and artist. She draws inspiration from within to create stories and narratives about obscure aspects of life. Sometimes surreal noir and other times concrete realities, she fashions her stories with a great deal of poetics. As a transgender woman living on the last great frontier of Alaska, she employs many of her experiences in her works of fiction, nonfiction, and poetry. She is the author of ten short stories, an anthologized story, a novella, and a poetry collection. She is most known for her *Ms. Mahogany Bones* and *thaMind Sol-Lady* tales.

Creep

Hold on. Wait a minute. Let me catch my breath, my feet are tired of having to run up them damn steps and get in the front door safe and in one piece. I have tell you like Fannie Lou Hammer said, "I am sick and tired of being sick and tired," of all this shit. What's the deal with all the creeps, lame no game having men in their cars all over Anchorage? I am so over all the gawking and honking car horns every time I walk down the block. I know I am a jazzy local celebrity, but this shit has to stop.

I guess I was about nineteen years old the day I walked in the house on a day like today, highly frustrated, to find my auntie sipping on a cup of coffee. She looked me over and situated me in the right frame of mind. She asked me what was the matter, and then I went all-in with my rant and chatter. "It's not that I'm out walking in a scandalous outfit with stiletto heels, but I am always getting harassed when I'm walking down the street."

"I'm sorry baby, but there is no love for a decent lady. I know, it's crazy, but that's why we called them honkies. And that ain't got nothing to do with them being white, either. Black and Latino men are flirtatious and nasty, too. You have to be careful and always alert because some of them will try to hurt you if you give the time of day."

So I follow her lessons, read the signs, and have participate in the stop sexual harassment protests sessions from time to time. As I was saying this shit ain't right, just like the other day, off Northern Lights. Just up the block and around the way, I am girl just trying to get to my house. Now, you know me, I am in my own muthafucking zone with my headphones on bopping to the beat of my own drum. This guy pulls alongside in his old rickety no muffler loud-ass car. I was surprise he could still start it and get it to run. "Hey Hey there

Hun!!!" with his lustful eyeballs popping out of his head. His left arm dangling and waving while his right had steadied the jalopy's steering wheel. "Oh Lawd . . . not today!" is all I could think of. I was not in the mood and definitely could not feel the fact that I caught a glimmer of his wedding ring. I told him he needs to leave me alone and go home to his wife with his undercover nasty behavior. And then I thought, well, more like I prayed, "Oh God please don't let this honky be my neighbor." My auntie taught me right, so I reached for my razor in my purse and slyly grabbed a hold of my mace. If he came any closer, I was ready to cut him deep and spray him in the face. He was gonna learn the hard way not to F with me. I watch T.V. and see all the newsreels; I was not about to be another transgender woman victim killed, sliced, and diced up on the side of the road in a trash heap, left for dead. I don't tell many people what goes on in my head, but I practice running in my heels and taking them off quickly to use the pointy part for a jab to the jugular of the rapist, stalker, or mugger.

This man and his slimy dick had no need to stop just cause he saw my fine sexy black behind walking down the street. Using peripheral vision, my head steadied the course ahead while I said, "Just keep on keeping on you creep!" Well . . . I didn't add the "creep" part but I made it clear that whatever he was selling I was not in the market for buying. He was horrid and just as old and crusty looking as his car. Even on a good day, he couldn't get far with me. Girrrrl, I didn't even give him an "E" for effort for trying.

This shit happens all the time to me, I ain't even lying. However, it don't stop there, I got mad stories to tell of similar situations and other encounters in different outfits. Take last Sunday for instance, I'm on my way home walking the distance from church and here comes another honky slowing down on the hunt with a sinister lurch. I was strolling down Spenard and 27 in my Sunday best, hoping I will still make it to heaven with swaying hips, switching from side to side. I know I'm not supposed to be cussing on a

Sunday after receiving the message of the Good Lawd but, "Aww Nawl!" this nasty muthafuka broke my stride, "Hell Nawl!!, I Don't Want A Ride!!!" If you had seen this honky, you would have thought the same and nearly died from laughing at this all too real, Lifetime movie scenario. He didn't have a car, just one of those bone-chilling-kidnapping-dark-gray-pick-up vans with an eight-track player for a radio. The only thing missing was a "Free Candy" decal sign to lure in some innocent naive child with his nasty plans. He was so morbid looking; he could be mistaken for the Addams Family's Uncle Fester. His real name probably was Chester the Child Molester.

Yes, I'm being prejudice and judgmental, but a girl has got to have her wits about her self if she wants to survive the strife. His creepy ass could easily have been the rapist with no respect for life. Either that or he was going to go home that night, drink a six-pack of cheap beer, kick his dog, curse his children, and beat his wife. All because he was mad that I told him, "Hell no you can't get with me. Leave me be or regret it. I don't play, so forget it. I quit kindergarten because they had recess. So keep on keeping on if you know what's best." You could see the disappointment and disgust on his face. As he sped off I got a good look and wrote down his license plate. Just in case he gets lucky with his evil smile and there is report about another missing child.

My auntie's words ring true; black men can be some low-down dirty honkies, too. Now this brother on 36th and C Street, last week, was actually nice looking but had no game. He had a nice car, but his rap was lame. Nevertheless it was more of the same, when he didn't get a response to his call, "Hey baby, what's your name?" while I'm walking home all classy, sassy, hips swaying again as I switch. "Oh it's like that . . . you Black Tranny Ugly Biaaatch!!!" That was it, the camel's back was broken from the last straw, I was not even playing or joking when I stopped my track, grabbed my razor and went back.

"Look here, you on the down-low nasty bastard. I am not a fag. I don't care if you are hot bothered and mad. I don't know what you think you are seeing, but my mama is a human being and didn't

158

give birth to no bitch. Maybe if you knew how to talk to a girl and didn't have a wack rap, you could get with this. Yeah . . . I know it is a given. I look good and work at Being Jazzy for a living. But I'm fed-up with all you honkies, white, black or whatever. Just keep on keeping whenever you see me walking down the street. I don't buy green bananas cause I don't have time for some creep!"

Yeah, my friend, I get tired of all the honkies, gawking eyes, and twisted necks; but the one that tickles me the most, the one I can not forget, is the skinny scruffy looking Latino dude last night on his bicycle. If I'm lying, I'm dying, it was such a bad approach I actually had to stop and give him the E for effort. Girrrrrl, can you believe, he was passing me by and had the nerve to repeatedly squeeze his little horn at me on his funky bicycle, "Olá Sweet Mama Sita." He was charming, yet ludicrous, ratchet, and ridiculous, so I gave him my name and digits. Okay . . . to be perfectly honest with you . . . to tell the truth, since he wasn't a jerk I brought his scruffy, bicycle-riding ass home and did him good like homework.

Shhhh-Be-Quiet

Remarkably beautifully, Ms. Mahogany Bones was welcomed everywhere with the exception of bars, buses, restrooms, department stores, restaurants, schools, churches, mosques, synagogues, and the library. The library wasn't a hostile environment; it was just Mahogany had a problem with being quiet. The staff may have known her name, if they hadn't said, "Shhhh-Be-Quiet" so many times. Wearing a gorgeous yellow summer dress with some yellow Sarah Jessica Parker sandals to match, Mahogany sat on the edge of the quiet zone, just in case folks came at her all sideways with mean, rude, and nasty attitudes. She kept her shades on to mask the hate crimes. With her head covered and the black shades on, it looked like she was either a spy or having a bad hair day trying to get an emergency appointment at the beauty salon.

Anastasia, one of her other transgender girlfriends, invited engaging gender police and immigrant-despising eyes with a *je ne sais quoi* type of attitude. Despite snarls and snares she flaunted her essence and accessorized it with luxurious handbags. Having been robbed that day, she was not at all pleased, and with a sunken face she sat at the library table across from Mahogany, who was able to lighten the mood by showing off her new Sarah Jessica Parker designer shoes.

They chatted flippantly under their breaths about all the malice that surrounded them, but the gravity of the conversation got really heavy when the Fellow-With-No-Swag and the Simple-Minded Jezebel walked into the library hand-in-hand. The Fellow-With-No-Swag and the Simple-Minded Jezebel had the audacity or were just too blind to see that they were sitting in the quiet zone next to the woman they had wronged.

Mahogany told Anastasia about the night she was waiting for her ride in front of the library. She had her headphones on and was dancing so hard that passersby mistook her for a drag queen street artist and threw money at her feet. She wasn't high and mighty acting, so she picked up the money and kept right on doing her thing until a fellow with no swag approached her. Because his britches sagged, he walked like a cowboy who rode four days with no saddle. Dazzled by her bopping behind, he started out with a weak pick-up line. "Hey Baby. Do you have the time?"

Mahogany glanced him over unimpressed and said, "I'm sorry, but I don't wear a watch, because I don't believe in giving some folks my time."

"Damn! Be that way. Fag!!!" said the Fellow-With-No-Swag. Enraged, she was not the type to forgive and forget it.

"Girrrl . . . and then this simple-minded Jezebel, she jumped me in the library in front of everybody. She beat me like a rented mule at school in broad daylight, Alaskan style! By the time she was done kicking my ass, I was all bruised with not *one* . . . but *two* black eyes! I went to the campus police and they looked at me all crazy. I tell ya' . . . folks don't like hearing truth, especially when it comes from a tranny."

"Well, I'mma go show 'em that we are not to be played with. Folks can't run us over and think we just gonna roll over, play dead, and be all meek. I think I might have to put my foot up his ass and slap her into next week."

Mahogany waltzed over to their enemies and confronted them. Anastasia looked on knowing there was no holding Mahogany back. Their enemies rose to their feet to spit out more nasty slurs and rude epithets and then . . . that was that. The library clerk heard a disturbance in the force, peeked over her glasses to see but missed it. In the blink of an eye the ruckus was loud, quick, and then Mahogany was gone like an empty tray of delicious banana split.

A week went by before the story could be told to the S.G.P.D. (Stankhorage Gender Police Department) during an interrogation about the incident at the library. Ms. Bones decided to be a good citizen, slid on a pastel blue vintage dress, and accepted the request for questioning. Fashionably late, she stood out in the suspect line-up for the Simple-Minded Jezebel to finger point her out. To Mahogany's surprise, Det. Kendrick Richard was *on* her case again. Switching his eyes from her legs to the issues, Det. Richard said, "It sure *is* nice to have you back in my interrogation room looking like a devil in a blue dress. There is a woman on the other side of that window, that says you assaulted her last week in the library."

"Is that so? Then why did she wait a whole week to say something?"

"Well, that's kind of hard to explain. She says you slapped her so hard that the next thing she knew, she had skipped over the past seven days. The doctors looked at her, but there are no signs of concussion or temporary amnesia. It just don't make no sense," said Det. Richard, shaking his head.

"Well, that's quite an interesting story, but it wasn't me."

"What do you mean, it *wasn't* you? We have library surveillance video placing you at the scene of the crime. Det. Bucky, please run the video for Ms. Bones." As if she wanted to put in a request for popcorn, Ms. Bones crossed her legs and reclined in the chair to watch the footage until it was paused. "You mean to tell me, this is not you in this lovely yellow dress?"

"Nope. It *wasn't* me. Do you know how many women wear yellow dresses?"

"Com'on now. Look, Ms. Bones, there is more evidence. Det. Bucky, play the audio testimony of the library clerk." While the tape played, Ms. Bones folded her arms and listened.

"Last Thursday, about high noon, Shhhh-Be-Quiet walked in wearing this gorgeous yellow summer dress with some yellow Sarah Jessica Parker sandals to match. Shhhh-Be-Quiet was sitting at the table with another crosser-dressing wannabe. That Fellow-With-No-Swag and that Simple-Minded Jezebel walked in and sat next to them. Everything was good so I went back to reading and then . . .

well you know . . . moments later I heard a disturbance in the force. I looked up and saw Shhhh-Be-Quiet slap that Simple-Minded Jezebel, and now all of a sudden, I am here today, and a whole week has mysteriously gone by."

Quietness upheld the interrogation room momentarily before Det. Richard broke it. "Sooo, Ms. Bones here is another witness that not only places you at the scene of the crime in a lovely dress, but stated that you slapped that Simple-Minded Jezebel into the next week."

"It *wasn't* me. That could be anybody. You know how many people they call Shhhh-Be-Quiet in the library?"

"Fine then, Ms. Bones. Det. Bucky, bring that fellow in here."

"It was *him*. That faggot put his foot up my ass!!!" said the Fellow-With-No-Swag.

"Like I *said* . . . it *wasn't* me." said Mahogany, yielding puzzling expressions from her audience and frustration from the detective.

"Now you are really starting to piss me off, Ms. Mahogany Bones. You mean to tell me that the video, audio, and multiple witnesses are all fabrications? Det. Bucky, get me those damn X-rays." Det. Richard held up a set of X-rays in front of the light. "Look, this is the Fellow-With-No-Swag and a shoe in his ass. Bucky, show her the shoe." Det. Bucky pulled the funky-smelling, fecal-matter-covered shoe out of the plastic zip-locked evidence bag. "For the last time Ms. Bones. Did you do it? This is a Sarah Jessica Parker shoe, isn't it?"

The detectives, accusers, and concerned citizens all knew she was definitely going to fall, crash, burn, and confess. Smoothly, Mahogany withdrew her electronic cigarette, mystically twirled it in the air, took a few pulls, and puffed out cool, mind-bending, vaporized smoke rings to dispel the hostile air and cast a spell.

"Yes. Yes, it is. And that is *exactly* why you need to go talk to Sarah Jessica Parker and not me." The interrogation was over. They had to believe her, because her truth was undisputed. Plenty of women wear yellow dresses, designer shoes, and are told to "Shhhh-Be-Quiet" in the library.

Furthermore, no one could explain how the Simple-Minded Jezebel got slapped so hard, she time traveled forward into—but still missed the next week. Although it was her shoe in the Fellow-With-No-Swag's ass, Sarah Jessica Parker was off being fabulous, so she had an airtight alibi.

The next day in the lobby of the library, Anastasia questioned Mahogany on how she beat the rap. Mahogany thought. She contemplated. Maybe a lie is what deserved to be told. People liked the truth, but truth was comfortable, easy and boring; whereas, a lie was shaky, hard and exciting. With her confident Jedi mind tricks, she could invert any lie into an undisputed truth. For she was an honest-to-gawd-good-woman.

"They just didn't know who they was messing with. I am not going to admit a damn thing. But now I can't go to the library anymore." Pointing to the library information desk. "You see . . . they got my mug shot up there."

In a new set of replacement shoes, Mahogany limped away, leaving her friends behind to read the sign. The posted flyer read:

Attn: Clerks and Staff of the Library.
Shhhh-Be-Quiet is Not Allowed Here.
She is Banned for all Eternity.
If You See Shhhh-Be-Quiet
Please Notify the Gender Police Immediately.

SHELBY
WILSON

Shelby "Mahogany" Wilson has been in Alaska for over twenty years. She is the vice president of Black Feather POETS Alaska, a nonprofit organization built on bringing cultures together through art. Shelby is a published poet, who started her poetic venture with Alaska Poetry League. In 2005, she was fourth runner-up in the Alaska Poetry Slam contest. Since then, Shelby has expanded her creative talents to include performance poet, workshop facilitator, writer, spiritual counselor, and motivational speaker. Her work has appeared online in *Daily Love, Vox Poetica, Fib Review, Eskimo Pie, Poetry from Wherever, Poetic Medicine, Moon Magazine,* and *Bent Alaska*. Her print work has appeared in *SaFire Magazine, Alaska Women Speak,* and in the anthology *In My Lifetime: Wonders*. Shelby produced and appeared on a spoken-word CD entitled *Lyrical Finesse, a Black Feather Production*. She has self-published a chapbook titled *Serenity,* and the poetry collections *Broken Wings, Mending Damaged Souls,* and *Verbal Stimulation, An Intimate Collection of Poetry*.

Misread Signs

I missed the sign that said OPEN for business
For good times APPLY WITHIN
I overlooked the sign that read FREE RIDES HERE
Forgive me for not understanding the rules
of etiquette for revealing attire
The clause that gave you the right to disrespect me
Just because I have large breasts and a big behind
I'm sorry if the media has lead you
To believe in a fantasy
But lies have been told
Your need for oral copulation and sweaty sheets
Has got you chasing false advertisements
I AM NOT A HO
I don't do service calls or lunch escapades
If you placed a price tag on me
Then I'm out of your league
I'm a queen and always a lady
I'm truly sorry but a mistake has been made
Please listen while I clarify
My sign says
APPLY BRAKES PROCEED SLOWLY

Fireweed

Fingers slipping between laced lingerie and skin
Gliding slowly over hips, thighs, calves
Feeling the cool Alaskan breeze over every stem
Shoulders, arms, wrists, hands
Dropping to the floor lowering lips,
tongue swirls around erect nipples
Hands scale over thighs as legs
guide in harmony against the wall
Breast against breast, lips on lips, hands free
Her pulse hastens
fingers grazing the tip of her pistil
Caressing and teasing the edges of her petals
from purple to red she blooms

LESLIE
KIMIKO
WARD

Leslie Kimiko Ward is the recipient of a grant from the Alaska Humanities Forum for her forthcoming memoir *1000 Cranes*. She has written and performed a thirty-minute monologue and one-woman-show based on similar content. Her first short story was published nearly fifteen years ago, in an anthology of lesbian erotic short fiction. She is a Creative Writing MFA dropout, with little understanding of the term exegesis. Leslie would like to thank her writing mentor, novelist Jo-Ann Mapson, for her stalwart advice and encouragement.

Nest

Standing in her mother's driveway, duffel bags in hand, Elsa takes a good look around, at the cottonwoods with their golden leaves, at the highbush cranberry's bright red bundles, the long-legged shadow cast by the water tower, and the jagged snowcaps on the neighboring wall of mountains. This landscape is as familiar to her as the arrangement of her mother's living room furniture, unchanged since the oak coffee table was as high as her chest, and her father's pillowy recliner doubled as a jungle gym.

Elsa will spend the winter in this house. With August nearly gone, her mother has already flown south, headed for arthritis-friendly desert country, leaving Elsa behind to wrap the old pipes in blankets, eat dinners off her childhood plates, and look after Little Big Bird, the chatty cockatiel.

The phone buzzes inside Elsa's front pocket. *Dammit*, she whispers, hoisting her heavy duffels to one hand, biting her glove off with her teeth so she can swipe at the screen. She checks the glowing picture. A sour face stares back at her. It's Mel. *Jesus. Already?*

Mel is Elsa's tenant and seasonal roommate, a chronically down-on-her luck, post-menopausal curmudgeon with no apparent friends or family in the state. Elsa rents Mel the spare bedroom in her own house, a few miles away. Over the past few winters, Elsa had grown tired of shoveling the snow on two driveways, tired of trekking up the hill each night to see if her faucets were still dripping, or if her roof had caved in under the snowpack.

If Elsa was being brutally honest, ever since her divorce, she had begun to loathe that tumbledown house. She'd only bought the house for its land: eight wooded acres just outside of Palmer, a few driveways down from the guy with his very own castle, complete with turret and vertical aluminum siding. Elsa had hoped to build her own cabin on the property someday, nestled between the birch trees. She planned to level the old house and haul it away for scrap, provided it hadn't already fallen flat on its own.

But this was all before Elsa got married, and before her new wife needed a dishwasher, and a linen closet, a greenhouse, and an affair. Between home improvement projects, Elsa used to flip through the pages of her log cabin magazines, the ones she kept stacked in her closet like vintage porn. Eventually, even the reminders turned sour.

The winters Elsa spent alone in her mother's house had helped to take the edge off. She'd started dreaming again, even renewing a few of her canceled subscriptions. Last summer, Elsa cleared a foundation, to the right of the greenhouse, in a spot where the morning sun could shine into her imaginary bedroom windows.

When winter hit, and Elsa burned out the motor on yet another snowblower, she decided she needed a tenant. She took an ad out on Craigslist seeking "a handy recluse with a steady job." What she got instead, was Mel.

"Found a yellow jacket nest," Mel coughs into the phone. "In the crawl space. You'd better come look at it. Don't want to get stung in my sleep."

"Shit, Mel. Do you go hunting for problems as soon as I leave? How big is the nest?"

"Big."

"Is it live?"

"Dunno. Didn't stick around to find out."

Elsa sighs. "I'll be over tomorrow. I've got to unload my bags and check on Little Big Bird." Elsa lumbers up the sidewalk. She jiggles her mother's floral-printed key in the latch. Opening the door, she is surrounded with the fading scent of her mother's lilac perfume. It mingles with the kitchen smells of leftover biscuits and warm flour.

Elsa drops her duffel bags at the foot of her mother's bed. She'll unpack later, she decides, eyeing the stack of empty milk crates left for her beside a teeming armoire. Forty-five years old, and still dressing out of milk crates like a college kid. Some things never change. It's the ones that do that break your heart.

The cockatiel chirps from his cage in the living room. "Jungle bird," Elsa calls out. "Who's a jungle bird?" Little Big Bird recognizes Elsa's voice and launches into a piercing series of open-beaked trills that bounce off the walls like a fire alarm.

The next afternoon, Elsa drives up the hill to check out the yellow jackets and the growing list of issues Mel has managed to compile over the past twenty-four hours.

In the kitchen, Elsa squats, and shines her flashlight under the metal sink. Mel stands beside her, takes off her shoes, and stretches her toes wide inside her socks. "Finally," Mel mutters. "Damn wrinkle's been rubbin' my foot raw all day."

"What's that?" Elsa asks, but Mel doesn't answer. She's already turned around, and is heading for the living room. Elsa gets down on her knees and reaches for the Allen wrench she left dangling underneath the pipe. She tethered the wrench there months ago, using a strand of green dental floss, in the hopes that she could encourage Mel to become more self-sufficient in the fix-it department. The garbage disposal clogs about every other week, but so far it hasn't broken so Elsa doesn't see the need to replace it. Instead, Elsa inserts the tiny wrench into the bottom of the machine, and gives it a few cranks. "Why didn't you fix this earlier?" she calls to the adjoining room.

"Couldn't," Mel grumbles, pushing against the arms of the Naugahyde lounger. "Ain't no way I'm takin' off my shoes at work." Mel tilts the seat back, and the footrest creaks in protest.

Elsa turns on the water. The pipes rattle. The faucet burps and spits before settling into a thin stream. Elsa flips the switch up, and a horrible clatter erupts from the sink. She quickly flips the switch down again, and the clatter tapers. Elsa waits, then reaches her hand inside the clammy disposal to feel around. The shape of the gears, the way they're set up to spin against one another, they remind Elsa of that carnival ride, the Scrambler. When she was a kid and her dad was alive, Elsa's family went every year to the state fair. "No screaming now," her dad would say. He took her on all the rides. Elsa always screamed anyway. That was half the fun. "You nearly squealed my ears off, kid," he joked, making a big show of it, gingerly patting the sides of his head, shouting "What?" and "Huh?" to Elsa's mother for minutes afterwards.

Elsa runs her fingertips along the edges of the metal gears until she gets to something sharp and out of place. Using her nails to loosen whatever it is, she fishes it from the sink. Pinched between her fingers is a rough hunk of gravel. *How'd that get there?*

Elsa runs the water and tries the disposal again. The empty gears rattle and whir. "I'm driving in to Costco tomorrow," Elsa says. "You need anything?"

"You're out of body wash," Mel tells her, punching the button on the TV remote, turning up the volume of a British announcer narrating a true crime drama. "And don't get that fruity kind. It stinks. Makes my nose itch, and I smell like salad."

For a while after Mel moved in, out of habit, Elsa kept replacing the empty household bottles: shampoo, laundry detergent, dish soap, salad dressing. It hadn't seemed strange until Mel started making requests. When Elsa was young, and she would whine about having to fold someone else's laundry, or pick up a mess she didn't make, her mother always reminded her: "We take care of the people we live with. It's not up to us whether or not they deserve it."

Elsa kept on buying the body wash. Something about the act made her feel useful. Mel's needs were simple. There were a lot of them, but every single one was manageable. Not like her ex.

Elsa types the words, *body wash, not fruity,* into a running list on her phone. "Butch up the body wash," she says. "Got it. Anything else?"

"Why's it always gotta be a gay thing with you?"

Elsa's pretty sure that if Mel liked people, Mel would be a lesbian. In fact, when she first moved in, Elsa had her figured for a closet case. She assumed Mel would come out once she realized Elsa was also gay, not that it wasn't obvious. With close-cropped silver hair, a penchant for Carhartts, cowboy boots, power tools, and a sharp eye for damsels in distress, Elsa would be an easy tell most places. But Alaska has a tendency to blow the fuses on general gaydar, especially out in the valley, where Instagrams of teenage girls sporting semi-autos, riding four-wheelers, or holding hundred-pound fish are about as common as bathroom selfies. In Palmer, women like Elsa are everywhere, and most of them are straight. In San Francisco, at least according to her friend, Tracy, a woman like Elsa would be in high demand.

"You should move here," Tracy told her. "You'd be a real heart-throb. A lesbian Clint Eastwood."

"And about as miserable as a wet cat," Elsa replied. "Why does anyone even live in California?"

"Oh, I don't know, maybe it's the winters full of sunshine? Or a never-ending supply of citrus?"

"Well, at least we have water. When's the last time you flushed a toilet?"

"Touché. I'll come visit next summer."

"Bring produce," said Elsa.

During Mel's first few months in the house, Elsa tried coaxing her out of the closet. She invited Mel to go dipnetting and hosted barbe-cues, all with her solid group of female friends, each of them sporting similar haircuts, sensible shoes, pockets full of Leathermans, and a col-lective appreciation for Susan Sarandon's glorious, age-defying rack.

It wasn't until Mel came home from work one day, complaining loudly about "some fucking dyke" who kept getting orders wrong at the warehouse that Elsa finally spelled it out for her.

"You do know that *I'm gay*, don't you?" Elsa said.

"That's disgusting."

"Homophobe."

"Dyke. Hey, did you get any toilet paper?"

"Shit," said Elsa. "Nope. Sorry. I'll get it tomorrow."

In time, Elsa quit trying to drag Mel out of the closet, and Mel stopped spending most of her time hiding in the bedroom.

Mel punches again at the remote, this time drowning out the sound of a Pizza Hut commercial. "Hate these stupid commercials," Mel grumbles. "Shitty deals are never true." Sure enough, at the bottom of the screen, in the all-too-familiar fine print, appear the words: *Alaska and Hawaii not included.*

Elsa pulls a warm bath towel from the laundry basket. Elsa's mother has a washer and dryer, but they're brand new, high efficiency, hold about three socks each, and take forever. Elsa prefers to wash a lot of clothes quickly, so she does her laundry here. That usually means dealing with Mel's clothes first, always conveniently left just inside the washing machine. Elsa gives the towel a sharp snap for a clean fold. A pair of hot pink bikini briefs go sailing into the air and flutter to the floor, landing in a heap at Mel's feet.

Mel stiffens.

A tiny satin bow, held on by a single stitch, shines from the top of the brightly colored bundle. Elsa stares at the panties, tightening her lips, and tries not to crack a smile. *Hot pink, Mel? Seriously?*

"That yellow jacket nest," Elsa fumbles. "Where'd you say it was again?" She turns, grabs the flashlight from the kitchen counter, and, stifling a laugh, takes several steps out of the room before Mel has time to answer.

"Crawl space." Even from the hallway, Elsa can hear the frown in Mel's voice. Elsa doubles over in silent laughter, clamping a hand over her mouth.

When she recovers, she grabs the rope hanging down from the ceiling. Tugging, Elsa feels a thin layer of crumbs and dust sprinkle onto her face. She is several steps up the aluminum ladder before she hears the buzz of a few stray fliers, stirred into action by the opening door. Elsa sweeps the eaves with her flashlight beam. It doesn't take long to locate the nest. It's a big one all right, larger than a football, tucked at the crook of a soffit. Elsa climbs slowly down the ladder and heads back into the living room. The panties are gone. Mel's eyes are fixed firmly on the television screen.

"I found the nest. It's a live one."

Mel nods, says nothing.

"I don't want to spray it," Elsa says. "Not in the house. I'm going to town for some dinner. I'll come back and take it out tonight. I'll probably need your help."

Elsa can see the whites of Mel's fingertips gripping the remote. "Sure," she manages, pushing the word through clenched teeth.

After dinner, Elsa hunts around the laundry room for appropriate wasp-killing attire. If it were up to her, she'd leave the nest alone, but if Mel ever got stung, she'd never hear the end of it. Elsa slides open a drawer and pulls out a roll of duct tape. She lays a few more articles of clothing on top of the washer, then digs through a Rubbermaid bin for the rest.

Later that evening, Elsa and Mel stand across from one another in the narrow hallway. Mel is holding both of her arms stiffly away from her sides while Elsa winds the shrinking roll of duct tape around one of Mel's wrists like a boxer. Elsa makes sure to close any gaps between Mel's leather gloves and her insulated Carhartt sleeves. It's getting harder for her to see the tape through the dark amber lenses of her snowboarding goggles. The steam from Elsa's breath keeps fogging up the plastic, now duct taped firmly to her newly crinkly, silver balaclava.

"Hurry up," Mel grumbles. "I'm sweating to death in here." Her voice, muffled under all of the layers of heavy clothing and duct tape, reminds Elsa of an astronaut.

"Oh, keep your panties on," says Elsa.

Mel jerks her hand away. "Gimme that," she says, tearing at the roll of tape still dangling from her sleeve.

Elsa picks up a broom and hands Mel a roll of heavy-duty lawn and leaf bags. "Tear off a few of these and triple bag them," Elsa says.

Mel gropes clumsily for the bags with her stiffly gloved hand. "I can't see jack shit. This is ridiculous. Why don't you just call someone?"

Elsa doesn't answer, but climbs up the rickety ladder, realizing that she can no longer hear the buzzing of the yellow jackets over the huff of her own breath in her ears, the steam of it rising and falling in front of her eyes.

In the attic, the two women creep closer to the nest. It's quiet, most of the fliers that were out earlier are tucked inside for the night. Elsa wonders how quickly they'll wake up. She hands the broom off to Mel, then carefully opens the mouth of the bags and reaches toward the nest.

AMY
GROSHEK

Amy Groshek holds an MFA from the University of Alaska Anchorage. She is a graduate student in the PhD program in English at the University of Wisconsin–Madison. Amy's work has appeared in *Alaska Quarterly Review, Contrary, Bloom,* and *Fence.* Her chapbook, *Shin Deep,* was published by Finishing Line Press in 2008.

What Goes Around Comes Over

When my girlfriend's other girlfriend
comes over for dinner with my housemate,
and my housemate, en route from the grill
to the kitchen, invites me to the picnic table,
I am not confused or upset. I sit
behind my sunglasses, tonguing
the cucumbers sliced to transparency
in the salad. I swallow the peppers
and lettuce, the peppered halibut,
and watch my girlfriend's other girlfriend
discuss with my housemate the making
of a replacement guard for a miter saw,
how her mannish hands approximate
the thought. I snap at my housemate
when she asks me to pass the bread, but I
do not weigh stabbing them both with a dirty fork
against bleeding myself in the flower bed.
So seldom these hot, backyard days.
Fresh is the halibut, soft as butter, soft
and salty, white as the clouds that are not
in the blue, blue sky from which the sun
burns us all without distinction.

The capacity for true love expires at age 25

At some point I quit trying to do good
and tried only not to do damage.
For every candle I'd lit,
every flower I'd opened,
there lay something dead behind me.
There is killing in all things,
I'd heard them say, especially love,
so I was terrified.
Out some window then
slipped my hope: dirty captive bird
taking back the perfect sky.
And all these years
this cage kept just for her.
With her the candles and blossoms
that covered the smell of the dead.
I was lighter then, or heavier.
How she flies.

Rubia Writes a Poem
About Light for a Contest

Light, that old word, worn bare by biblical
metaphor—it turns a poem to stone.
Knobbed cliché, light, and its cousin, white,
sewn in fringes to black-and-white Westerns
my father watched as a child. Silly fool,
to believe that good guys dressed in white,
to believe in men entirely good or bad.
But the world has taught him. But light. But white,
adjective with which my Mexican girlfriend
labels the selfishness common to uninformed
Northerners. Nevertheless, light! My hand
on her thigh, my pale neck draped
with her black curls. Being gay makes me less
white, she says. Less. In Anchorage they speak of light
like a famous acquaintance. *In November the light
goes away*, they say, or, *Today I saw the sun*. Miracle
and cruelty, the daylight so far north.
Generous, careless, ubiquitous—true celebrity.
Light. White. Blessing unto the blessed
in their houses with big windows. Waking
the not-so-blessed to labor or exposing
their progress home at the end of third shift. Yet,
light! Don't you want it? Don't you sit
in the sun and read on a February day?

Dinner at Her Place

When she takes my hand
and tries to kiss me
I'll say I'm busy,
my lips are resting,
do I hear someone
breaking into the living room?
I haven't yet finished
my wine, I'm only
halfway through *Fossils of Texas*,
I have a prearranged call
to my house
in five minutes
from China.
There is the moon, dim
in the long June dusk,
the way she drops her eyes
to her empty hands.
But I've hurt enough women
to start a commune:
just crossing the room
I stub my toes on regrets.
We could be long and deep and glorious.
We could be life's one brilliance
purchased with a thousand failures.
My cat has developed
hepatitis.
Are those Navy SEALs
on the rooftop?
If I don't go out
and start the engine
my truck will explode.

Pearly Everlasting

When the dean says she understands completely
she means there isn't enough money, and anyway,
she disagrees. Go back to your computer, sort the emails

of your students, arrange for their tour of the rooms of books
they will never have time to read. No one
can see anymore, through the winter steam of the city,

overpowering moon and stars, the desperate aurora.
And in "Interrupted Meditation" when Hass is told
that "there is no key, not even the sum total

of our acts," he thinks of love, sees the end
of his marriage, his wife in tears. "I don't love you,
she said. The terrible thing is / that I don't think I ever

loved you." What I thought, reading the poem,
was how I watched a room of faculty, for half an hour,
expostulate the filing of a form. Tonight I'll stand

before my students, buttoned into my pantsuit,
fulfilling a contract in exchange
for health insurance. He was right, Hass, your Pole,

and then you found not even love
could answer him.
So you sang out the name of a weed,

the common name of a weed against
the whole world because you couldn't say
there isn't any key. Plastic

tray of the registrar's unprocessed forms,
black and finely dusted. Manicured nail
my reading student draws across the line,

wrapping word after word in glossy beige.
Spruce. Aurora. Pearly everlasting.
Anything not to say we make it so.

GABRIELLE BARNETT

Gabrielle Barnett has been a frequent contributor to *Cirque Journal*. She has also placed poetry and nonfiction with *Alaska Women Speak, Wild Voices, POL,* and *Contact Quarterly*; her poetry was recognized in *F Magazine*'s 2014 statewide writing contest, and her nonfiction won a 1993 Alaska Press Club award. With a PhD in Performance Studies from NYU, she taught as contingent faculty at UAA from 1993 to 2013. She calls the coastal forest and mountains of Turnagain Arm home, seeking balance between the pulls of modern city life and the wish for a quiet backwoods retreat.

Mountain Man

James set two mugs, a jar of jam, and platter of toast, all ends cast off from otherwise eaten loaves, on the sturdy drop-leaf table. Idle gossip had been brewing along with the coffee, woodstove warming the A-frame against a steady drizzle damp, low clouds still funneling through the pass.

Passing the toast to Jo, he apologized, "I eat so simply now; it's such a bother to haul a lot of food out here. Got my dried bulk items, and learned to like cabbage. I do miss the rhubarb. Died off this year. The chickens give me plenty of eggs. Mostly I drink water."

Pausing to stoke the stove and light a bowl in a pale, stone pipe, he returned to his rambling monologue on the exhale, grateful for an audience after a stretch of solitude.

"Just look at my skin. It's the diet, the pure water. Still so clear, and at my age. And the sauna, to help flush the toxins, sweat them out. You've got to flush those toxins, honey. Eat simply, drink lots of water, and cleanse; cleanse the colon, cleanse the liver, cleanse the blood, cleanse from the inside out. Honey, just let it go."

"Here I am, late summer again," Jo mused, "still just a weekend visitor, taking refuge from the city, fleeing another disaster with a woman who doesn't get me." She looked around, relaxing into the familiar surroundings. Underfoot, signature fragments of blue circle and red stripe speckled the hardwood floor, courtesy of the school gym rebuild. A seated Buddha surveyed the scene, complacent and inscrutable as usual, from a perch atop the spiral stair. Behind the old cast-iron stove, stacks of cups, plates, and jars, waiting for the eternal backlog in the enamel sink to clear out, buried a wooden counter.

"I could give you a hand with those dishes," she offered, accepting pipe and lighter from her host.

"They can pile up a bit more; it's not yet worth heating water," he replied.

As soon as the summer swelter set in back east, she had started longing for this place. She missed seeing timberline on a regular basis: somber conifer spires breaking up the bright mass of birch and aspen leaf. She missed the cabin under the contours of that beloved rock face, daubed all muted orange, rose quartz, and dusty yellow, crevices filled with clumps of mossy tundra jagging down from ridgeline. But an unexpected loneliness confronted her when she arrived.

"Seems like half the state cleared out with the crash," Jo reflected, passing back the pipe. "Anchorage feels so empty."

James agreed. "Hardly anyone there worth visiting."

He poured himself a cup of coffee.

"Yeah, I guess the half that stayed is sticking close to home, putting down roots, digging in, just trying to get on with things," said Jo, spreading jam on a slice of toast.

"I'm spending less and less time in town myself, nowadays," James explained. "I go in for the laundry run, try to pick up the food drop, mostly for other folks out here in need. I do what I can. So many just barely making it these days."

"Looks like you finally got that bulb wired to the solar panel," Jo noted, refilling her own mug.

"Should give me light through October and again come February," James acknowledged proudly. "Sun won't be clearing the ridge mid-November."

"Mid-November I'll be deep in my big city routine, riding the F between Brooklyn and the East Village," she laughed. "Hard to believe that's real when I'm here."

"I'm thinking of spending the winter outside again; plant another crop of garlic on the family land in Alabama. Last year's crop paid for the trip, with a little left over. Organic garlic is fetching a good price these days. Got to get that greenhouse started. Still hoping to put in tulips this year. Lots of tulips. If only I could get ahead for a season, I know this land could pay for itself," he sighed, lighting yet another bowl.

Over the years James had remodeled the place, starting by digging out the cabin floor several feet down, and adding a root cellar under the kitchen, accessed though a trap door. He pushed out a wall upstairs, creating an alcove with a dormer window, to let in light as well as free up some headroom. Downstairs, he set in a small octagonal picture window to catch the view up valley. An extension to the original arctic entryway served as storage space for just about anything that could handle freezing. A wooden deck off the west side, out the sliding glass doors, invited summer guests to look out over sunsets and the brackish water of Dragonfly Pond.

"Always so many chores waiting," he continued. "Haul, build, split, lay in, mend, feed, stack. Envy those damn cats, always napping when there's work to be done."

As the pipe changed hands again, talk turned steamy, moving beyond the new root cellar and leaky roof to the running feuds, both domestic and neighborly. Who left who, why, when, and how. Deals and hearts broken. Convoluted disputes over property lines and rights of way. Custody suits and court proceedings, escalating beyond divorce.

Fueled by a full pot of caffeine, the rumor mill churned. James loved to test, needle, and bait, whether bantering and bitching in the kitchen or working the massage table. He could be catty, even vicious when jealous, detecting a sore spot, honing in on the vulnerability, and digging hard. Jo had watched James burn the bridge to his last long-term lover this way, when he showed up with a woman, suspected to be a girlfriend in the making. James knew how to out that screamer of a spot inside the big toe, or the knot hiding under the scapula, that possessive streak, that lurking hang up over body image, that trip about sexuality, that nagging doubt about being woman enough, or man. Most of the time he knew when to back off;

after preying on the pain a while, he'd admonish, "Stop holding on, that's baggage you don't need, honey, get it out of your way, let it go."

So why couldn't she shake her ex's edict: half and half, could swing either way women were a waste of time. Only real dykes from now on, she had said. If not being 100 percent lesbian 100 percent of the time made her suspect, she was better off on her own. She didn't like seeing herself as a potential traitor to the lesbian nation. She felt unfairly disqualified, cast into a limbo land of in between and nothing at all. It hadn't threatened her last boyfriend that she was also into women, so why couldn't the women in her life be just as open?

James interrupted her brooding, unexpectedly veering onto raw emotional turf of his own.

"The grandmother, that bitch, went and called DFYS. All over a little weed. And my thing for men."

Jo had never met the child, just seen photos. James and Benjamin outside the cabin. James and Benjamin going to town. James and Benjamin smiling for the camera.

"Don't make me no pederast. Men aren't boys. We're talking about a two year old."

There it was again. Prejudice. Making a whole class of people guilty by default, that deep-rooted assumption that gays are up to no good whenever children are involved.

"When are people going to wake up?" she scoffed in his defense. "Where are the stats on guys messing with underage chicks? Look at Annie, felt up by her mom's new squeeze. Did some time, and he's back on the scene, still lusting after those new teen tits."

James shook his head. "Too much hot-blood in that Harley-riding man."

Jo tried to piece James's life together, getting nowhere figuring out her own. He was notorious for lying about his age, getting caught in inconsistencies from one rendition to the next. But by her best estimate he was more than twenty years her senior; pushing fifty to her still twenty-something. Upstairs, in the strictly shoes-off loft, carpeted thick and kept uncharacteristically clutter-free, a large painting capturing him as a much younger man, joyfully nude, hinted at a life left somewhere behind. On one of her early visits, James had shared the contents of a flimsy cardboard box tucked in the upstairs dresser: Kodak memories dating back to the days of black-and-white glossies.

"They're calling it neglect, abuse, child endangerment," James continued.

A strapping fresh-faced Marine posed on a public lawn somewhere in Kerouac's America: perhaps a clue to the undesirable discharge that first redirected his career, long before Stonewall, long before AIDS, the Gay Men's Health Crisis, and Silence = Death.

"The mom entrusted me with him; I relieved her of a burden she was not ready to bear. I could see she couldn't cope."

During his bohemian Atlanta days, in shorts and an unbuttoned polo shirt, he tossed thick, curly hair, flaunting the taut, tanned body of which he remained so vainly proud, warmly greeting beehived young women and mod young men at the door of a bustling coffeehouse. Again too alternative for the time and place, he had to move on; that time anti-war activity got him run out of business and town. "Surely he'd already suffered enough discrimination for one lifetime," Jo thought. "Surely it could stop now. All of it. Surely all narrow-mindedness keeping people out, keeping people apart, stopping gay men from parenting, dumping bi people in one closet or another, could just stop."

"She was too young; she had no support. No father in sight. And where was the grandmother then? I'm the only parent that child has really known."

A brief relocate to the Haight took him west, but finding that mecca already on the wrong side of trendy, he left. He wanted to go to India, but that required too many vaccinations and visas, so he headed north instead, looking for land to go back to, seeking freedom and peace, self-reliance and community away from it all. Winding up in Anchorage, he fell in with the start-up health food crowd, established a massage business, and bought property in the

Talkeetnas, complete with blueberry bog, forested acreage, and an eroding bluff overhanging a braided meander and flood of a glacial river.

"I took on that child when no one else wanted him. I gave him love no one else had to spare. It was the right thing to do. It was something I could do."

With the right company he'd sashay to Leonard Cohen until the cassette player batteries died. With the right weather, he'd go about all his chopping and sawing, baking and planting buck naked, reveling in his best birthday suit, so out of place there was no question he belonged.

"So I have got to defend myself in court. Against projections and conjecture. Justify myself. That's all the thanks I get. Because now she wants him. I don't know if I'll ever see that child again."

Jo searched for something worth saying. "It's so unfair. Court sounds kind of scary."

"She doesn't have a case, really. Nothing but hearsay. Another reminder that this is all temporary anyway. Attachment brings suffering. That's the human condition. Best get on with those chores before we lose any more of the day. We can fire up that sauna later, put on a pot of soup."

With conversation and coffee drained to the dregs, damper closed, and pain set back on its shelf, James pocketed the pipe, absent-mindedly stashing what was left of the weed behind a jar of Granola. Leaving the cabin unlocked, tended by a host of Ganeshas, Shivas, Buddhas, and the stray Devata, collected from import shop, thrift store, and garage sale, he loaded up rototiller and chain saw, to lurch on up the dirt road, shifting beat-up green pickup into low for the steep climb: a fading Southern queen keeping the homestead dream alive, just barely in the bush, highway hum always drifting down valley with the clouds.

TEEKA A. BALLAS

Teeka A. Ballas has worked as a freelance writer and editor, and staffer and stringer for newspapers, international wire services, travel publications, and radio. The cofounder of *F Magazine*, Ballas has worked tirelessly for seven years as editor and publisher of Alaska's only volunteer-run, independent arts and culture publication. As of 2015, she has placed the magazine on hiatus while she focuses her attention on working with her partner, Dawnell Smith, on a multimedia project that entails an art documentary, a dual memoir, and an audio slideshow collectively titled, "Exhuming My Father."

Carrots, Peas: *in D minor*

She releases the bite on her lower lip to blow a renegade strand of hair from her eyes. With a swift wave of her right hand, she moves the pan of braised ptarmigan in reduced crushed juniper berry and red current juices to the back burner, and with her left hand guides her roux of most beloved imported ingredients to the closer flame: butter, rice flour, a dash of paprika, two grinds of sea salt, four pinches of Aleppo pepper. She gradually adds the homemade vegetable stock. With one hand she whisks without pause, a hint of music between each beat. With her other hand she drops finely chopped carrots and peas into a sunken pan of hot caribou fat to brew a hash; then diced onions, zucchini—all from the garden—into a dry stir fry pan, tossed over a low flame to sweat them together. A continual lift and twist of her wrist throws the contents into the air and catches them.

It's a cacophony, a discordance of motion. I play a game with myself, trying to intuit her next move, but it's dizzying for me to watch her hands. Instead I watch her feet. Bare and cracked, they hardly move. Only a slight shift of weight from one to the other indicates the mayhem delivered by her upper torso. Her ankles slim, her calves thick from combat, plaid cotton boxers come down just past her buttocks, rounded, firm. I want to lunge into the kitchen, press my breasts against her back and bite on her ear, tug on her ponytail, and laugh—but I know it would only disrupt the flow. Our flow. The rhythm in her head. Her manic cooking, her panic. Her fear of sleeping hungry.

In the cities where her story began, there are those who have it worse than us, those who live in the shadows cast by wealth.

They fight for rotten scraps. They shed tears, wring hands, gnash teeth so gnarled they can only suck and gum what food they find. She tells me stories about those she lived among, what she had to do to survive. Sometimes I tell her to stop talking about it; I am laden with guilt for the contrast of our lives. I was born and raised in Anchorage—a city with different social ills than those Outside. I had the luxury of summers and the great outdoors sans concrete, suffocated earth. Very young I learned to fish and hunt, gut and tan. My palate is simple like my cooking, if I couldn't catch my food I might starve, too.

She has an inherent ability, a gift, to look into a cupboard even an impoverished city dweller would see as bare, and as an outrageous throe of movement and attitude, adorn a plate with piquancy and lusty appeal in under an hour of aerobic culinary activity. She says poverty taught her to cook. Poverty and eating scraps off rich people's plates when she worked busing tables for wages so low that a full day's work didn't afford her the price of an aperitif.

Sometimes when I watch her work, I can see the impressions left behind—a shadow in her eye, a twitch in her brow, a turn in her lip. When she is so buried in those moments, I resent not just her history, but how she squanders the moment by living it only as a means to defeat the past. In those instances, she cannot see me; she cannot see the ease in which I swing my axe; my perfect posture as I brace, draw, and release; the gracefulness in my cut and clean. It is as though I am posturing for a blind artist. It is as if I am only living between her seconds, between the notes she's humming in her head while she wields and blows.

This incessant motion of hers is not relegated to the kitchen. It's how she moves through life—it keeps her from noticing the hollow, the void—the place where anger and pain reside. She's at war with her demons, the ones who determined for her before she was old enough to cross the street alone what the outcome of her life would be. The sexual reprobates whose acts buried within her a path that would know only struggle, doubt, and false footing.

I don't always know how or where I fit in her life, but I take solace in knowing I am not the problem. I am not her past. I am now. I get to sit here with her. Eat the cuisine she creates out of food we harvest and I catch. Feel her tears fall onto my shoulder at night when she thinks I am sleeping. Listen to the monsters growl and churn inside her while she slumbers. I want to pick up my rifle and shoot her demons, but have learned the best way to help her fight the bastards is to hold them down when she needs to kick them.

Sometimes, when the volume is turned up in her head and she's immersed in a burst of activity, her tongue lashes out at me. I am not a fighter, I'm a hunter. So I stand aside and bide my time. I have a hunter's quietude, a fisherman's patience. Eventually, in short time, she comes around, wraps me in her earnest embrace, lets me taste the wealth of my fortitude, reminds me why I wait.

A hush is unfolding in the kitchen. Each burner's flame is extinguished. Discarded culinary effects are placed in the sink. Her feet move more than her hands. They dance between spaces as she removes two plates from the cupboard. Two glasses. A bottle of sour wine made by neighbors. She begins to hum, then sing . . . and I release the breaths I've been hoarding.

"My darling lives in the green," her voice soft in sound but firm in texture.

"She wants to be . . . ah la la . . . with me."

A pool of copper brown, spicy roux. A scoop of vegetable hash doled atop.

"But darling . . ."

Notes rise and embolden.

"I've no time to be deceived . . ."

A twirl and spoon of blues.

"By the sweetness of desire."

Ptarmigan placed gently atop . . .

"Ahh . . . All I've got is time for sweet . . . sweet . . ."

A trill and fade.

"Sweet ed-di-bal . . ."

Delicate swirls of deep red, tart rhubarb syrup.

"She wants to taste my sweet ed-di-bal . . ."

Carrots and peas . . .

"Sweet ed-dah-bal love . . ."

She spins the plate down in front of me. Places on my mouth soft lips with sour wine lingering upon them.

For now, we feast.

Cupid's Arrow

red makes the buffalo hit the fence
the tourist's social camouflage
drives it to fury

its passion imitated
she paints
brushes and strokes

flush pastels across my body
moon indigo over my face
a pouting lip
a rounded tear

slipping through her memories
her laughter momentous
full of texture and strength

holding me up
high in the air
safe from the buffalo's rage

SANDY
GILLESPIE

Sandy Gillespie, writer and artist, lived in Alaska for twenty-two years. She worked as a professional artist and arts administrator and exhibited extensively in Alaska, including solo shows at the Anchorage Museum and the Alaska State Museum in Juneau. Her work is in the permanent collections of these institutions and the Museum of the North in Fairbanks. Gillespie currently works out of her Minneapolis studio. She holds an MFA in Creative Writing from UAF and continues to teach online for the Kachemak Bay Campus of UAA.

The Trees Tell the Story

They walked among us—listening deeply to the ruffling of birch
leaves, the ting
  of aspen leaves. They smiled at the spruce, tapped the trunk of
  the largest—the one that would stand as sentinel at the top of
  the driveway. Before they brought chain saws and bobcat, they
  invited friends. To come. To listen. To dedicate this place in
  love. They brought gifts—tokens of the earth from other loved
  places. They brought stories and laughter. Dogs and cats. They
  consecrated this
  space in their own way, understanding that the sacred
  already breathed here.

When they began to build, they did this with respect. They took
down only
  enough trees to live amongst us. They saved our severed trunks.
  Split them into logs and stacked them for winter.

We welcomed them. We danced in the wind, bending as if we were
60-foot palms
  swaying along a sundrenched coast. We sang until our leaves
  fell, then rustled hellos as they walked from cabin to outhouse
  to campfire. We heated them in woodstove and fire pit—listening to their stories and the stories of friends who gathered
  around the fire.

When they were ready to build a studio on the second ridge they
had to take more
    trees. Clear a larger space—creating required more floor space
    than living. This time a concrete base—and the need to hire
    help to stand the larger walls. We didn't mind—they still re-
    spected us, would save our trunks for heat and be grateful. But
    something had shifted in their hearts.

We wanted to lift them up—high into our boughs—to let them see
what they had
    built—together. How beautiful, how holy this ground. But they
    were busy. They focused on the workspace, lost the heart space.

When one left for a winter in Homer, we stood in silence and held
the space. We
    waited for her. She returned to say goodbye. She left an image
    of herself under willows outside her studio. She left the ashes
    of beloved beings near the campfire. She left her heart's beat,
    the sigh of her breath. We hold her. We wish her peace and the
    grace of knowing we remain.

MORGAN
GREY

Morgan Grey, despite growing up in Nebraska, has always felt the pull of the sea and been fascinated by the legends of the seal people that span the North Atlantic from Norway to Iceland. She is working on a novel about June's selkie family in Prince William Sound. In the late 1970s Morgan was a founding member of the Lincoln Legion of Lesbians, a radical dyke collective that organized conferences, concerts, and other events promoting lesbian community and visibility. She was a volunteer and later office manager for the lesbian journal *Sinister Wisdom*. She received her MFA in Creative Writing from the University of Alaska Anchorage and is a former Executive Director of 49 Writers.

Breakers

The regulars had already claimed their tables by the time Bren arrived. The evening was young, and the bar would soon be packed. She stowed her knapsack and coat on the pile next to the low stage, then pulled out her fiddle.

Chris looked up as he strapped on his uillean pipes. "Long time no see."

Eric paused from misting his bodhrán. He pulled her into a hug. "What's kept you away for so long, sweetheart? We've missed you."

Bren eyed the spray bottle in his hand and pulled away. "Family business, you know. But now I'm back in action." After three months of being a good girl, she wanted to cut loose. Time to get back to her life, her music, and finally get laid.

"There will be broken hearts in Anchor Town after this weekend, methinks." Chris pressed his hand to his chest in a dramatic flourish.

Bren scowled. She tightened her bow and stroked it with rosin.

"They always fall in love with her. It's sad, really. Such a hot body, and such a cold heart." Eric spritzed her before returning his attention to the drum.

Bren pretended to ignore him as she tuned her fiddle, but his words stung.

Della joined them and pulled out her tin whistles. "Good to see you, Bren. Thought you'd completely disappeared, this time."

Bren nodded. "It's good to be back in town." She ran through a few scales to warm up while she scanned the gathering crowd and weighed her options. Mostly straight couples tonight. A blonde sitting by the windows tried to catch Bren's eye. They'd spent an unremarkable night together the last time Bren had been in town.

As a rule, she avoided emotional entanglements by spacing out her dates with the same woman. Casual and friendly was her motto. Anchorage was too small to deal with a string of unhappy exes. But she might be willing to reconsider the blonde tonight if nothing better showed up. It had been three months, after all.

Chris gave the cue for a fast jig. Bren lost herself as her music meshed with the other musicians, rising and falling together or in counterpoint, taking turns with leading and supporting. The rhythm felt more intimate than sex, the communion deeper than with any lover. Music is truth. Why care about the rest?

At first break, she wove through the crowd. People patted her on the shoulder, saying "glad you're back," and "you've still got it,"—things she could barely hear over the din of conversations and clinking bottles. She shouldered up to the bar next to a tall lass with ebony hair who'd come in mid-way through the set. Bren ordered a beer and winked at the girl. "Hi, I'm Bren." She leaned in close, stretching up toward the woman's ear to be heard over the noise. The woman smelled of good soap and faint musk.

The girl nodded, her short dark hair fluttering with the motion. "I've heard of you. You're pretty good."

"I could give you a private concert later."

The woman raised an eyebrow and twitched up a corner of her mouth. "Sounds like fun."

Bren returned to the stage, chugged her beer, and picked up her fiddle. Eric counted out the beat for the next song. Bren opened a medley of Scottish reels, then wove arpeggios around Della and Eric's voices.

After the second set, she packed up her fiddle and said good-bye to her friends. The dark-haired woman sat near the door. A scraggle-bearded guy perched on the chair next to her, his lips close to her ear. He slid his hand to her knee. She lifted it to the table.

"Let's get out of this place." Bren reached out toward the woman, who smiled and clasped her hand. She pulled the girl to her feet and into a quick hug.

"I feel like dancing at Myrna's," Bren said as they stepped out of the club and onto the street. "What do you say?"

"Over on Fifth? Sure," she said. "I'm Shay."

They turned the corner onto Fifth Avenue, passing a couple of baby-faced hookers shivering in their miniskirts and cropped jackets. The steady beat of disco music blared as Bren opened the door to the gay bar. Every table was full, and people stood two deep at the bar. The place reeked of spilled beer, sweat, and the dirty-sock stench of poppers. The bartender—an old friend of Bren's—let her stash her fiddle and knapsack behind the bar. Bren bought two beers, which she and Shay downed before maneuvering onto the packed dance floor.

The first songs were long and fast, the beats pounding through Bren's viscera, flowing red through her arteries, telling her body how to move. When the music turned slow and romantic, she pulled Shay close and laid her cheek on the swell of Shay's bosom. There were advantages to being short.

They paused after a few more dances and several beers. Shay's chest glistened with sweat in the deep V of her silk blouse. "Want to go back to my place?" Bren lifted her eyes to Shay's face, busted. She grabbed her stuff and together they walked to Shay's car.

The next morning, Bren felt more relaxed than she had in months. Good music, good dancing, good sex, and a few beers, just what a girl needed sometimes. She glanced at the clock as she padded into the bathroom. Ten already. Time to head back home, to the island.

Shay stirred as Bren came out of the bathroom. "You're dressed already?" she asked. "What's the hurry?"

Bren shrugged.

Shay stretched and sat up, the sheets falling to her lap. "Let's have breakfast at Gwennie's."

Bren turned away and closed her eyes for a moment. There was something about Shay that felt safe. She gave herself a mental shake. "Sorry, can't do it." She grabbed her fiddle and backpack on the way to the door. No matter how good the sex, or how well they connected, she never stayed for breakfast. Breakfast led to talking and talking led to questions, questions she didn't want to answer, like where are you from, how did you come out?

Bren didn't like to speak of her own coming out because, back home, she wasn't out. She lived most in the island Alaska town where she'd grown up, a place where everybody knew her. But they only knew so much. She kept her love life far away from home.

Her first time, ten years earlier, she learned the hard way why she had to be so strict. It was a rare day, hot and sunny. In the evening she hiked around the island to an isolated beach, and sweaty from the exertion, she stripped and jumped into the freezing ocean. When she surfaced, Bren noticed a woman on a rock at the waterline, watching her.

Bren stood naked in the splash of the waves. Her heart was pounding and her stomach tense. She stared back at the woman. The salt spray reddened the woman's broad cheeks, and the sea breeze liberated light brown strands from her short ponytail, several curly tendrils fluttering around her square face. She was the most beautiful woman Bren had ever seen.

"Did you see that seal?" The woman nodded toward the spot close to shore where Bren had been.

Bren shook her head, her gaze returning to the woman.

"It was swimming right there. At first, when you came out of the waves, I thought you were a seal." The woman laughed. "Maybe you're a selkie!"

"What's that?"

"Half seal, half woman." And then the woman's smile turned sly. "Are you?"

Now Bren laughed, her cheeks went hot. "Maybe."

That night in the woman's tent, Bren discovered that sex with women came as naturally to her as gliding through the sea. The woman's body smelled of almonds and vanilla, spiced with smoke from the campfire, as she gently turned Bren to face her in the sleeping bag. Their breasts touched. Bren's nipples hardened until they hurt, her body stiffened.

The woman brushed her fingertips over Bren's cheek. "It's okay," she whispered as her lips brushed Bren's. Bren felt the heat of her own body surge from her core, like a riptide, threatening to pull her deeper. She closed her eyes, trying to steady her ragged breathing as the woman's hand slid lower. Her touch against Bren's skin felt as good as swimming in a shallow lake on a hot day, the rinse of the water and the warmth of the sun caressing her. No, it was better. Bren had never known anything like the play of the woman's skin against hers, her tongue tasting Bren's body, her fingers teasing out swelling ripples of pleasure. She fell asleep in her lover's arms. She dreamed of seals.

Bren awoke to the sound of a motor followed by the scrape of a hull on rocks and the splash of feet in the water. The sound of voices—the woman responding to several men. Bren held her breath to hear the words. Damn, it was her father, searching for her. She shivered in the morning chill as she threw on her clothes and crawled out of the tent.

The image of her father's face burned into her memory: the relief of finding her safe shifting to disgust as he took in the scene. He ordered her to the skiff and told the woman—who was camping on private land without permission—to leave the island. Bren watched the woman strike camp as the skiff rounded the point and headed home.

Later she sat by the water for a long time, the incoming tide breaking wave after wave upon the beach. She never again saw the woman who had awakened her desire, the desire that pulled her to the city and to women. But Bren always returned to the island. The deep pull that she felt for this place. Each wave calling her home.

Now, years later, Bren existed between two worlds, never comfortable in either. She loved the city, the excitement and stimulation from the throngs of people, the strange sights and smells, playing music sessions with the band, and best of all, her nights with women.

But there was also the pull of the sea, the place she belonged.

Back in Anchorage a week later, Bren stood at the bar during a break between sets. "That chick," the bartender tipped his head toward Shay as she walked in the door, "has been looking for you every night this week."

"Hey, baby," Shay sidled up to Bren, bending close to her ear, "it's nice to see you again."

Bren stiffened. She'd hoped to avoid a scene. But here was Shay, still smelling of good soap and herbal shampoo, her moist breath tickling Bren's ear, her hand warm and solid on Bren's arm. What the hell, Bren thought as she put her arm around Shay's waist and pulled her close. She nuzzled Shay's neck. "Likewise."

As the days lengthened into summer, Bren spent time with Shay almost every weekend. There was truth in the joke about lesbians renting a moving van for the second date. The remarkable thing about Shay was that she hadn't pushed their relationship. Bren allowed herself to be lulled by the pleasure of Shay's company and her easy-going ways.

"We need to talk," Shay said one night as they got ready for bed.

"Can't it wait?" Bren asked as she pushed Shay onto the mattress. She straddled the tall woman, pinning her arms to the bed as she nibbled at her collarbone. Shay bent one leg and twisted, flipping Bren onto her back.

"I don't get you." Shay's shoulders slumped as she sat on the edge of the bed. "You're all passionate, but you disappear every morning."

"Gotta get to work. It takes hours to get there—the drive to Whittier, the boat to S—" Bren felt a familiar sinking feeling in her gut. She'd had this conversation too many times. "The boat to the research station out in the Sound."

"That's an excuse. We've been seeing each other for months, but always on your terms. You don't give me your phone number. Hell, I don't even know where you live. You know all about my life, but you tell me nothing about yours." Shay pushed herself off the bed. She strode to the doorway, turned and leaned against the frame. "You're totally out. Everyone knows you're a dyke. What are you hiding?"

"You know how it is in little towns. I have to stay closeted at home."

"And where is 'home,' exactly?"

"I like you, Shay, but don't push it." She stood and gathered her clothes. "I don't do commitment. I made that clear from the beginning."

"I'm just asking for some honesty."

Bren pulled on her jeans and T-shirt.

"What are you doing?" Shay's face twisted, and she began to cry.

Bren's heart pounded as she grabbed her pack and brushed past Shay as she headed out the door. What she needed was the sound of the waves. If she could just get close enough to hear the break.

LAURA CARPENTER

Laura Carpenter survives Alaska winters by sledding, running in studded shoes, and drinking chai lattes. She works too hard for the largest museum in the state and plays just as hard with her daughter and (now legal!) wife. Her publications include *Curve, The New York Times, Anchorage Daily News, Alaska Pride Blog, Naked Ptarmigan, NorthView, Inside Passages,* and more.

Mirror, Mirror

Amber never thought she would have children. A dog, perhaps, that came with a girl she dated. A cat, more likely. In those days of late mornings and later evenings, when possibilities dragged on like warm beer, she saw friends hitch up with moms and shook her head of well-sculpted hair, laughed, and hit the gym.

Children? No. She was not the motherly type.

Or, rather, she wasn't seven years ago, before a long-haired, long-limbed brunette named Mallory caught her eye and stole her heart. Mallory was allergic to cats and eager for kids, and Amber (blind, swooning) would have given her anything. Mallory, a smart siren not easily caught, dragged Amber from her tidy condo and plunked her down in a house with a yard. Before Amber registered what was happening, she had traded her Skidoo for a stroller.

As Amber looks at the bathroom mirror coated with toothpaste spittle, she thinks about that woman she was, the carefree gal who danced with all the chicks in the room and was still up at dawn to run ten miles in subzero temperatures. She remembers the freedom of those single days, the time, the clean floors, the sex, the glory. She looks at the young elite runners and skiers now, in their short shorts and high-tech gear, and they don't even see her. She's invisible to them. Her current coworkers don't know the medals she's won, the podiums she's graced. She's just another mom out for a jog.

"Mommy!" A little girl with wild curly hair slams into Amber, knocking her slightly off balance and jerking her from her stupor. The broken hippopotamus toy found on one of their walks and the homemade cape reappear on the bathroom counter before Amber, along with long brown hairs, a half-rinsed Hello Kitty toothbrush, three fairy cups, and a crumpled washcloth. Amber's hair gel squats among Mallory's lotions and beauty products, like a stump in a field of fireweed. The toilet isn't flushed and a mild stink wafts to her nose.

"You be the bad queen," her daughter says, handing her a paper crown and a butterfly eye mask. "I'll be the good queen and Mama will be my child."

Shaking off the memory of her single self, Amber slips on the mask and crown. She raises her hands, her fingers curled like claws. She laughs her best evil queen laugh. "Muwahaha!"

Her daughter squeals with joy and points her plastic wand at Amber, blocking a curse and casting a spell of her own. "You can't get my baby, Bad Queen!"

The pretend curse strikes Amber. "Aaaaaaaahhhhh!" she wails dramatically, crumpling to the ground.

The good queen dashes off to protect her "baby," who is doing dishes in the kitchen. Amber gets up off the floor with more groans than she'd like and tries to remember what she was doing in the bathroom in the first place. She has no idea.

She starts to wipe the counter but catches her reflection in the mirror. Paper hearts attached to pipe cleaners pop out from the pink crown. Who would have thought that someone could get her to don pink? Or an outfit made entirely of fleece? Her waist and hips have gained at least twenty pounds in the last five years. It is barely 8:30 on a Saturday morning and she's been up for two hours. The sun won't be up for another two.

Who is this woman staring back at her? Who is this person who knows all the songs in *Frozen* and can find Piggie and Gerald books in the library in three swift steps? Whose trophies collect dust in a corner? Who thinks a hot date is collapsing on the couch in front of a movie? What happened to the stud who got a phone number every time she stepped off the dance floor?

The house is too quiet. Amber holds her breath and cocks her head to the side, as alert as a fox. Her heart quickens. She opens her mouth to call out "Everyone all right?" when peels of laughter erupt from the kitchen. Amber breathes out a sigh of relief and listens to the magic in their giggles, magic not found anywhere else, not on the trail or at the bar.

"She has awoken!" Her daughter shouts from the hallway, sounding so much like Mallory that Amber nearly bursts with love.

Amber looks back at the mirror, at herself as she is right now, a thirty-seven-year-old woman who will not win any races this season or set any records. Instead, she will get more colds than she'd like to count. She will take her daughter to preschool, and then go to work, cook dinner, convince her daughter to go potty, read stories, sleep too little, and repeat. And repeat. She will get sex once a month (if lucky). She will forget to comb her hair some mornings. She will not fit into her favorite pair of pants.

But she still has her strong chin, her biceps, her drive to be the best.

"Mommy, stop staring at the mirror and come play with me."

Amber grins. She doesn't have to win races or collect numbers to be worthy. She's married (legally!) to the sexiest woman she's ever met and mom to the sweetest, silliest kid. She doesn't miss the lonely nights or the empty days she filled with beer and workouts, aching with a void she could never satisfy.

"You just try to get away from me, Good Queen!" Amber growls in her bad queen voice, which sounds remarkably similar to her pirate voice.

The good queen shrieks and darts away.

Amber grabs the broken hippopotamus toy off the bathroom counter. "You can't stop me! I have the Hippo of Power!"

KATE PARTRIDGE

Kate Partridge received her MFA from George Mason University, and her poems and lyric essays have appeared in *Colorado Review, Carolina Quarterly, RHINO, Better: Culture & Lit,* and *Verse Daily.* She lives in Anchorage, where she teaches at the University of Alaska Anchorage, co-edits *Gazing Grain Press,* and serves as account coordinator for VIDA.

Model

As if the name isn't enough,
she insists that I stand on the porch, too,

to look at the beaver moon,
which is indeed pale as the rings

around birches along the river, or bright
enough to light them, and barely obscured

by the early evening streetlights and sirens,
the icicles grafting onto each other

in regimented curtains. Here
and there, one takes an abrupt turn

where it's been dripped on—
sudden left elbow tapering out.

My friend says nothing can be done
about the icy intersections except patience,

but he also recommends wrapping
a turkey in bacon, so take your best guess.

The term fishtailing makes me wonder
what it would be like to be propelled

by sudden shifts from behind or to wade
across a street completely submerged

in fins. The ice seems suddenly preferable.
In fact, we snap off ice spears

from the roof and compete, perhaps
not as safely as one might, at hurling them

into a snow bank, where they remain
wrapped in snow as though modeling

the rule for treating impalements:
leave the object in place.

Earthquake Park

Someone has taken care
that all the edges should be jagged:

fence posts cut in descending steps,
path split by a constantly-shifting

line up to the edge where houses
shrugged off into the ocean, remaining

ground rippling across trees locked
upward. From a rock along the inlet,

she observes the planes landing,
crossing before Susitna and selecting

the international landing to the west
or the local airfield to the north.

If she can identify all of the objects
in the sky, she believes in order.

Beneath her, the rocks boast
cartoon faces and phone numbers,

the recovery of ancient method
almost reverent to the location.

Another woman scampering further on
the ridge slides down the mud bank

into a stand of grass, a collapsed circle
outlasting the animal that formed it.

M 4.0, 21 km S of Knik-Fairview

Otherwise, a static day—
the snow huddled against the mountains,

the bike trail puddled over root-carved ravines,
we decided to go to war or not.

When we left, Ben gave me a field guide
in a bar we frequented. I didn't read it

but went to a preserve to learn
to recognize my neighbors—

the bears fielding blueberries
from the paws of a young keeper

pitching them over the deck,
the caribou fencing, antlers clacking

like hockey sticks. In the gift shop,
a stack of pelts, fleshed and stretched;

a child stroking them and murmuring,
"Poor reindeer. Now he's dead."

DAWNELL SMITH

Dawnell Smith works in a cubicle by day, a shared desk pod/family room at night, where she crafts columns, reviews, and articles for daily and weekly newspapers, quarterly magazines, blogs, and other digital chalkboards. When not on quad skates, working on art projects, running errands, and getting outside, she makes essays, poems, short stories, and other mixed-genre pieces. She won a Rasmuson Fellowship in 2015, and is currently working on a collaborative memoir and video/audio project with her partner, Teeka Ballas. She lives in Anchorage with her partner, teenage boys, rescue dogs, crickets, renegade shrews, and lone gecko. (She feels bad about the gecko; it's cold and the tank seems limiting.) Her derby name is WickedSpeedia.

What Would Derby Do?

Dear WWDD,

I hate my job. It's not the work I do. It's my boss. She's passive aggressive, a micromanager, a social fail. Yep, a great combination. She treats me like a fucking child. We get paid shit, but we do something decent. She just doesn't get the "decent" part when it comes to her staff. My boyfriend says I need to stick it out a year. We're broke. But I dread the walk to the office from the parking lot. I've started showing up late to avoid her. And when I do run into her, I feel like throwing up. It's just a stupid ordinary job, and she's just a stupid ordinary bitch. Why does she make me feel like crap?

Jobba the Hunt

Clearly, you can ditch it, tough it out, or hit the bitch where it hurts. That's the obvious advice. That's how I would have responded a year ago, but I got the wind knocked out of me. I feel trapped in a noisy washing machine with my kneepads and wrist guards in the soak, agitate, spin, and repeat cycle.

My *WWDD* advice blog came to me like the big bang, a self-made extension of my derby career and a vehicle for moving from retail to publishing. I figured it could go viral, help pay some bills, keep me relevant in the badass community. That was two years ago, and the blog blew up by year one—the likes, shares, invites, comments, and nudges by social media hounds went off the chain. Even now, the blog's reach keeps hitting all-time highs despite my bout of writer's block. I feel less like a witty advice columnist and more like an imposter every day. You know, the old friend who gets called every six months by the ever-heart-broken slosh who thinks it's cool to vent until 2:00 a.m. because they used to share a dorm room and get hammered twice a week.

I've come to a complete stop and derby can't abide a standstill. Wheels must roll, any direction, any speed—fast, slow, imperceptible, backwards, lateral, powerful, graceful, on toe-stops, in the air, over a roller girl pile-up, through a blockade of hips and limbs. If you get stuck, get used to it; do anything to get out of it; try anything to keep the forward motion. Do not let it get in your head.

It's playing offense and defense simultaneously. If a blocker opens a hole for a jammer, the other team's star might slide on through. It's all timing and intention, awareness and response, communication and contact. Let your girl through and then slam the door on the other chick.

Roca knew this as well as I did. She wasn't loud, she didn't curse, she never tagged people on Facebook and Tumblr after a game, because watching derby wasn't a social event for her. She paced. She twitched. She anticipated how the blockers should pivot and brace, when the jammer should accelerate, how the lead jammer could fake and cut to the inside lane for a clean pass. She would identify the flaws in each team, the limitations of each skater, the untapped strengths of the under-recognized. She never tied a skate in her life or asked me not to, but Roca understood the game. She absorbed it tactically, strategically, metaphorically.

Offense and defense: The day she left, she dropped a love letter into my skate bag. I wasn't surprised, I just wasn't paying attention; she didn't have to drive through my wall because I left the lane open.

Strangely, I don't recall the timbre of her voice anymore, though we talked day and night the first year, but when I close my eyes I can see the curve of her fingers around a pen, the slope of her hand poised on the keyboard, and her first hesitant, frustrated moments before a flurry of loops and lines, key strokes, and returns. She studied anthropology, dabbled in poetry, stayed connected with people around the world. She called them, wrote notes in her hand

and scanned them into emails, drew her own happy faces on round bodies with many arms.

I unfold her last letter, Verdana with addendums and tangents in her own script, English and Spanish. I carry it in a hideaway pocket of my sling bag with the coffee-stained napkin carrying our first collaborative poem. The creases of both parchments fall back into place when I fold them. Enormous messages made tidy and small.

The afternoon we wrote our first poem, we headed out as partners rather than women on a date. I grabbed her writing hand in mine, "You know, we should chat, hang out, fall in love, even argue, because it works, because it's fun, because it's real, even seamless, but let's avoid having a 'conversation,' okay? 'The talk' never sits well with me. The 'sit-down' always comes off as another request for me to give in to what I don't want and give up what I do."

Roca clutched my two stunted hands in her one long one, holding a coffee mug in the other, and leaned from her chair to kiss my neck. I loved her for that—the way she could hold her tongue even as her mind raced.

My father used to say, "Let's have a talk," so we would sit, and I would never speak and he would never confess.

"Maybe we need to sit down and talk this out," my mother would beg, and we would sit, she and I, in our trusted silence.

"Can we just sit down and have a conversation?" my latest lover would suggest when lust gave way to my needing some space, and we would sit, hearts in transit, until I left.

People in control don't ask or hear or reflect, they tell, presume, and justify; the one-way communication they call an agreement. I learned this before I could read. There are things communicated in flesh that can find no voice, things said, accused, and demanded without dialogue, without any acknowledgment but the civilized skirting of what needs erasure, restitution, or at least a, "can I get a witness?"

I survived by standing in the shadows and saying nothing. When the shit hit the fan and splayed across the haunted walls of our family dollhouse, my shame held my tongue hostage and saved me. Even then, as that child still formed by imagination, I convinced myself that I would grow up and declare in dramatic courtroom fashion the truth of the wrongdoer, the strength of my character, the proof of my worth. But the loss of innocence is less about what you lose, and more about you can't repossess.

Even if you put the thief away for life, you'll never get back what they stole.

Dear WWDD,

I think I did something bad. I was drunk. I can't remember.

Anon

I keep my Roca memorabilia tucked away in a travel trunk. The poems, love letters, stories, even shopping lists and vacation plans, little reminders of films we want to see. I dust them off sometimes and try to extract from memory and evidence what really happened. It's easy to remember only the bits of conversation we care to, but the letters, notes, tombs, diaries, Craigslist ads, cryptic lines in the "I saw you" personals outlive those interpretations. They force you to reposition and reconsider. They make you relive the past by re-interpreting it.

As a kid, I used to leave scraps of paper under my brother's door as warnings, but he took them as threats. "Do not go downstairs," I would write. I wanted to warn him about the hell breaking loose, but he later told me he assumed I wanted to keep him from something good, maybe ice cream or a good TV show. No matter how often he walked into the maelstrom, he still doubted my motives.

He never heeded those notes, but he tucked them away. We shake our heads and laugh sardonically at the misunderstanding, and the intended camaraderie we only now know. Perspective of a thing deepens when you experience more angles of it.

I guess those warnings were my first attempt at giving advice.

Later in grade school, I kept a poker face as I passed notes and delighted at how I could incite a drama by knowing what observation to make, how to make it, who to keep in the loop, and how to redirect backlash before the brunt of my words come falling back on me. My middle school savvy led to a college prep advice column, "Ivy League," with encoded messages for the "in" crowd about where to get the best weed and how to get free pop from the vending machine. I concocted a system for my target audience to find the information they needed by scanning the bullshit of the day with headlines like, "The Top Five Study Habits for Getting into College," "What to Wear at an Interview," "How to Start a Club," and "The Pros and Cons of Study Groups." When you offer the advice, you control the questions by controlling the answers, and my fallback inquiries were always, "Who are the influencers?" and "How can I protect myself by making them need me?"

In college applications a few years later, I described my column as "visionary." It makes sense that I'm back at the keyboard twenty-five years later where I can pose (or impose) a view of my chosen sport, the derby life, the spectacle of the game.

On the track, you might get laid out and knocked on your ass, belittled and dismissed, made heroic and mighty. You might get blindsided. You might not be good enough, strong enough, experienced enough, young enough, fit enough. You might discover your calling. You might stink. You might look fat in your uniform. You might get your confidence back. You might end up in the "in" crowd and regret what it turns you into. You might find your soul mate.

Ah, the ways the derby love bubble can pop.

Dear WWDD,

My marriage is a pile-up right now. We went from occasional sex to no sex. We went from kissing each other hello every morning to barely saying goodbye and even that's a chore. He says I spend more time with derby than I do with him. He thinks I care more about my derby schedule than our family. It's not that I don't see his point, but you know: Derby. Because it's where I can fuck up or jam like a rock star, and either way I still have my skates and my wives and my thing.

I love him, I really do. His family's fucked up and he got the ass end of the deal, but I thought we worked that out ages ago. I thought we were managing it. I thought that with the kids close to moving out and our debt finally paid down, I could finally do something for myself, that I can do something that makes me a little fucking special for a change. Now he's basically saying, "Derby or our marriage, you pick." If I back off the oval to save my marriage, can I still save myself?

Love Un-Handled

A year ago I would have answered with a rapid-fire "play or get off the track" meme with a hardcore Sigourney Weaver *Alien* shot bolstered with some faux metaphysics: "The oval is the metaphor for life, the wall a symbol of cohesion, and teamwork the gel that holds it together. Why keep your man in the line-up if he won't even put on skates?"

Just like that, I'd get a few hundred "likes," dozens of shares, retweets with snide one-liners, and comments bemoaning my lack of compassion, recounting another rash of pity parties, hating on my choice of words or themes. No shit, if you read them out loud, the feeds would sound like an epidemic of AM radio personalities bouncing off the hermetic studio walls. Roca used to roll her eyes when I dropped a blog post because she could see the mediocrity round the bend.

"You can think harder than this," she would say, scrolling down my posts and viewer responses.

"It's just a thing," I'd shrug. "I've got too many letters to over-think it."

"Well, you can write better than this, too," she'd say and get up to get on with her own business.

Every blog (over 100,000 fans and climbing!) made a new beginning for me, though. I learned how to twist a tweet into a one-sided manifesto sound byte every bit as shearing as an ass cheek across cement. To every "She's got kids, debt, and a heap of ex baggage, but she slays me when she skates. Should I ask her out?" or "Sure, size doesn't matter, until you're upended at the knees and gasping for air at the bottom of the pile," I would construct a *WWDD* blog easily broken down into 140 characters: Jam's on, baby, if you can't put on the #star when told to throw down for the team, then take your #FishnetDerbyEntitlement to the stands.

Once the blog blew, I spent more hours posting, updating, blogging, tracking analytics, responding to letters than I did dreaming, romancing, even skating. Roca encouraged me early on, helping lift it off the ground and give it traction. She got me doing something I cared about again. She convinced me that taking the basic tenets of roller derby—the attitudes, rules, tactics, strategies, legacy, sports scene, and sideshow—to build metaphors and meaning would matter. She said once, "What better way to help people deal with a sucky love life or lousy job than advise them to 'dump the douche and put on your skates.'" (Crude words rarely fell from her lips, but she meant them when she said them.)

Pimping out the "get on with your life, we've got your back " message helped me subvert the wearisome song and dance of query, submission, rejection and replace it with instant gratification: Followers, likes, retweets, comments, favorites, shares, you name it. The blog made the 100 best blogs in Daily Tekk and I got invites to tournaments, boot camps, and conferences. I went from being a bookstore assistant manager with a dead-end job in Anchorage to a minor celebrity on tracks and in roller rinks all over the world, from Oklahoma, Florida, and Kodiak, Alaska, to Germany and Taiwan. I drank sake with trilingual military wives and smoked dope with rednecks in the back of 1970s American trucks.

I stopped hiking, reading books, or planning escapes. I stopped joining the give-and-take dialogues we used to spend all night unraveling. Everything came out in short, biting sentences, truncated and rambling, one after another.

"Stop talking to me in blog rants," Roca said weeks before she vanished in the virtual fog.

"JFC," I said.

"What, you'll be sending me emoticons tonight and calling it making love tomorrow?"

Roca began walking the lower slopes of the Chugach Range alone; we began to snip at each other about who should have picked up the box at the post office or changed the oil in the car. Where Roca once called me on my horseshit and played poet to my documentarian, she turned inward to an interior hum. We stopped talking, yes, but I stopped listening first. We both forgot to care.

She soon tired of my workaholic, derby-holic all-nighters and my way of taking whatever we talked about and circling back to my latest blog post, engagement analytics, and what we needed to do to push its visibility. I knew things were messed up, but I kept putting it off, dropping it to the bottom of my chore list, conspiring instead to write a blog post about how derby can take over your life.

By then, though, Roca had stayed long enough. She didn't look broken up or weepy. She didn't leave in sobs. She just looked done. She packed her bags in front of me, quietly gave me instructions for keeping the garden and fish alive. She may as well have been talking to a smart phone, though, because I only gave her directions to the easiest route out.

I always unravel the letter and expect more: "I'll miss you. I'm excited for you. I'll always love you. Roca."

Maybe that's why after the first read I managed only an impulsive Tumblr video montage of epic derby fails with a flippant side note: Uh oh, my mother o' rants means the single life for me, bitches. More track time, more me time, more *WWDD*."

Hey WWDD?!

Totally miss you. Can't believe the stuff you say, LMFAO! Shit girl.
I think you're my all-time MVP derby crush!!!!
    So. How do I tell my derby wife that she stinks? I mean, a LOT.
I mean, how do I tell her, "You stink and it's not in the every-
one-smells-in-derby kind of way?" Because, damn, she needs to
take care of that shit.

Derby love. Xoxo
P.S. Text!
Hanna Satana

With derby, you can couch surf. You can find a sounding board for dangerous plans. You can ask for a loan and stay for dinner. Where there's a derby, there's an array of women and men who skate, run line-ups, referee, keep track of the score, do the color commentary, raise the funds, and pepper the sport with verve, grit, and community. You can reach out to a league in any state and most countries, small towns and large: Spokane, Baton Rouge, Austin (of course), and Fairbanks, Melbourne, Germany, and Taiwan. You can build vacations around derby. You can plot a worldwide tour as long as you can afford the time and expense, and as long as you show up ready to play. You'll get hit, flail, and lay it out on the track, but that's part of the payoff, the bruises and chafes and dislocations.

Pain isn't the issue. It's whether and for how long you have the patience for it.

We all toy with our own tolerances eventually. I started early by jabbing myself with an upholstery needle to watch the thick, red pearls rise and slide down my arm. I can still find the scars if I stretch my skin. But I graduated to another kind of hurt quickly when I met my first crush, a boy. I was sixteen, but I told him nineteen.

We went out for a few months, I don't remember how long, but I recall the way his roughness coaxed out of me a monstrous, hungry, brutally free thing and how I loved how it lashed out and seethed. In that place, as that being, I could own my hurt and hate and longing; and it seemed right and fair that it could spit and unleash what I could never do on my own but that had been done to me.

We didn't last, of course. He came over one night with friends to party.

"Fuck you," I said casually.

He had fucked me plenty of times without my wanting it by then, and I felt my ribs tightening even as I held my whatever stare. They hung out for a while and talked about what I could handle and still keep the same cold stare. Awkward minutes passed until they shrugged and left. The next day I gave the kid his walking papers, his empty wallet, and the lighter he left on the step.

I kept the cigarettes.

Roca used to orchestrate romantic gestures out of the ordinary. She'd send a text, "Tonight, cheese and bread in bed while streaming the nationals," and I'd get home and find the latest game on the laptop and a platter of bread, cheese, and spices in oil.

She grew up a strict Catholic girl with a come-and-go father who whipped her at every unsavory thought—his, not hers. She made it north in her twenties via Mexico City and Brownsville, Texas, because she wanted to touch the past by walking through it and study the collision of nature and culture.

I'm an Alaska-grown child who never left except here and there, but I spent most of my days outside in the wilderness, the neighborhood, the parks, and trails. Inside felt like a trap to me, so I stayed out for as long and as often as I could, summer and winter.

Roca and I figured our differences would help us align, but parallel paths never entwine.

The last night I spent with her, I came home after practice and found her watching *Koyaanisqatsi* again on the laptop. Uninterested in the film and too tired to sleep, I curled up against her and ran my hand over the curve of her ribcage, the dip at the base of her back, and then I put her hand on me and touched myself. We had slept together for nearly two years, but this time she pushed my hand sharply and snapped.

"What the hell? I'm watching a movie. Can't you just watch a movie?"

I could care less about the film. I felt exhausted, but ramped up; worn out, but turned on. I wanted to fuck or go to sleep, because sometimes that's how it goes with a body driven by untended and unknown sorrows. The sting of her rejection did not sit well with me.

"Don't think I'm going to conform to your idea of how and when and where to make myself feel good," I said. "This is my bed, too. You think things are fine, but I'm not getting what I want or need. You say we just have to work some shit out, so work them out. You're the one who drank the Kool-Aid and can't see your way out of self-loathing—not even now that you're Out and estranged—and it doesn't mean I have to go along for the ride."

I stood and pulled on my robe, pulling clothes off the floor and folding them, putting them in drawers. "It's the plotline of all time, right? First they tell you how precious you are, how precious love is, and then they feed you their shame about who you are, about your body, about what you look like, about what you do with it, about who you touch and share it with. All those words on a page, words from the pulpit, words from your so-called family carefully crafted to make you feel like shit.

"If they can make you stop giving yourself pleasure, let alone have sex with your partner, on your own time, for your own pleasure, without fucking hating yourself for it, well they can make you do anything. They own your ass. And that's what this is about, right here. The big mind fuck that owns your ass and makes you feel crappy about yourself and shitty about me and shitty about sex, so you put out desire like a bowl of dry cereal, and you know what? It tastes like a big fat fuck you to me and every other queer who didn't get brain washed . . ."

I spoke bitingly, as if driven by the subterrain of my heart and the need to claim the yes and no, the wrong and right, the will and won't for myself in the safety of her heartbreak. I spoke as if sharing it with my followers, as if performing for my "friends," as if trying to keep up appearances to the people who kept me silent because they could.

Roca sat in bed as the light from the computer screen swept across her pupils. She did not look angry. She did not look afraid. She did not look hurt. She looked ready to go. Our final jam, and we didn't even get on the track.

> *Dear WWDD,*
>
> *I'm just not feeling it these days. My game is off. I can't stand the drama. I think I've just burnt out or done what I need to, but I worry. It's easy to become irrelevant. What does the post-derby life have in store?*
>
> *Ender's Pain*

It's not that I decry faith and love; it's just that I put a lot of currency in bliss. I figure there's sorrow and pain enough in the world that you may as well engage what feels good while you can. I know what my body betrays. I see the scars every day.

WWDD used to get me high as a kite with a welcome ego-boost. Now it's a way to offset my long, boring workday with furtive posts on my smart phone. I sure as hell won't make the World Cup derby team. I joined the sport late. I'm in my late thirties and already worn out—inflamed hips, headaches, TMJ, lackluster sleep—the stuff born decades ago and churned into heavy cream. It's the miles and the way I traveled them.

I hear about people all the time, people who have dreams, plans, plots unfolding like storybooks, their long-awaited retirements with retirement pay, their long road trips with long-lived lovers letting go of all they built to quest the last of their designs:

the Hawaii bungalow, a cabin in the woods, cruises and grandchildren and temp jobs to boost the vacation fund. The thirty-odd years of saving and scraping and scrambling for opportunity and reserves, and it didn't come easy, and they're stiff in the joints now, but they still get around nicely, they're still loved and in love.

Roca used to say, "Do people know the chances, the odds, their blessings? Do they know how much we watch them in awe?"

Those people who grab onto life's arc and ride it out of the tangled forest floor to a place where they can see through and beyond the roots and weeds and trees—yes, the people who muddle through and around me and all that I've hoisted up on my shoulders or crunched underfoot, who have a clear sight line of all I want and long to see— the view from the clearing, the 360-degree sigh of belief.

Dear Olena,

Just want to touch base. I miss home, but I am well. I miss our laughing, our hikes.

I wasn't sure if I could make this move without you, but I made it and I feel connected to myself again. I'm in Turkey now, a village called Ayder near the border, but I guess everywhere is near a border here. I work at a teashop and teach English. This is a place of history, and you know how I adore history.

Here, the mountains look lush like home and it smells like the spring when we took the ferry from Skagway to Sitka. It's not the same, but there are waterfalls, meadows, peaks, and travelers. I am one of them.

I can speak a little Turkish now, enough to order pastries and make small talk. I met someone, too. She is Turkish. It is more dangerous here for us, but to everyone we know, we are close, close friends, and that is where it sits for now. She has decided to call me Raki because it "is close enough," and our conversations are "intoxicating." She is always playing with language. We are always messing it up and laughing, all the ridiculous translations.

It's funny, we don't speak each other's languages well, and she doesn't speak Spanish at all, but we fumble through and somehow learn through the fumbling and misunderstanding to communicate, even when the words scramble into something other than what we mean.

You and I fumbled a lot, too. Words can be such untethered things. Communication is like history that way—we hate memorizing the details, but if we don't hold onto it, we repeat the same mistakes.

I do not know many people here, so I feel lucky to have found someone eager to repeat, repeat, and repeat again the same words and phrases until one of us gets it right or until it doesn't matter, usually the latter. By then, we are drunk on our giddy misinterpretations and on to the next lesson.

I want you to know how much I miss our walks, how much I miss you. Write back if you can.

Ser la roca está, mi amiga íntima.
Roca

It's been a week since I sat at the keyboard, and days since I dared hold a pen.

I go to the track, put on my skates, breathe. I feel that old dread mounting again, the buzz of anxiety, the wash of sensory anguish, old traumas mired in new. I cannot discern the difference. I join the wall of blockers and shift as it moves. Or I take the jammer cap and wait at the line. The whistle blows, my visible field narrows, my muscles angle toward the gaps between blockers, my speed gains at turn one, my thighs drive toward the inside lane, body hitting, evading oncoming hips and shoulders, anticipating the force of what's sure to come, the past compressed with the future here in this moment on a track where the damage is witnessed, tallied, and shared, and the hardship heralded in hematomas and sheared skin.

This is what derby would do. This is all it can do.

VIVIAN
FAITH
PRESCOTT

Vivian Faith Prescott is a fifth generation Alaskan, born and raised in Wrangell, Alaska. Vivian is of Sáami, Irish, Suomalainen, and Norwegian descent (among others). She lives in Sitka and part-time in Wrangell at her family's fish camp. Vivian has an MFA from the University of Alaska and a PhD in Cross Cultural Studies. She's the author of a full-length poetry collection *The Hide of My Tongue* and two chapbooks: *Slick* and *Sludge*. Her linked story collection is forthcoming from Boreal Books. Vivian's poetry has appeared in the *North American Review, Drunken Boat, Yellow Medicine Review*, and *Cirque* as well as other journals. She was recently awarded a Rasmuson Fellow in poetry for 2015–2016. Vivian is a co–founding member of the Blue Canoe Writers, a multicultural writers' group in Sitka, Alaska, and she co-facilitates a teen writers' group at Mt. Edgecumbe High School.

The Minister's Wife

I went to bed with a woman—
the minister's wife, on a Salvation Army
retreat. In the cabin, there were only two beds—
two women to each bed and we settled in,

sharing the frayed gold bedspread.
And in the morning I revealed
how she wrapped her legs
around mine, and snuggled closer

to my warmth . . . I smiled
and her brow furrowed. She jerked
away, apologized for offending
me—my body—as her body searched
for heat.

And I wondered if that night, she too
crossed the reverie, legs entwined,
lips and tongues spending the night
in all our soft dreaming.

Tales in Fairyland

Tales in Fairyland

We hiked up the muddy trail beside
Indian River because she wanted
to show me her favorite place.

We trudged through puddles, over damp moss,
tree roots, beneath the spruce canopy
until we reached the gravel bar

of the alder-lined river. Our feet clacked
over rocks, slipping down beside the bank.
We ducked our heads under the branches,

where stones smoothed to finer sand.
There surrounded by trees, she pointed
—A fairyland, she said,

showing me where she once pitched a tent,
set up a cook stove, where she'd sat
writing in her journals.

I stood with her imagining this place
as it really was—a place she'd fled to,
where she wept and huddled in the rain

the day her father tried hexing her fairies out,
yelling her into the corner of our living room—
queer, fag, lesbian, queen, dyke—

That same day I stood watching her flee,
my daughter, running towards these woods—
clipping fireweed blossoms with her wings.

Can I touch your Chinese Hair?

Long ago, back in Distant Time, before time was time, before there was a *me*, before there was a plot and arc, before I discovered that I had a spine and a text and illustrations and maps, there was the creation story. When I was in college, I would go walking around at Pikes Place in Seattle and tourists would ask to touch my hair. Just like when I was doing tours in Alaska.

Can I touch your hair?
At first, I let them touch my hair for a dollar but it didn't make me rich, it made me poorer, so I decided to trade stories. *You can touch my hair if you tell me a story.* In the beginning, I got some lame stories, some really bad ones, but not all. Camille was the first person that I let touch my hair in exchange for a story. Camille was from Utah and she was Mormon. She'd always wanted to be an Indian, to touch an Indian, to kiss an Indian, and low-and-behold, here one was. But I was a girl, though I think that intrigued her. So she told me a story of how her father was an asshole. I know all about asshole fathers. She told me how she had to wear granny-style dresses and how her father had always told her to be submissive to men. She was supposed to have lots of children. One night, when she was sixteen, she snuck out to go to a party with a friend. Her father caught her and locked her in the hall closet. She hates the smell of boots, she said. For that story I let her touch my hair and when I did, leather scent dusted my pages.

What kind of person are you?
I took a poetry class at UW and the professor asked what
ethnicity I was? Actually, she just said, "What are you?" When
I said, "Sáami," she gave me a blank stare and I know she was
trying to think of something to say . . . there was a long pause,
even longer than I'm used to. So I said, "You know, indigenous
peoples from Scandinavia?" "White Indians?" I didn't want
to say the "L" word and I don't mean lesbian. I tried talking
around the word. I went over the tundra and down to the lake
and back up and around again. I stood up and circled that
professor a couple of times. I pounded a drum and nearly
fell over in a trance and finally I said, "LAPP. Have you ever
heard of a Lapp? Laplander? People recognize that name. Yes,
I'm a dumb-short-ragged-person. That'd be me." But, you
know what? She didn't know what a Lapp was, either. And I
was struck silent. How else was I going to explain who I am,
or was, or will be? The conversation pretty much fell off dock
and I made some kind of an excuse to leave the room. The
next day I saw the professor in the hall and she said to me, in
fact she blurted it out: "You're all over the Internet." She was
thrilled. I was real. I was true. I wasn't lying. Google made me
real. She was smiling and so excited and I said to her,

"Do you want to touch my Sáami Hair?"
and she did. I let her touch my hair and when she did, I
reached up and held her hand there and she curled her
fingers through my hair. It felt good. Very good. I said let's go
to your office and she led me down the hall and around the
corner. We went inside her office and she locked the door and
pulled down the shade and I said, no, leave the shade up, so
she pulled it back up again. And she took an Indian weaving
off the wall and laid it on the floor. I don't know if it was an
authentic Indian weaving from India or the Americas or if it
was from China but that's okay because I am all those fibers
anyway. And she didn't let go of my hair the whole time.

Can I see your card?
I think they always mean they want to see my BIA card or
my tribal card or maybe my green card but I always pull out
my DNA card. Usually I have to take the card out whenever
I cross a border like whenever I go from Southeast Alaska
to Anchorage, or when I go to a meeting, or when I have to
stand up and say something publicly. Sometimes, I take the
card when I go into the grocery store. I had it laminated.
It's a custom card created from a study of our Sáami DNA,
a diagram that looks like a sun. We are people of the sun. I
have the U5b1b proof laminated with my smiling face in the
center of its universe. It's proof that I was born from those
people. Heck, I'm a born-again-Sáami or maybe I'm a Sáami-
born-again. I hate the church reference. They persecuted us,
tried to destroy our culture. The missionaries did the same
thing to my Tlingit relatives. You must be born again to enter
the KINdom. So maybe Christians need a card, too. Proof
that they've gone down on their knees and checked the box,
something about blood-of-Jesus-quantum. Check. Check.
Check.

What's a Sáami?
My mom and I learned how to make an oval drum. I'm
learning about all the symbols on the drum now. We have
to research the information at museums in Scandinavia
because when the drums were confiscated, they put them into
museums and now we have to ask permission just to touch
them. We have to use gloves when we touch them. They're
afraid of our oils, our fingerprints, our D . . . N . . . A . . . our
Sáami motif: mtDNA haplogroup U5b. Sounds like a punk
rock group, eh?

You look exotic. What kind of Indian are you?
I'm the kind that comes from a detailed phylogeographic
analysis of one of the predominant Sáami mtDNA
haplogroups, U5b1b, which also includes the lineages of the
"Sáami motif" that was undertaken in 31 populations. The
results indicate that the origin of U5b1b, as for the other
predominant Sáami haplogroup, V, is most likely in western,
rather than eastern, Europe.

Can I touch your Indian Hair?
The researcher promised that it was a noninvasive form
of gathering biological information. It's just dead skin.
With 99.999 percent accuracy he yanked my hair, pulling
the strands, stuffing them into a plastic Ziploc bag. Right
then and there he analyzed the root bulb, told me a story
of Y-DNA, linking me to Asia and a story of haplogroup
I, linking me to Europe, and of U5b1b connecting me to
the Berbers. Even though it was a complicated story, full of
tricksters and fornicators, it was a good story so I let him
touch my hair again. This time he didn't pull it out. Instead,
he leaned in and sniffed my hair. He said it smelled like a
New Year, or maybe gunpowder.

Do you want to touch my Chinese Hair?
Well, we don't know if we're Chinese but we might be. We
had a relative that worked in the canneries in Wrangell,
Alaska, who came from China. Maybe he intermarried with
our family. Maybe I have Chinese cousins.

Do you want to touch my creation story?
This story began with a young woman, me, who went off to college to study ology to become an ologist. She learned everything she could about Greeks so she could understand the colonizers' Western worldview like why she had to memorize the birth of Zeus and not the story of how Raven stole the sun, or how the Wind Man created the tundra just for her Sáami people. She specialized in over 400 ology stories: heliology, phycology, trichology, odonatology, nephology, and more. But even today she resists stories with beginnings, stories with a middle motivation, and an end that makes sense, a story that's so clear that you can see a salmon egg on the bottom of the stream. Warning: *These* stories are not fairy tales. *These* stories are not for children.

Before the World of Men and Boys, There Was the Land of Girls

Our fingertips drew glyphs
on one another's backs:
      Spiraling Venus' hand mirror,

my girlfriends and me, in the dark
at church camp, tracing the shield
      and spear of Mars.

One girl lay on the floor, the others
      gathered round chanting—

Light as a feather, stiff as a board.
Light as a feather, stiff as a board.

And with two fingers each placed beneath
her body, we levitated her higher and higher,
      offering our passages—

before we felt the weight of men, when our bodies
were made of air, when girl-flesh tickled
      without shame,

when we lifted our girlfriend up—all breast buds
and knobby-kneed, raising her toward
      the Divine.

JERAH CHADWICK

Jerah Chadwick is a former resident of the Aleutian Island of Unalaska, where he raised goats and wrote poetry while living in an abandoned World War II military compound for seventeen years. In 1988, he began teaching for and directed the University of Alaska extension program for the Aleutian/Pribilof Island region. He holds degrees from Lake Forest College, Illinois, and the University of Alaska Fairbanks. His work was chosen for an Alaska State Council on the Arts Writing Fellowship, and his poems have been published in numerous journals and anthologies in the United States, Canada, and Ireland. He is the author of three chapbooks as well as a volume of poetry, *Story Hunger*.

Cold Comforts

Boiling water in a scorched can,
first bubbles breaking
where an ash floats
fracturing the surface. Soon I'll steep
and pour black tea, savoring
this moment of attention, the cabin
creaking refusal to gusting winds
that have all night grasped
at everything. Some days
I'm as inarticulate and restless,
as needing to be held.
Days when I'm warmer
chopping wood than burning it,
sourdough collapsing in its crock,
wood stove ticking like a sprung clock,
overloaded. Like some Crusoe finding
only his own foot prints in snow
and following them, I know I am living
off my life the way the freezing
survive for a time. Cold
driving me into the dazed
blur of other bodies, the fleeting
warmth of fever as I strip
my clothes, stumbling
through blizzard, the exposure
of letting go.

Legacy

Morris Cove, Unalaska

"A woman behind each tree,"
the soldier joked
of feeling horny
at the sight of spruce, saplings
they planted around their huts
to relieve the erosion,
loneliness, a longing
interminable as the tundra.

Forty years later
a single stunted tree stands
out from concealment,
from a ravine picked with care
up the hillside. The banks
between it and the collapsed buildings
windbreaks, the camouflaging grasses
flattened by drifted snow.

Beyond the boundaries
of this camp, the historical
fact of courts-martial, I imagine
a man set apart by desire,
some chastened Whitman,
his only poem furtive, this
forearm and fist of a tree.

Returnings

1.
Salmon rush the stream
into rapids. White wings
of gulls, eagles, and ravens
shadow their splashing,
the flash of fins'
riffling circle and streak.

Crowding the bank,
fireweed flare and fume
seed in spinnerets
that drift in swirls of light
on water the salmon
know after years at sea
as source, freshened
sense of even so few
parts per million.

And from millions spawned,
thousands thrashing the gamut
of mouth and gravel.

Like Li Po's poems
set aflame and afloat,
this charged current,
the shallows like
shreds of burning script.

2.
Burning script. How many stories
and the tongues that told them, ash?
Our history, scattered sparks,
glimpses.

What had been done to us
we did to each other. Listen

like the blind who must
hear their dreams, these spaces
between our words a distance
we'll cover with our hands.

Survivors to have made it
this far, I reach
for you, here

where we began, are
beginning again, this bed
where we kiss with our eyes open.

Lesson of Bread

Our wool socks steaming
by the tiny stove, we poise
over tea, encountering the animal

smell of ourselves
in each other. The tea itself
incidental but necessary,

cooling in our mugs. We sip
and stare at our hands,
our drying pant legs, the stove

steeping in the room's
sourdough air. *How people
used to meet,* I think,

*yes, keeping yeast starter
alive in their clothes,
breaking isolation*

*like bread, a trail
going only so far. This is
my body, the least*

I would have you know.

A Sense of Direction

Crust gives way to powder,
to waist-high drift
as we trek homeward—
hills magnified
with headwind, the strain

of supplies in our packs. Climbing
out of our tracks to pull you
from the deeper snow,
I press ahead, falling
behind
again to follow

through the glazed depths,
the sinking grate and jar
as we lift our feet
and step on through the thinning
air of exhaustion.

For what must be miles
both of us staggering
forward and back,
overtaken by the numbing
expanse, the provisions

and heavier boots
of our own pasts,
we plunge and falter,
breaking trail, each
leading and led.

Stove

Some black grub
grown enormous
it exists to consume
becoming a potbellied husk
smoke swarming above us
as we hurry for fuel.

With thick gloves
we stoke the coals
the harnessed heat
our honey.

Nothing is sweeter
than to stand close
opening our coats
to sit, keeping
our distance as it hisses
and steams turning
our dough to bread
our skin to blisters
in the bargain.

Like a baby
it must be fed
and fed. We doze
and wake, filmed
with sweat, toss it
paper, planks, afraid
to find it cold.

It is our changeling
our burden, the little
bit of hell at the heart
of our household.

The Life to Come

Some days the dough
takes on the humid
sheen of your shoulders
and my hands ache, trapped
air sighing and catching
as I work the back
of your thighs, your buttocks,
again, feeling them
slacken and firm.

Then driving the dough
back into itself,
I fold and turn, press
against and away,
drawing out the raised

warmth of your hips,
the wedge of your pelvis
beneath my cupped palms,
remembering
pliancy, the guiding
slip of your hands
over mine.

Beating down what becomes
our bread, I think today
of that logger diving
with a mouthful of air
toward his pinned friend
who laughs and drowns
balking at the intended
kiss, how we keep
to ourselves, wrestling
the diffused weight
of a world, our own
held breath.

MEI MEI
EVANS

Mei Mei Evans is the author of *Oil and Water*, a novel based on the events of the Exxon Valdez oil spill, which was a finalist for the PEN/ Bellwether prize as well as the first novel published in the University of Alaska Press Literary Series. She is Professor of English at Alaska Pacific University and co-editor of *The Environmental Justice Reader*.

Going Too Far

1.

It was late in the day when Tierney and Robert crossed the Alaska–Canada border at Beaver Creek. They were both so pleased with their accomplishment that they decided to continue hitchhiking together to Fairbanks the next day, where Robert would apply for a job on the new pipeline and Tierney would look for whatever work she could find, wherever she could find it. She figured she was doing Robert a favor by hitching with him since guys traveling alone or in pairs often had a hard time getting rides, and he definitely provided protection for her—everyone knew what could happen to girls who hitchhiked alone. Besides, Robert had a tent, which was vastly preferable to the sheet of plastic under which Tierney had tried to sleep her first few nights on the road, before she met him on the Yellowhead Highway.

Her body was coated with dust from the unpaved Al-Can, her hair so dirty that it had begun to clump. As promised now, in a clearing beside the highway, Robert snipped off her long locks with the tiny scissors on his Swiss Army knife, and Tierney loved the unaccustomed weightlessness of short hair. New look for a new life, she thought, patting her head happily before realizing how horrified her father would be. He was always commenting on her hair, "long and beautiful, just like your mother's."

Robert's hair was not a problem for him since his head was completely shaved, matching his clean-shaven face. After several days together, she still thought he looked a lot younger than twenty-three. He said his bald head kept him cool, but whenever he made the mistake of removing his now-filthy Red Sox ball cap, mosquitoes and flies swarmed his head. With his broad chest and wide smile,

Tierney thought Robert bore an amazing resemblance to the guy on TV commercials, "Mr. Clean," except that Mr. Clean was some kind of giant and Robert was pretty short for a man, only slightly taller than she was at five foot five. In any case, his baldness was just one of the things about him that Tierney had begun to find irritating. Another was that he'd believed her when she told him she was eighteen. In her opinion, if he was really as old as he said, he should know when a sixteen-year-old was lying about her age.

The border crossing, a single, small concrete building, made Tierney think of the kind of isolated military outpost featured in old movies. On the Alaska side, a thick layer of new asphalt welcomed travelers with the promise of a smoother journey than the unsurfaced, bone-jarring road from Canada. The women's restroom in the still-new complex had both hot and cold running water and large mirrors on two walls. Tierney shampooed her hair with the liquid pink soap in the dispenser above the sink and proceeded to wash every inch of her body with wadded-up paper towels. Her new haircut dried in no time flat while she ducked under the electric hand dryer that was mounted to the wall, fluffing her new shag with her fingers. She loved the way she now resembled a unisex rock-and-roll celebrity. If I were just a little taller and didn't have boobs, she observed proudly, people would think I was a guy. Her face and arms were tanned from being outdoors; her eyes were bright. Her dad would say she looked as healthy as a horse. Tierney was so elated by the chance to wash herself and so happy to have reached Alaska that she resolved to be nice to Robert for however much longer they traveled together.

In fact, she was in such a good mood as they walked away from the border and into this new land, that she even found herself laughing at Robert's stupid jokes. Honestly, for a Harvard graduate, sometimes he didn't seem too bright. Robert pointed to their next destination on his road map, a town called Tok. "Tick-tock," he said. "The mouse ran up the clock." Tierney noticed what looked like mossy pincushions of tiny pink and white flowers growing beside the road. It thrilled her that she'd never seen anything like them before and had no idea what they were called. It may be true that Alaska is technically part of the US she thought, but it's "terra incognita" to me. The term was one she'd learned this year in her eleventh grade history class.

It was probably just her imagination, but Alaska this evening felt colder than Canada had this morning, as if the snow here had only melted within the last day or two. The air was chilly and clean, the countryside tinged with the barest haze of green, even though it was already mid-June. Alaska hadn't even been part of the US when Tierney was born, although it became Number 49 just a year later. She and the state of Alaska were practically the same age! Well, how do you like that? She could perfectly picture her father uttering the stock phrase, feigning surprise before breaking into his crooked smile. Tierney realized with a pang that she missed him; she would have to call him the minute he got home from his honeymoon.

Robert was in a good mood, too. He offered to buy her a burger at the next roadhouse, by way of celebration. Like the other road-houses they'd seen, this one resembled a plywood shack with a gas pump out front, and the handful of patrons at the bar all appeared to be locals. Tierney and Robert left their packs inside the door, took seats at a small table, and once they'd given their order to the middle-aged bartender who doubled as the waiter, they studied Robert's map to be sure they took the right road to Fairbanks in the morning.

When their food arrived, Robert cleared his throat and pronounced himself "impressed" that Tierney's parents had let her travel alone. Something about the way he said it made her think that he'd been pondering this information ever since they'd met, and that while he strongly disapproved, he wanted her to know he was open-minded. He reached for his hamburger.

She decided to tell him the truth. "First of all, not 'parents,' plural. My mom died when I was ten—six years ago—so it's more like my dad and his new wife." Tierney kept her eyes on Robert to make sure he did the math. She dipped a French fry in the ketchup she'd squeezed onto her plate. "They're on their honeymoon right now, as a matter of fact. Mexico."

"They don't know you left?" Scandalized, Robert forgot his manners and spoke with his mouth full; a gobbet of half-chewed food fell onto the edge of his plate, where they both stared at it.

"Yuck." Tierney made a face. Robert hastily covered the soggy remnant with his unused napkin. "Nobody knows anything yet. At least, I don't think they do," she said. "I figure I have about a week before the shit hits the fan. Once they get back from their trip, I'll call them."

"So you're basically running away from home?" Robert held his burger in both hands, no longer eating.

"I guess so. Basically." Tierney shrugged. "Makes it sound worse than what it is."

"Which is what?"

"Just, you know, time to be on my own. Make my own life."

"Don't you think you're a little young?" Robert still wasn't eating.

"Not really. My folks eloped when they were seventeen."

"No kidding." Robert finally took another bite of his food. "Mine were almost thirty before they tied the knot." Tierney was relieved that he'd decided to change the subject. "They took me to Mexico once," he continued. "The Yucatán Peninsula. Also to Guatemala."

Tierney tried to think where Guatemala was, deciding it was most likely in Brazil.

"And they took me to Europe after my high school graduation," he added. "This is my first time in western Canada, though."

"Dang. You must be rich."

"Not me. My parents. They paid, and I had a great time." Robert grinned, as if the finances of travel were inconsequential.

"Are they paying for this?"

He shook his head.

"Buy me a chocolate shake," she said, not asking.

"NO."

They both laughed.

"So you're an only child, too?" Robert asked. "Like me?"

"I have an older sister, but she's married. They already have two kids, and she's pregnant again."

"What does she think of you leaving?"

"She doesn't know. They live in Rapid City." Tierney looked at him. "It's in South Dakota. I live in North Dakota."

"No other relatives?" Robert insisted. "What about grandparents?"

"One grandfather, but he's an alkie. My dad refuses to have anything to do with him."

They finished their meal in silence. Tierney wiped her mouth with her napkin. "That was really good," she said. "Thank you."

"My pleasure."

"Do you have a girlfriend?" Tierney asked as they waited at the bar to pay the check. "Why not?" she pressed, when he shook his head.

"Do you have a boyfriend?" Robert countered.

"No."

"Why not?" he teased.

"Don't want one," she said. "Don't get any big ideas."

That night Robert gave her a quick good-night hug in the tent. Tierney tensed, wondering if he was going to try something, but he turned away from her in his sleeping bag and soon fell asleep. She decided he was just a harmless, friendly guy. Besides, now that he knew she was underage—jailbait—she doubted that he'd mess with her. Tierney thought about her dad and mom, wondering if they'd both felt an immediate attraction the minute they'd met at that long-ago summer dance, if each had thought about the other, "This is the person I'm meant to be with." Not for the first time, Tierney wondered if that's how it was going to be for her: knowing right away that some guy was the one she was destined to marry. She had yet to meet any boy who'd had anything even remotely like that effect on her.

Her father was really going to be pissed when he found out she'd left. Pissed and hurt. But then again, it wasn't Tierney's fault that he had chosen fakey, too-much-makeup Helen over his own daughter;

Tierney knew she and her new stepmother would never in a million years be able to coexist under the same roof. Her dad sometimes complained about how stubborn Tierney was, claiming she went "too far." Like the time a few years ago when she refused to eat any of the rabbit stew that their neighbors had shared with them. He scolded her for wasting food, insisting she remain at the table until she finished her portion, but by ten o'clock, when she was still sitting there, her food untouched, he'd finally sent her to bed. Or the time this winter when she hadn't talked to Helen for a whole week in protest of Helen's scolding her for something Tierney couldn't even remember now. "You made your point, missy," her dad said tightly. "Can you please just give it a rest?"

Now, she wondered, would he think that in traveling to Alaska, she had literally gone too far? Had she passed some point of no return? How could she explain to him that the idea of Alaska had struck her out of the blue but had been so alluring that she couldn't resist? How were you supposed to know how far was too far until you tried it, and wasn't it also true that what might be "too far" for one person, would be just right for someone else?

In the morning, Tierney gathered from their next driver, another lone male in a truck, this time a dark-green pick-up, that Tok was pronounced "toke," prompting a giggle from Robert before Tierney grasped the reference to smoking weed. She frowned at her traveling companion, thinking he should grow up. Then she wondered if Robert might be a pothead. The driver was very quiet at first, and as the miles passed beneath the wheels of the truck, revealing one light-filled vista after the next and almost no sign of human habitation, Tierney felt deeply content and oddly at home. The land appeared to be every bit as unsettled as she had hoped.

"A person could get lost out there," she said gleefully, indicating a wide flat valley fringed with dark trees that extended all the way to a distant range of silhouetted saw-toothed peaks.

"People do get lost here," the driver said with a frown. Although her first impression had been one of an unkempt middle-aged man, Tierney now noticed that the driver's beard was in fact neatly trimmed, his fingernails clean, and that he wasn't nearly as old as she had supposed. He smelled of soap, not sweat. "Two fellows from Germany overwintered in an abandoned trapper's cabin on the Yukon last year," he told them. "They built themselves a raft and tried to float out after the river broke up, but only one of 'em made it."

"Drowned?" Robert guessed.

"Apparently. But accidentally or on purpose? That's the real question."

"What do you mean?" Tierney felt the hair prickle on her neck.

"How do we know his buddy didn't do him in? Sometimes winter has that effect on people." The driver chuckled.

Tierney shifted uncomfortably. When, after a moment's delay, Robert also snickered, she elbowed him to make him stop.

"My name's Ned, by the way. I'm just funning with you." The driver glanced at Tierney. "But people do get in trouble up here—all the time. Right now lots of folk, like you two, are coming into the country because of the pipeline. There's bound to be some tragedies before it's all over."

"How long have you been here?" Robert asked him.

"Almost eight years," Ned said. "I came up for college, UAF, and fell in love with Fairbanks. Fell in love with my girlfriend, too—now my wife. We built our own cabin. Sixteen by twenty-four." Tierney could hear the pride in his voice.

Robert leaned forward, the better to converse. "Really? Like a log cabin?"

Ned nodded.

"No kidding," said Robert admiringly.

"Everybody up here builds log cabins. It's no big deal."

"I would love to do that," Robert said.

"Maybe you will," Ned said. "Stranger things have happened in the land where the mountains are nameless."

Nameless mountains, Tierney thought. It was a perfect description for this enormous rugged place.

Robert suddenly leaned forward. "Look!" He pointed to the side of the road where a large, somewhat ungainly animal was standing knee-deep in a shallow pond, lifting its head from the water, a mouthful of pale green vegetation dripping from its jaws. Tierney couldn't believe how big the moose was.

"Wow." Robert sounded like a little boy.

"Lots of meat on that one," Ned said. "Seriously," he continued after another mile, "you two should take care. Some real screwballs are coming north these days. Schemers and dreamers. And ne'er-do-wells, sorry to say." He nodded toward Tierney. "A lady hitch-hiker went missing outside Anchorage a few months back. Troopers still don't have any leads."

Once again, Tierney shivered. This guy seemed perfectly nice, but what if he were some kind of psychopath himself? She tried to remember if they'd passed any other vehicles since they'd climbed into his truck. There was actually nothing to stop Ned from pulling off the road and murdering them.

Instead of exercising caution, however, Robert continued to act like a puppy-dog, practically fawning over their driver. "Have you ever done any survival stuff up here?"

Ned grinned. "You mean, on purpose?" In a more serious tone, he added, "People who spend much time here don't usually go looking for ways to make it harder than it already is. Oh, every now and again, a European or a Japanese shows up who wants to walk solo across the Alaska Range or something crazy like that."

Robert continued a little breathlessly, "You know that movie that came out a couple of years ago with Robert Redford: *Jeremiah Johnson?* About a mountain man?"

"Can't say as I do."

"Have you seen it?" Robert asked Tierney, who shook her head. "I love that movie," he sighed. "I'd like to try to live like that—off the land."

So that's what had drawn Robert to Alaska, as well as the lure of the money to be made on the pipeline. What was it that drew her, Tierney wondered, beyond a fresh start in a new place?

Ned smiled again and shook his head. "Not my thing. I just want to finish my doctoral thesis and get a decent job."

As he and Robert compared notes on their educations, Tierney wondered what it might be like to finish high school in Alaska. So far, her focus had been on getting to Alaska; now she considered what would happen if she stayed. Her dad would shit a brick if she dropped out of school, especially since she only had a year left.

"You two trying for pipeline jobs?" Ned asked.

"I heard you have to get a union card first?" Robert sounded unsure of himself.

Ned shook his head. "If you don't already have the card, and you're not already residents, and you aren't Alaska Native, which I take it you're not, you should probably forget about it." He glanced briefly at Tierney. "Are you Native? You might be able to pass. But if you're not an enrolled member of a tribe, I don't think it will do you any good."

"I'm not trying to get on the pipeline," Tierney protested. "*He* is." She'd only ever had one paying job, besides babysitting, and that was working weekends this past school year as a bus-girl and dishwasher at Milly's All-You-Can-Eat. She was beginning to wonder if Alaska was as much of a man's world as North Dakota. If so, she might have a hard time finding work.

Robert nudged her. "We could be better off looking for jobs in Anchorage than in Fairbanks." He looked flushed and unhappy.

"Okay," she said. "Because I really, really need to make some money."

"Anchorage is a lot bigger than Fairbanks," Ned said. "You two should have no problem finding work there."

"So if that's the case, we're going to need to backtrack a little." Robert suddenly seemed like a much younger, more insecure version of himself. Get a grip, Tierney willed him telepathically; you're a college graduate, for Pete's sake. This is not the end of the world.

Ned slowed the pick-up and did his best, since there was no shoulder, to pull onto the side of the road without driving over the lip of it. "We would've been glad to put you up for a few days," he said, "but really, I don't think you have a snowball's chance in hell of getting on the pipeline." Once they'd gotten their backpacks from the bed of his truck and set them on the ground, he handed Tierney half a bag of raisins, an unopened family-sized Hershey bar, and some reddish-brown strips of what he said was home-made caribou jerky. She figured he could tell they were hungry. "Good luck, you two."

They spent several hours there, swatting at the occasional over-sized but sluggish mosquitoes, eating most of the raisins and all of the chocolate, and gnawing on strips of jerky.

"This is so good," Robert enthused. "Caribou. Wow."

He played his harmonica; Tierney wished she had a book. Barely ten vehicles passed them the entire time.

Finally a beat-up sedan, its rusty front bumper attached to the car's hood with a twisted coat hanger, pulled over. Three people shared the front seat: two unkempt young men flanking a dusky-skinned middle-aged woman with long black hair, who looked as if she were twice as old as the two scruffy white guys. After loading their backpacks into the trunk, Tierney and Robert climbed grate-fully into the back seat, voicing their thanks. Tierney smelled the sour sweetness of beer immediately.

As the driver gunned it, the lady in the front seat hoisted a six-pack to her shoulder and asked without turning around if they wanted any. Olympia. Oly. Tierney's dad's brand. She and Robert both declined politely. Tierney noticed lots of gray and white strands in the curtain of black hair that hung before her.

"Sure?" the woman asked. "It's free." She laughed hoarsely, and Tierney wondered if she were drunk. Out of politeness, Tierney re-frained from stealing a glance at Robert but sensed that he, too, was ill at ease. If they hadn't just spent such a long time waiting for a ride, it might have been smart to pass this one up. The two men turned out to be something called "roustabouts" and when Tierney asked what that meant, the taller one, riding on the passenger side, swiveled his head toward her to explain that they worked on "rigs" in a place that sounded like Lower Kuginlit. Was that an Eskimo village? Tierney wondered. And was the lady from there?

Before Tierney could duck his hand, Tall Guy reached back to stroke her cheek, saying, "Pretty little thing. You want to sit on my lap?"

The driver laughed raucously. "Good one, Surfer."

"Drilling rigs?" Robert asked, leaning forward abruptly, which caused Surfer to withdraw his outstretched arm. Was Robert actually trying to protect her, or was he just taking an interest in the conversation? "Do you need a union card to get hired?"

"No way," the driver said. "It ain't exactly the pipeline." He and his fellow worker guffawed loudly. The driver chug-a-lugged his beer, dropping the empty bottle onto the floor at the woman's feet, where it clinked against what sounded like another empty. "Matter of fact, me and Surfer here just put in our applications for the Big One, the biggest, baddest construction job in the history of the world." He wiped his mouth with the back of his hand. "But everyone and his brother wants a job on that mother." He and Surfer stared at each other before bursting into laughter.

"You're a fuckin' poet, Wendell." Surfer swung his face toward the back seat again. "You two coming from there, too? Fairbanks?"

"Squarebanks," quipped the woman as Robert and Tierney shook their heads in unison.

"Squarebanks is a fucking circus," said Wendell. "I need another brew."

Surfer uncapped a bottle of beer for his fellow roustabout, then tipped his own bottle to his lips and swallowed before turning to the occupants of the back seat again. "You two want to party with us in Tok?"

"No!" Robert sounded alarmed. "I mean, thanks anyway, but we've got to get to Anchorage."

"Having a baby or something?" Wendell asked, making his friends in the front laugh again.

Tierney wondered where the heck one would party in Tok, the ghost town she and Robert had passed through earlier in the day with Ned.

"Anchorage!" Surfer exclaimed. "Now that's a party town! Yessiree Bob."

"Well, shit." Wendell braked, bringing the car to a stop in the middle of the road. "Why didn't you say so?" He began to turn the vehicle around. "We're just drinkin' and drivin'. Might as well take you to Glenallen as Tok, get something going at the Highlander." So saying, he completed the U-turn and stepped on the accelerator, heading back the way they had come. Catching Tierney's and Robert's anxious looks in the rearview mirror, he explained. "There's a cut-off."

"Gonna get my high at the Highlander," Surfer crooned. "Oh, yeah."

The woman leaned her head against his shoulder. It turned out that Maggie, or "Magpie" as the men called her, was Athabascan. "Indian, not Eskimo," she clarified. "Not the same."

"The same but different," Wendell added.

Maggie slapped him on the arm. "Different!"

When the first six-pack was exhausted, Surfer reached down to produce another. The three in the front seat were clearly already under the influence, Tierney thought, wondering how much longer Wendell could safely drink and drive. Fortunately, there was next to no traffic on the road, and the sky was still too bright for headlights despite the fact that it was getting late. Maggie fell asleep against Surfer while Wendell continued his uneven acceleration, often straddling the centerline.

They made it to Glenallen at nightfall, which Tierney figured must mean it was close to midnight. Despite the hour, the light seemed merely shaded rather than really dark, and she knew that the sky would soon begin to brighten again. Wendell skidded into the unlit parking lot of a plywood-clad building marked only by a hand-painted sign: "Hi-Lander here." He turned off the ignition and for the first time turned in his seat to regard the two hitchhikers. "Party with us," he said again, leering at Tierney with bloodshot eyes. "We need another lady. We're tired of sharing her."

Robert did a great job of thanking them for the ride while insisting that he and Tierney really had to get to Anchorage and were going to keep traveling through the night. He and she hurriedly removed their packs from the trunk and helped each other slip their arms through the shoulder straps.

Surfer, stretching his back outside the car, leaned in to shake Maggie, who had slumped over onto the seat. "Come on, Magpie. Wake up, dammit."

"Just leave her," Wendell said.

"What if she pisses herself again?"

The two men argued awhile before deciding to remove their unconscious passenger from the car. One pushing, one pulling, they extracted Maggie with difficulty and carried her awkwardly between them to a grassy strip that ran along the front of the dark building, where they arranged her on her back on the ground.

Tierney and Robert lingered to watch.

"We can't just leave her," Tierney whispered.

"She's really drunk."

"Shouldn't we at least tell the police? There's police in Alaska, right?"

"We should probably stay out of it," Robert said. "I mean, it didn't seem like they were holding her against her will or anything. It's not too cold; I think she'll be okay." The two roustabouts entered the nondescript building, strains of country-western music briefly escaping the opened door. Robert tugged on Tierney's sleeve. "Let's go."

Tierney walked slowly to the road, before stopping to crane her neck in an effort to locate the shadowed shape on the ground that was Maggie. "What does that even mean, they 'share her'?" she said indignantly.

"I know; it's gross." Robert kept walking. "But I can't believe he drove us all this way when they were headed to Tok. Saved us a lot of time." He turned onto the shoulder of the highway, stopping when he realized Tierney no longer followed.

Casting a final look at Maggie, Tierney told herself it would soon be light, that someone would discover the sleeping woman and take care of her. They'd give her a place to stay, lend her clean clothes, and feed her until she was ready to return to her village. Still, Tierney turned away reluctantly. "You don't really want to keep going, do you?" she asked Robert once she'd caught up with him.

"No," he said. "I'm beat. But I definitely didn't want to party with them. Did you?"

They walked in silence, observing the small but neatly arranged homes of the town, their interiors dark and silent at this hour. Tierney withdrew from her sweatshirt pouch the plastic bag that held the last of Ned's jerky, and they chewed hungrily on the few remaining scraps of dried meat. Whether they wanted to go further that night or not, not a single vehicle drove by in the time it took them to walk from one end of the community to the other. They set up Robert's tent as soon as they found a wooded spot that offered concealment from passing traffic. "It would be horrible if they picked us up again tomorrow," Robert said, crawling into the tent.

"I know. Let's make sure we get on the road early. While they're sleeping off their hangovers." Tierney followed Robert inside. Considering that she'd had scarcely any physical exercise for days, she still felt exhausted. She spread out her nylon sleeping bag and shirked her sweatshirt, bunching it into a pillow. Robert removed and carefully folded his flannel shirt, setting it where his head would rest. They both slipped into their sleeping bags dressed in jeans and T-shirts. Once they were lying side by side facing the top of the tent, pale daylight filtering through the green fabric, Tierney said. "I wish it would get dark once in a while. Enough to get a good sleep, anyway."

Robert said nothing for a minute before facing her. "There's something you should know."

"What?"

"I'm thinking of turning around, going home."

"But we just got here! You haven't even tried to find a job." Tierney stared at him.

"If I'm not going to work on the pipeline, what's the point?" he said petulantly. When Tierney said nothing, Robert added, "My parents want me to go to law school."

"I can't believe you." She stared at the top of the tent, waiting for him to say more, but the next sound she heard was his soft snores. She lay awake for a long time despite her fatigue, wondering if he was going to abandon her in the morning. What would she do if he did?

When she awoke sweating only a short while later, the inside of the tent was as warm and humid as a greenhouse. Robert was still sleeping beside her, but he had thrown aside his sleeping bag and removed all of his clothes except for his boxer shorts. Tierney scrambled out of her sleeping bag, as alarmed by his near-nakedness as she was by the stifling heat. Her commotion woke Robert, and he smiled at her sleepily. "You might want to take off your clothes," he said.

"No way," she said, gathering her sleeping bag and sweatshirt into a bundle, unzipping the tent, and pushing her things outside ahead of herself. "I can't believe you did that!"

"Did what?"

"Took off your clothes." She stood in her socks outside the tent, taking in the brightness of the sun. Incredibly, it was as if sunset and sunrise had occurred simultaneously and the day was already well underway.

"It's hot!" he said, poking his head out.

Tierney picked up her sleeping bag, looking for a place to spread it on the ground. "I should have known better than to travel with you."

After a pause, Robert said quietly, "Have I really been so awful?"

Tierney shook her head wordlessly. Now he was going to try to make her feel sorry for him. "I'm sleeping outside from now on. And I won't be traveling with you much longer, just so you know."

276

"Suit yourself," Robert said. "I think you're overreacting." He zipped the tent closed behind her, the camping equivalent of slamming a door.

"I can't believe you," Tierney muttered again, flashing on an image of the unconscious Maggie-Magpie, laid out on the ground beside the bar. Why did guys think they could do whatever they wanted when it came to a female, with no regard for how their actions might make her feel? Wide awake, Tierney pictured herself walking back to the Highlander to check on Maggie but shuddered when she imagined Surfer and Wendell, even drunker now than they had been earlier, figuring out that Tierney was on her own. And what did she have to offer Maggie, anyway? Suddenly, Tierney realized she was under siege by a cloud of small mosquitoes. The insects swarmed every inch of her exposed skin, probing her face, neck, arms, and hands. They found her ears and mouth, all the while emitting a relentless, high-pitched drone. Tierney hurried to pull on her sweatshirt, arranging its hood over her head, tying the drawstring so tightly that only her eyes and nostrils were exposed. Then she kicked with her stocking feet at the fallen branches, twigs, and other duff that littered the ground in order to clear a space for her sleeping bag. She spread it out quickly and crawled inside, breathing hard as she pulled the zipper all the way up. She used her fingers to swipe insects from the few square inches of her face that were still exposed, during which time the swarm went for the back of her hand. She was sweating profusely and knew her body heat would attract more bugs. She felt twitchy, itchy, and hot.

Then she inhaled a mosquito that was drilling into her lip and imagined that others had breached her sweatshirt hood and were probing her scalp. She slithered out of the sleeping bag, swatting her face and head so hard it hurt. Goddammit. This was all Robert's fault. "Open up," she said. "I'm coming back in, and don't you dare try anything."

In the morning, he was as usual annoyingly cheerful, acting as if he'd never had a change of heart about finding work in Alaska and never letting on that he'd stripped almost naked just a few hours earlier. The mosquitoes were still thick and fierce, so they packed up in a hurry. Once they were ready to hit the road, Robert helped Tierney hoist her backpack, his hand brushing her shoulder. "Don't touch me," she growled, so tired she wanted nothing more than to sleep in a real bed, inside a real house with screened windows.

"Relax," he said, adjusting his own pack and looking around to make sure they had everything. "You made your point."

Tierney headed for the highway, clutching what was left of the bag of raisins Ned had given them. Once she reached pavement, the number of mosquitoes immediately decreased. She had already taken off her pack when Robert stepped out from the thicket. "I wonder where Magpie is," he said.

"I can't believe you didn't even try to help her," Tierney said, opening the bag of raisins.

"Neither did you," he retorted, setting his pack alongside hers.

"Yeah, but you're a guy. Males are supposed to protect females. Maybe they don't teach you that at Harvard?" She watched him clench his jaw. "I think it would be best if we split up when we get to Anchorage."

"Fine," Robert said. "Whatever you want. Suit yourself."

She nibbled on a few raisins, but he declined her offer to share them by shaking his head with a hurt expression. Suit yourself, she thought, cramming a fistful of them into her mouth.

The very first vehicle to come along that morning stopped for them, which Tierney interpreted as a good omen for her decision to separate from Robert. Neatly groomed Dennis, in a small Ford Pinto hatchback, wore an open-at-the-collar, button-down business shirt and was headed all the way to Anchorage. After she had clambered into the back of the compact car to huddle with their backpacks beneath the hatchback, Robert slipped into the bucket seat in the front. Dennis seemed disinclined to talk, which made it a perfect ride to Tierney's way of thinking; she fell asleep almost immediately, awakening only as they entered the city, in time to glimpse a small airport with dozens of little planes in a variety of colors tied down around the perimeter of its airstrip. They passed used and new-car dealerships, liquor stores, bars, retail shops and restaurants—but all the business fronts without exception appeared drab and devoid of decorative touches. Tierney spotted only one enterprise whose name had any obvious connection to Alaska: The Gold Nugget, a pawn-shop. She saw countless parking lots, not a single tree, and very little grass. It appeared that only a handful of buildings stood more than two or three stories tall. In short, the fabled city didn't feel very cos-mopolitan. As a matter of fact, it seemed to bear a certain utilitarian resemblance to Williston, Tierney thought. She and Robert, who had scarcely spoken all day, exchanged a glance, seemingly of like mind that Alaska's biggest city was a big disappointment. Now that they had actually arrived in Anchorage and discovered how unattractive it was, Tierney felt a lot less confident about separating from him.

At their request, Dennis dropped them at a grocery store. Thanking him, they hoisted their packs and entered the Safeway, where they found weathered flyers taped to both the outer and in-ner doors. The photocopied pages featured a blurred picture of what looked like a high school yearbook photo of a girl with wavy hair: "MISSING: Karen Ann McMasters, 19 y.o. Dark-brown hair, hazel eyes. Ht. 5'2" Wt. 110 pounds. Last seen Eagle River exit, Glenn Highway, 8:00 p.m. March 30. Call with information. REWARD," followed by the phone number for the Alaska State Troopers. Was this the lady hitchhiker that Ned had mentioned? Tierney thought Karen Ann looked younger than nineteen. Following Robert in-side, where they set their packs in a corner beside an assortment of brooms and dust pans, Tierney decided not to raise the subject of their parting ways just now.

She had been craving milk and intended to buy herself a quart, but when she found that it would cost her triple what she would have paid at home, Tierney changed her mind. In the produce sec-tion, Robert held up a puny bedraggled pineapple and said, "Guess how much?"

Tierney thought for a moment, deciding on an outlandish amount. "Three dollars."

"Six!"

Despite their expense, Robert selected some hard salami, cheddar cheese, and three apples; he offered in a gesture of peace to share his loaf of bread and bag of carrots with her. Tierney, meanwhile, calculated that a single large jar of peanut butter would probably offer her the biggest bang for her buck. They paid for their purchases, reshouldered their packs, and made their meal at a picnic table beside a small empty playground across the street, still scarcely talking. In fact, Robert seemed uncharacteristically subdued, so once Tierney had used his Swiss Army knife to spread peanut butter on a couple pieces of bread, she grabbed a carrot and wandered off as if intent on exploring the little park.

She contemplated the cement and asphalt that paved everything, the seemingly slapped-together buildings and otherwise undistinguished architecture that might have been found almost anywhere in the USA. How could Anchorage's residents let their hometown— the major metropolis of wild Alaska—languish as such a singularly unattractive community? Because, no two ways about it, Anchorage was butt-ugly. Tierney took a bite of the carrot and realized she had zero desire to linger, let alone to look for work here; it would defeat the whole point of leaving home for uncharted wilderness.

She nestled herself into one of the swings, nibbling on her sandwich. For the first time, she was pierced by homesickness. Strangely, she didn't miss her dad as much as she missed her best friend, whose parents had divorced, resulting in Janice and her mom relocating to western Montana after Christmas and forcing poor Janice to change high schools mid-year. Tierney missed the waitresses at the restaurant, all of whom had always shared their tips with her. She even missed chain-smoking Milly, the crusty owner of the All-You-Can-Eat.

All you can eat, Tierney thought. Is this how it feels to bite off more than you can chew?

Where was Maggie-Magpie right now? Please, let her be safe. Tierney, who took pride in the fact that she never cried, found herself perilously close to tears and swallowed her food with difficulty. Maybe Robert was right; maybe they should both go home. As much as Alaska itself thrilled her, she had yet to meet anyone with whom she could really relate. She was sick to death of only getting rides with men, even if some of them had been nice. And even though she was ready to part ways with Robert, she was afraid to hitchhike alone.

She rejoined Robert at the picnic table, where he sat scrutinizing his road map, his cheese and salami sandwich untouched. She took a seat opposite. "What would you think of going here?" he asked at last, carefully avoiding her eyes as he pushed the map toward her, his finger indicating a black dot that lay directly below the larger dot that was Anchorage and immediately alongside the vast light-blue swath that was the Gulf of Alaska. Seward. "It's only about a hundred miles away." Still not looking at her, he added, "I'm guessing it might be a fishing town."

"I for sure don't want to stay here," Tierney said. "This is not the real Alaska."

"I know what you mean," Robert said, smiling for the first time and reaching for his sandwich. "Let's go for it!"

Tierney nodded, wondering why he always had to take such big mouthfuls.

2.

It was a long hot trudge through the city to get back onto the highway. Cresting a hill, they passed a looming billboard-like structure fronted by an empty parking lot. "It's a drive-in theater!" Tierney exclaimed.

"I wonder how that works in a place where it never gets dark," Robert said.

They had already lost count of the number of cars and trucks that passed them; Tierney thought it possible she'd seen more vehicles in Anchorage than she'd seen the entire time she'd been traveling. But it wasn't long after they'd stuck out their thumbs that a sleek, black Lincoln Continental, the kind of luxury car that never stops for hitchhikers, pulled over. As they jogged up to it, lugging their packs, the driver's side window lowered automatically with a discreet mechanical whir, releasing the unmistakable odor of marijuana smoke.

A pretty African American girl with an afro, who looked barely old enough to drive, beamed at them, while from within the car Tierney could hear high-pitched female laughter. "Hi, there," the driver said. "We're going as far as the Funny Bone." She tugged at the collar of her orange turtleneck, as if she were overly warm.

"What did you say?" Robert set his pack down at his feet.

"We're going most of the way down Turnagain Arm," the driver said. "Raven Creek. Where are you headed?"

Tierney spoke up. "Seward."

At this, the three other girls—all of whom were white—giggled. "It's on the way," one of them said. "Definitely on the way," another chimed in. Like Tierney, these three wore hooded sweatshirts. More laughter.

Tierney and Robert glanced at each other. "Sounds good," Tierney said as he nodded. The trunk of the car opened mysteriously and soundlessly on its own, which made Tierney laugh. They set their packs in beside an assortment of brightly colored paper shopping bags and stepped back, expecting the trunk to close on its own, too.

"You have to do it," the driver called, so Tierney gave the trunk lid a good hard push.

Since the car's four occupants were all crowded into the front seat, the cavernous back seat was empty. The interior smelled like marijuana, and everyone but the driver acted stoned, Tierney thought, judging from their continuing hilarity. Once Tierney and Robert had gotten into the car from opposite sides and shut their doors, the girls introduced themselves, but the only name that stuck in Tierney's head was that of Pearl, the driver, who quietly concentrated on propelling them down the highway while the other three kept up an animated babble. All three girl passengers had their hair pulled back in ponytails. Tierney wondered if they were cheerleaders. Did Alaska have cheerleaders? Did it even have football?

The car glided silently out of town, descending toward a distant body of silty, gray ocean that was walled in between the flanks of steep, snow-spattered mountains. As they put the depressing city behind them, Tierney felt her enthusiasm returning. Soon she could see white birds flitting above a marsh, lots of them, swooping and darting at high speed. Here and there across the opaque dark water, she noticed chutes of dirty snow overflowing the gullies at the base of the sheer slopes. The setting reminded her of pictures she'd seen of Scandinavia. Fjords.

One of the girls ejected an eight-track cassette from its player beneath the dash and inserted a new one. Soon Tammy Wynette was belting out "Stand By Your Man," and the threesome in the front were swaying together to the beat, bellowing the chorus.

"Only you would dance to that, Trish," the blonde closest to the door said when the song ended.

"Beats dancing to 'Wichita Lineman,'" the brunette retorted and even Pearl laughed.

"You know why I always pick Glen, don't you?" the same blonde said.

"Why?"

"Because his songs are the shortest."

"You never told me that," the other blonde said, slapping playfully at her seatmate. "Shoot! I'm going to start dancing to it, too."

"You can't! I've got dibs. Tell her, Pearl."

The marsh ended abruptly in a wall of rock cliffs on one side, ocean on the other, and the highway itself funneled into two lanes, with no shoulders to speak of. Tierney could see rock debris at the base of the cliffs, some of which had tumbled out into the roadway, and she realized for the first time that a set of train tracks ran a little below and parallel to the road on the ocean side.

The back seat was so roomy that Robert had reclined in his corner, canting his body. Now, looking at Tierney inquiringly, he laid both ankles atop her lap and stretched out. She crossed her arms so she wouldn't have to touch him, but she didn't push his legs away, and in a few minutes, true to form, he was asleep. How could he sleep at a time like this, when they were passing through some of the most dramatic scenery in the world?

Mile after mile, the sinuous road followed the contour of the coastline. The girls in the front seat kept up their banter until one of the two blondes turned around, and Tierney saw that she was not really as cute as Tierney had at first supposed. The girl's eyes were set a little too close together or something.

"What's your name?" she asked Tierney, and the others stopped talking to listen. One of them lowered the volume on the tape deck.

"Tierney."

"What kind of name is that?"

"She was a famous movie star. Back in the day. My parents really liked her."

"What about him?"

Tierney looked at her slumbering seatmate, whose mouth hung slightly open. "Robert."

"Is he your boyfriend?"

"No! No way. We just decided to hitch together for a while." Tierney lowered her voice. "I don't even like him all that much." Something about the weight of his legs on her lap changed, as if Robert had heard her. Well, so what? It was true, wasn't it? Served him right for going naked on her last night.

"Where are you from?"

Tierney told them, then asked about each of them in turn, learning that Trish, the brunette, was the only one of the four who had actually been born in Alaska. Angela and Donna Sue, the two blondes, had moved north with their families when their dads were stationed outside Fairbanks with the military. They'd been friends since junior high. At nineteen, the three were still technically teenagers, but Pearl, twenty-five, was a recent transplant from Las Vegas.

"Pearl's a celebrity," Trish said seriously. "She's an exotic dancer, the real thing."

"You guys live together?" Tierney asked. "What do you all do?"

"We dance," Pearl said matter-of-factly, catching Tierney's eye in the rearview mirror. "At the Majestic. In Seward."

In response to her blank look, the small blonde explained to Tierney, "Topless dancing. At the Majestic Bar and Grill." She said it with pride.

Tierney recoiled involuntarily, immediately shaking her head to try to make it seem as if her reaction had just been a muscle spasm. When she glanced his way, Robert's eyelids were scrunched closed.

"We live together, share a house," Trish continued. "We take turns cooking, though some of us are better at it than others." The two blondes pushed at her, protesting this assessment of their culinary skills.

Tierney wasn't at all sure how to process this information. Did "topless" mean that they were prostitutes? But they were so young! And they seemed so healthy and happy.

"We're not hookers," Pearl said firmly. "And no one dances bottomless. Not ever."

Tierney really needed Robert to stop faking sleep, so she pinched his calf. "What?" he said irritably, swinging both legs to the floor as he sat upright.

The girls turned their attention to him. "Hiya, Bob."

It turned out that the group had gone to Anchorage on a shopping spree, in search of "costumes." They explained that their boss wanted them to come up with sexy dance outfits, which they said really just meant two-piece swimsuits. "Pearl and Cleo sew some of their own costumes," Donna Sue explained. "You should see them. Sequins and everything. But we," she said, indicating the younger trio, "we basically just wear bathing suits."

"Yeah," Angela said. "Her and Cleo are the stars. They have real acts. The rest of us just dance."

"If that's what you want to call it," Pearl said, shaking her head disapprovingly, which elicited objections from the others.

They were now on their way back home to Seward, with a stop planned at the Funny Bone to have a drink with their dancer friend Cleo, to show her the fruits of their shopping expedition. "'Cleo' is short for Cleopatra," Pearl said. "Really. That's what her mother named her."

"She's our queen," Trish said, and Tierney wondered if she didn't detect a note of sarcasm.

"You guys should come in with us and meet her and Gavin, her old man," Donna Sue said.

"He's a hunk," Trish commented, "a steamroller, baby, 'a churning urn of burning funk.' Sorry, Bob. Girl talk."

When they reached the Funny Bone and got out of the car, Tierney was surprised to discover how small Pearl was. Petite. But definitely what you would call stacked. Tierney saw Robert's eyes grow wide when he noticed Pearl's Dolly-Parton bust. She was quite a beauty, Tierney thought, with her sparkling eyes and curvaceous body. Trish, the tallest and most slender of them all, was a looker, too, with her lithe figure and sprinkling of freckles. Her boobs, however, did not seem particularly noteworthy for a topless dancer, and although the taller of the two blondes was what you might call "well-endowed," the other was essentially flat-chested. Shucks, Tierney thought, she herself had more up top than two of these girls did. Were they really topless dancers or were they pulling her leg?

The Funny Bone was a weathered log cabin with a sagging roof and unwashed windows; Tierney stood with the others immediately inside the entrance of the surprisingly crowded establishment, her eyes adjusting to the dim lighting, and realized that the floor was not a real floor at all, just hard-packed dirt littered with sawdust and discarded peanut shells. The place had a smoky, sweet-sour smell from what she supposed was years of spilled drinks and the residue of cigarettes. The crowd was almost all men, many wearing cowboy boots and a few even sporting Stetsons. A number of them were bellied up to the busy bar. Tierney noticed that the relatively few ladies present seemed to be all of a type: big hair, painted fingernails, lots of makeup, each one forming the hub of attention for a cluster of men. The women reminded her of Helen, her new stepmother.

"Notice all the pointy-toed footwear?" Trish said to Tierney.

"I had no idea there were cowboys in Alaska."

"Not Alaskans—pipeliners," Trish told her. "Most of 'em are from Texas and Oklahoma. The Funny Bone has suddenly become one of their favorite watering holes."

Tierney now saw how the rear of the building opened into a newer, more spacious, more square, and better-lit addition that housed a couple of pinball machines, a pool table, a jukebox, and a dozen or so small tables with chairs. It had a real floor, covered with checkered linoleum, and the walls were unpainted plywood, as if the extension were newly constructed. At one of the tables, a statuesque lady with straight, dark, shoulder-length hair and bangs had risen to her feet, waving both arms overhead.

When their ensemble had entered the building, the men at the bar turned as one to check them out, the conversation momentarily subsiding. Now the patrons began to press toward the new arrivals, their voices clamoring, "Buy you a drink?" As they surged forward, Pearl deftly led her entourage to the waving woman in the back room, leaving the men to mutter surprisingly bitter comments: "What the hell." "Don't go bein' like that." A few straggled after them, but most turned back to the bar, murmuring, "Shit" and "Damn."

Whether it was because her short hair made her look even younger than she was or because they assumed she was with Robert, the men ignored Tierney altogether. Uncertain whether to follow the others, she lingered behind with him. But Robert apparently felt no such corresponding allegiance to Tierney; without so much as a glance, he abandoned her in favor of making his way to the bar. She hurried to join the dancers.

Tierney saw that Cleo wore a thin, velvet headband across her forehead, accentuating the severity of her ruler-straight, dark bangs. She looked like she was kind of old, definitely over thirty, and resembled, well, Cleopatra. Tierney noted the lady's stately figure and pointed breasts, wondering why she was wearing such outmoded attire: a long-sleeved ruffled blouse with a high collar and a full, floor-length skirt. A tall, powerfully built, red-haired man, sporting a Fu Manchu moustache, stood with his arm around Cleo, hoisting a mug of beer to his mouth. He wore a leather vest over a tight T-shirt, his torso and arms as muscled as a bodybuilder. Tierney had always thought the Fu Manchu was a really dumb facial hairstyle, but this guy pulled it off; no doubt it helped that he looked like someone you wouldn't want to mess with. She wondered if he and Cleo were hippies.

When everyone got done hugging each other, Pearl introduced Tierney to the couple, who shook hands with her as Pearl explained about giving Tierney and Robert a ride to Seward. Gavin's huge hand was coarse and calloused. "Old man," it was now clear, referred to boyfriend or husband—not father. Drawing out his chair, Gavin insisted that Pearl take his seat, saying he would get some more beer.

"Gene Tierney?" Cleo said. "What a beauty she was." She appraised Tierney. "And you, too, from the looks of it. Who does your hair?" Everyone laughed at that, and Tierney felt her cheeks flush. She hastened to explain about the dusty Al-Can.

"Are you going to audition?" Cleo asked her.

"For what?"

"We can put her in the Donna Summer wig," Cleo said to Pearl, who laughed. "She'd look adorable in that leopard-skin pantsuit."

Tierney saw the other three girls roll their eyes as they snugged chairs around the small table and urged her to pull one over, too.

Addressing the group, Cleo asked, "How do you like my outfit? I call it 'The Schoolmarm.' The skirt has snaps, so I can whip it off with a flick of the wrist."

"What about the blouse?" Pearl asked.

"Snaps, too," Cleo said, tugging on her ruffled collar to demonstrate how quickly she could disrobe.

The blonde girls shrieked with mock horror, and one of them reached over to stay Cleo's hand, but not before Tierney had glimpsed Cleo's impressive cleavage.

"Is that a *corset?*" Pearl asked, her eyes wide.

"The real thing," Cleo said proudly. "I found it in that vintage clothing store. I figure we could set up the stage like a one-room schoolhouse," she continued, refastening her snaps. "The guys'll love it."

"They'll eat it up," Trish said drily. She covered her mouth with her hand to direct a whispered comment to Tierney, "I swear, sometimes I think she gets off on her costumes more than the guys do."

Donna Sue was telling Cleo in great detail about their successful shopping expedition. Cleo planned to follow them out to the car when it was time to go, so they could show her their new dance outfits. Gavin returned grasping two pitchers of beer in one hand and a stack of plastic glasses in the other. Setting everything down, he began to pour, while Donna Sue and Angela, whom Tierney now thought of as "The Blondes," passed the filled glasses around the table. When she declined any beer, Trish kicked her leg lightly and said under her breath, "Take it. Be polite." When Gavin proposed a toast to his "beautiful wife" and everyone raised a glass, Tierney was glad that she'd followed Trish's advice.

"Can anyone stay over?" Cleo asked the assemblage. "Gavin has to go back to Valdez tonight. I could sure use a hand."

The two blondes exchanged a look. "We really want to get home," Angela whined, avoiding Cleo's eyes.

Pearl addressed Cleo directly. "I promised them we'd go back tonight."

"What about you?" Cleo asked Tierney. "Do you and your man want a place to stay for a few days? Room and board in exchange for chores?"

Tierney realized that she had never, not once, thought of Robert as a "man," implying as it did a kind of maturity she thought he lacked. She looked around, but couldn't see him anywhere.

"What's his name?" Cleo asked. "He looks cute."

"His name's Bob," Trish said.

"You and Bob can sleep in the new guest house," Cleo said. "It's got a double bed."

"He's not her sweetheart," Trish said.

"Yeah. We're actually headed our separate ways." Tierney flushed. "Soon."

"Splitting the sheets, huh?" Cleo said.

"It's not like that," Tierney insisted, flustered. She reached for her glass and took a long drink, successfully deflecting further conversation. She hadn't realized how thirsty she was, and the beer tasted surprisingly good, so she drank some more, aware that Trish was watching her with amusement.

Tierney again searched the crowd for Robert, but again she failed to locate him. Maybe he was in the restroom? She relaxed a little when she remembered that their packs were still in the trunk of Pearl's car; he had to be nearby.

"I'll stay," Trish volunteered. "I don't work until Friday." She raised her beer to Tierney. "What do you say? We can hitch down to Seward together."

But what about Robert? Tierney was reluctant to voice her uncertainty. She'd already declared that he meant nothing to her, so why was she hesitant to make a plan that excluded him? "Sure," she said, glancing from Trish to Cleo and Gavin, "I mean, if it's all right with you." Maybe she could do her laundry at their house. And call her dad in a couple of days on their phone.

"Cleo will work your fanny off," Pearl warned. "But it's fun if you like to get physical."

Gavin was telling pipeline stories. It was hard to know how much of what he said was true even though he swore he wasn't making up any of it. He told them about the unimaginable kind and quantity of food that was regularly available to the workers at the pipeline camps: steak, King crab, baked ham, roast beef, mashed potatoes, multiple flavors of ice cream, salad bars, homemade bread, muffins, cookies, pies, and cakes. Gavin said there was no limit to how much you could eat and that a lot of guys would take two steaks from the cafeteria-style serving line, but then, discovering themselves full after one, would slide the second off their plate right into the trash. "Unless they decide to use it for bear bait."

Pearl said, "Bear bait?"

"Some of the guys from the lower 48 set out garbage on purpose, hoping to lure animals into camp so they can claim they had to shoot them in self-defense." Gavin's eyes flashed. "Don't worry. Some of the rest of us make sure the assholes come to regret their actions."

Resuming a lighthearted tone, he described how he and a handful of his pipeline buddies had tried to play football recently on the tundra above their camp, but after two of them sprained their ankles within the first few minutes, they gave up. Tierney felt the beer going to her head and soon enough, she was braying with laughter along with the others—especially when Gavin recounted how a friend of his, on a bet, had stripped naked to "streak" through their construction camp, wearing only bunny boots because of the snow and ice that still lingered on the ground. Bunny boots? Tierney pictured plush Bugs Bunny slippers, which made no sense. Gavin said his friend was five hundred dollars richer for his prank.

Tierney felt more relaxed than she had since leaving home, but still she continued to cast her eyes about in search of Robert. Finally, she spotted him leaning against a wall, engaged in conversation with another clean-shaven young guy, both of them holding bottles of beer. Taken aback by their easy familiarity with one another, Tierney thought for a befuddled moment that Robert must have run into someone he knew. It wasn't only that the two young men were both somewhat small of stature or that they appeared to be close in age; it was like they had a previous acquaintance with one another.

Maybe the other guy had gone to Harvard, too, she finally decided, or perhaps they had discovered they knew someone in common.

"I'll be right back," she said, slipping from her chair. Tierney needed to tell Robert that she was going to work for Cleo for a few days in exchange for room and board and would then hitchhike on to Seward with Trish. It was possible she'd run into him there, depending upon how big Seward was, but she wanted him to know that this looked like the end of the road for her and him. As she threaded her way through the mob of inebriated men that packed the front of the bar, she wondered if Robert would be upset with her.

"Excuse me," she said, trying to push past a pockmarked, over-weight customer in a velour leisure suit who blocked her way. Instead of moving, however, the man reached out and seized her wrist, drawing her close enough that she could smell his stale breath and feel how tautly the skin was stretched across his potbelly, like a pregnant woman. Repulsed, she tried to pull away, but he tightened his grip. "Give me a kiss," he demanded drunkenly, puckering up.

Trish appeared out of nowhere, karate-chopping the man's bent elbow so that he released his grip on Tierney's arm. Tugging Tierney away, she said loudly, "We gotta go. Right now!"

The man stood swaying unsteadily, rubbing his arm. "Why you gotta go?"

"Go where?" Tierney asked, even as Trish dragged her out the front door into the parking lot, where Tierney stared at her, stupefied.

Trish burst into laughter. "You should see your face."

The fresh air was a tonic after the stuffiness inside. Tierney breathed deeply, feeling how muddled her thinking had become from the beer. "He doesn't even know what hit him," she finally said, giggling. She followed Trish around two corners of the building to the side farthest from the highway, where an empty fire pit was surrounded by standing rounds of firewood set up as stools, and one large log on its side, stripped of bark, apparently served as a fireside bench.

"His name's Max," Trish said, sitting down in the middle of the log, facing the blackened depression in the ground. "He can be a real pest. He shows up at the Majestic every now and then. Always wants to date one of us and won't take no for an answer." She produced a slender joint and a book of matches from her sweatshirt pouch and grinned. "Wanna get high?"

"No thanks. I think I'm already drunk."

"Come on." Trish patted the log beside her while carefully licking both ends of the marijuana cigarette and setting it between her lips.

Tierney took a seat. "No thanks. Really. Pot just puts me to sleep."

Trish scowled. "You know something? You really need to loosen up." A few seconds later, as she lit the joint and inhaled deeply, her face was transformed with happiness. When she extended the burning cigarette to Tierney, Tierney raised it to her lips, taking an abbreviated puff but dutifully drawing the smoke into her lungs. She remembered the ramshackle collection of shacks she and Robert had passed through—Tok—and felt a little shocked to realize that that had happened only yesterday.

Finally, Trish exhaled. "Are you running away from home?"

"It's more like quitting a job before you get fired." Tierney watched Trish take another extra-long toke. "My dad remarried. I don't really get along with the new wife."

Trish nodded, extending the joint to Tierney while holding her breath. Exhaling slowly, she said. "My parents are divorced, too. It sucks."

"My folks didn't divorce. My mom died." Tierney handed the joint back without smoking. "I really don't want any more of this."

"When?" Trish sucked deeply from the roach before delicately stubbing out what was left of it.

"Six years ago. I was ten. She died of an infection."

Trish was carefully dabbing the burnt end of the joint with a spit-moistened finger. "That really sucks," she said, tucking the roach behind the matches in the matchbook and slipping them back into the pouch of her sweatshirt. "You're only sixteen? I was sure you were older."

"Because I'm so sophisticated, right?" Tierney was overcome by her own wit.

Trish laughed so hard that she snorted like a pig, which made them both convulse even more. "Almost peed my pants," Trish gasped, dashing behind the closest bush, where she dropped her jeans and squatted to pee.

Tierney followed suit a short distance away and they returned to the fire pit buttoning their pants at the same time. "Now we're pee sisters," Tierney said. "Get it? Like blood brothers?" They each took a seat again on the log, this time facing away from the fire pit.

"Pee sisters?" Trish shoved Tierney so hard that they both slipped onto the ground. Soon they were tussling playfully, as if they'd known each other for a lot longer than a couple of hours. Trish surrendered first. Breathing hard as she released her grip on Trish's arms, Tierney felt exhilarated, and not just because she'd prevailed in their contest. She offered Trish a hand up. "Do you know why it's called the Funny Bone?"

The two took turns brushing off each other's clothes. "I do. Unfortunately." Trish refastened her dark, wavy hair in its plastic barrette. "Do you know what an oosik is?" At Tierney's blank look, she explained. "It's the penis bone of a walrus, maybe a foot and a half long." She held her hands approximately eighteen inches apart.

"What? A *walrus* penis? Is this a real thing, or are you shitting me?"

"If you shut up, I'll tell you."

"It's a real *bone?*"

"They keep it behind the bar and when a *cheechako* comes in—"

"What's a *cheechako?*"

"Stop interrupting! It's someone like you. A newbie to Alaska. Anyway, the bartender hands the oosik to someone who doesn't know what it is, and tells them to make a wish while they rub up and down on the oosik as hard as they can to make their wish come true." Trish watched Tierney's face.

"That's disgusting!"

Trish shrugged. "You asked. That's how the Funny Bone got its name. Guess what, though?"

"What?"

"Lots of bars in Alaska have oosiks. Stupid, right?" Trish squinted at the sky, which was still very light but no longer bright. "It's getting late. They'll be wanting to get down to Seward." Smiling at Tierney, she said. "We'll have fun at Raven Creek. Cleo and Gavin have a really groovy scene, man."

"Are they hippies?"

"I guess so. Maybe. Why?"

"No reason." Tierney thought about how everyone she knew in Williston badmouthed hippies, but she wasn't sure why.

"You'll like it," Trish said again. "Anyway, I'm ready to take a break from Angela and Donna Sue. The lezzies. They really get on my nerves sometimes."

"Wait. Are they really lesbians?" Where Tierney came from, anyway, being a lesbian if you were a girl was just about the worst thing that someone could say or think about you.

"They act like it."

"But acting like it is not the same as *being* it, right?" Tierney peered into the other girl's eyes.

Trish laughed. "What are you talking about?"

Angela and Donna Sue appeared together at the corner of the building. "What are you doing?" the two blondes said accusingly, almost in unison. Tierney and Trish laughed so hard that Trish doubled over and Tierney crossed her arms over her stomach because each time she gasped for breath, it hurt.

"Are you high?" Angela demanded.

"God, Trish," Donna Sue added.

"What's going on?" Trish finally managed, wiping her eyes with the backs of her hands.

"They're in there talking about Watergate," Donna Sue said, rolling her eyes. "We got bored."

"What're they saying?" After months of seemingly nonstop news coverage, each revelation about the White House scandal more shocking than the last, Tierney realized she hadn't heard anything about Watergate since she'd left home. What was the president up to now? Her dad called him "Tricky Dick." Were they still conducting those impeachment hearings?

Angela and Donna Sue could not enlighten her. "I don't understand why it's such a big deal," Angela confessed. Tierney watched the two girls carefully, wondering why Trish had accused them of being lesbians.

The four of them trooped back into the Funny Bone. No sooner had the door closed behind her than Robert confronted Tierney. "Where were you? I've been looking all over." Angela and Donna Sue made their way back to Cleo, Gavin, and Pearl, but Trish stayed with Tierney.

Robert introduced his new friend, Lance, and Tierney found herself shaking hands with possibly the best-looking boy she'd ever met. He even had shiny, white movie-star teeth. Trish inserted herself, offering Lance a dazzling smile and proffering her hand as if she were royalty. Robert was telling them that Lance worked at a "fly-in wilderness lodge." "He's pretty sure they'll want to hire me, too, since they need to build two more cabins this summer and some other stuff." Robert sounded really eager. "I'll learn how to build with logs!" In a more serious tone of voice, he added, "The plan is for me to drive back to Anchorage with him tonight, so we can talk to the owner first thing in the morning." He searched Tierney's eyes uncertainly. "Sorry."

Tierney's first reaction was indignation that Robert had gone ahead and made plans without even discussing it with her. Then she marveled at the way both she and he had more or less simultaneously stumbled on separate solutions to the problem of splitting up. She told him what had transpired for her among her own newfound friends. Robert smiled broadly when he realized that Tierney wouldn't be alone, and his obvious relief touched her.

"Sounds good," he said. "I'm happy for you."

"Me, too. I mean, I'm happy for you, too." Tierney noticed that Trish had maneuvered Lance into a less crowded space a few feet away and was talking to him earnestly, her hand on his forearm. Gee, she didn't waste any time, did she? For his part, Lance looked relaxed but not nearly as engaged by the conversation as Trish; it was as if he were accustomed to pretty girls throwing themselves at him. Tierney knew that the odds were slim to impossible that someone like Lance didn't already have a girlfriend.

Robert said he needed to get his pack from Pearl's car. "Me, too," Tierney said, and as if on cue, Pearl appeared, leading the other group out of the bar. She and Robert joined the procession and once outside, Tierney introduced him to Cleo and Gavin.

Pearl unlocked the trunk of the Lincoln; the blondes displayed their purchases to Cleo while Robert and Tierney retrieved their packs, setting them on the gravel. Lance and Trish emerged together from the bar, Trish still talking his ear off.

Robert hooked an arm through one strap of his backpack and shouldered it, turning to Tierney. "I guess this is it, then," he said. "Good luck, okay?"

She surprised herself by offering him a hug made awkward by the presence of the bulky pack. She felt like she should say something, but found herself at a loss for words. "You, too," she finally managed. Detaching himself from Trish, Lance led Robert across the parking lot to an older-style red pickup, and using both arms, Robert swung his pack up and into its bed.

The girls were replacing the shopping bags in the trunk of their car. As the red truck pulled onto the highway and gained speed, Tierney noticed that Robert never looked back.

"Farewell, Sir Lancelot," Trish sighed under her breath, so that only Tierney could hear her. "Goodbye, Bob. Good riddance, Thingamabob."

Tierney turned on her angrily. "His name isn't Bob. It's Robert."

"Are you going to cry?"

"No," Tierney snapped. "No, I'm not. Are you?" Trish could be fun, she thought, but she might have a mean streak, so Tierney had best be on her guard.

3.

Cleo and Gavin had their own emotional, full-body goodbye in the parking lot beside their extended-cab truck. Tierney knew that a big truck like that cost a bundle. In fact, Tierney noticed, a record-setting number of new or nearly new trucks filled the Funny Bone's parking lot. She guessed they belonged to the pipeliners inside. The Lincoln's trunk remained open; Pearl explained to her that Gavin was driving himself to Valdez that night, so Cleo, Trish, and Tierney would ride with Pearl and the blondes as far as the Raven Creek bridge, at which point the three of them would continue on foot to Cleo and Gavin's "homestead." Trish helped Tierney maneuver her pack into the trunk and Pearl closed its lid.

Without discussion, Cleo took the front passenger seat; the four girls squeezed together in the back, Trish and Tierney sandwiched between Angela and Donna Sue. Tierney was glad she got to sit beside her new friend. As Pearl started the car, Cleo remarked casually to no one in particular, "That Lance looks like a real Prince Charming."

Pearl glanced at her, laughing. "You better not let Gavin hear you talking like that."

"I have a feeling he plays for the other team," Cleo said.

"Me, too," Pearl agreed.

Tierney came to attention. What other team?

"What are you talking about?" Trish demanded. "He's not a homo."

"How do you know?" Cleo said mildly.

"Because."

Tierney kept her eyes focused straight ahead. First, Trish had called Angela and Donna Sue lesbians; now Cleo was saying Lance might be homosexual. Was it because they were topless dancers,

298

she wondered. Did that make them see everything in terms of sex? After all, Cleo had assumed she and Robert were sleeping together when nothing could have been further from the truth.

Then Tierney remembered waking up in the tent to discover Robert all but naked beside her. Was that really just last night? So much had happened in a single day! She thought of Maggie-Magpie. Where was she now, and was she okay? Tierney realized she would likely never know what had happened to her.

She noticed she was getting used to the shady light that passed for midnight. "Does it ever bother you guys that it never gets dark?"

Cleo spoke without turning. "Six months from now you'll think it's nothing but dark." She laughed at her own cleverness.

It made Tierney feel good that Cleo assumed she would still be here in half a year.

"It's almost solstice," Cleo said. "We should make a fire on the beach on Sunday."

"Solstice bonfire!" Donna Sue said excitedly. "Hot dogs!"

"S'mores!" Angela chimed in.

"What's the big deal with solstice?" Pearl said, giving voice to the question Tierney was too shy to ask. They had broken through the screen of trees to an open stretch where Tierney could see the dark ocean and the looming wall of mountains again. Now, in the late light, the water beside them glinted silver, like mercury.

"The longest day of the year," Trish said. "A big effing deal in Alaska."

Pearl glared into the rearview mirror. "I said 'effing,'" Trish protested.

"Watch your mouth."

"Eff you," Tierney heard Trish mutter ever-so-softly under her breath.

"Alaskans have to make hay while the sun shines," Cleo explained. "Work our tails off when it's light and warm, and then hibernate when it's dark and cold."

"Hibernate and sew costumes?" Pearl teased her.

They were crossing a bridge. Tierney looked at the churning stream that ran between the wooded mountainsides on the left to meet the ocean on their right. A lone fisherman stood almost silhouetted at the mouth of the creek, holding his rod with its tip pointed out to sea, reeling in slowly. "What's he fishing for?" she asked.

"King salmon," Cleo said. "Gavin caught a nice one this morning."

Pearl slowed, steering the car into a pullout. When Cleo got out, Angela and Donna Sue scrambled for window rights to the front seat.

"Shotgun!"

"I said it first!"

Pearl lowered her window, speaking to Cleo. "See you in a few days." Calling to Trish, who was helping Tierney extract her pack from the trunk, she said, "Behave yourself." Finally, directing her words to Tierney when the two girls joined Cleo at the driver's side window, she said, "You're welcome to stay with us in Seward. Have fun."

Cleo and Trish both offered to take a turn with her pack, but Tierney, anxious to prove herself, insisted on carrying it alone. In any case, Cleo needed both hands to hitch up her skirt to keep it from trailing on the ground. The three crossed the highway and set off single file down the muddy trail, hiking alongside the milky glacial water that coursed at a powerful, clamorous clip just a few feet away. Realizing that she had not yet strayed from the road system in Alaska, Tierney was thrilled by the prospect. The three said little, concentrating on maintaining their footing on the slippery trail that followed the stream bank—a task made more difficult by the fact that, because they were in a narrow valley, it was now actually quite dark. Tierney walked directly behind Cleo, watching carefully where the older woman placed her rubber-booted feet. The smell in the air when they'd gotten out of the car had reminded Tierney of fertilizer, but as they left the ocean behind them, she began to sniff something bright and sweet, a plant smell she'd never encountered before.

"What is this?" she asked. "It's yummy."

"Balsam poplar," Cleo said, indicating a grove of large trees on the opposite hillside. "It's the buds. Best perfume in the world."

Before long, they reached the bend in the stream where Gavin and Cleo were building their homestead in a level glade of young birches. The largest of several buildings was a simple tall frame house with an ample deck, behind which Tierney could see a steeply triangular snow-covered peak. Smaller structures were arrayed on either side of the main house, and Tierney thought she could make out a garden plot between the house and the stream. Even in the semi-darkness, you could tell how tidy everything was, how all the buildings were plumb, unlike the many collapsing, dilapidated structures she'd so far observed in Alaska.

Cleo directed Trish to show Tierney the "guest cottage." "The bed's made up with fresh sheets," she said. "See you in the morning." With that, she turned at a fork in the footpath and strode toward her house.

When they reached the building they were to sleep in, Trish lit a kerosene lantern that sat on a stump immediately outside the door. Tierney set her pack down on the plywood floor in the entry, which was crammed with equipment: handtools and long-handled gardening implements, two chainsaws, a rototiller, gas cans. An entire wooden crate appeared to contain nothing but work gloves. The place smelled a little damp but the odors of leather and gasoline were familiar, making Tierney think of home. Trish kicked off her muddy sneakers, instructing Tierney to do the same. Then she carried the lantern into the next room, where a large mattress on a low wooden platform lay covered with a blanket and a zipped-open sleeping bag. Several unlit candle stubs lay in saucers on the windowsill above the head of the bed, along with two thick new candles and a box of kitchen matches.

"Is there a bathroom?" Tierney asked, spotting a roll of toilet paper standing on a shelf.

"The biggest one you've ever seen." Trish smiled. "It's called the great outdoors. There's an outhouse for pooping, but you can pee anywhere the rain will wash it away. Do you need to poop?"

"No!" Tierney was embarrassed. She tore some sheets of tissue from the roll and stepped back into her damp shoes before heading out the door. "I guess they don't have a telephone, either?" she said when she returned. "How about a washing machine?"

"No phone, no electricity, no running water," Trish said. She fished in her sweatshirt pouch for the roach and lit it, almost burning her nose in the process. She inhaled deeply. "Here," she said, handing it to Tierney, who now wondered if Trish was a stoner. Although she had little interest in getting high, Tierney also didn't want to argue about it. She figured that one or two hits might even help her to sleep.

"I have to call home pretty soon," Tierney said. "My dad and his wife get back in a few days. I mean, he's going to be freaked out enough that I'm gone. I have to at least let him know I'm okay."

"We can hit a pay phone on our way to Seward." After Trish had smoked the roach down to nothing, she popped the tiny remnant into her mouth and swallowed it before pulling her sweatshirt over her head and unzipping her jeans. "Wait 'til you taste Cleo's cooking," she said. "You'll flip." She stepped out of her pants and sat down on the edge of the bed to remove her socks before slipping between the covers.

Trish was so casual about undressing. Tierney had always been shy about taking her clothes off in front of others. She blew out the candle and quickly removed her outer layers. Clad only in T-shirt and undies, she slipped into the chilly bed beside Trish.

Trish immediately rolled toward her. "It's freezing," she said, spooning Tierney.

Unused to being touched, let alone held, Tierney tensed. She wasn't sure if she liked this or not.

"God," Trish said, wriggling. "That Lance is so sexy! Just thinking about him makes me horny." She was quiet for a minute. "Don't you think he's good looking?"

"I guess so," Tierney said. "But don't you already have a boyfriend?"

"Not right now. We broke up. Again." Trish rolled away and lay on her back. "Anyway, I don't want to talk about Ryan. He's boring."

She didn't say anything for a minute or two. "I know Lance isn't a fairy."

"How do you know?"

Trish laughed. "I wouldn't be thinking about him like this if he were!" She turned toward Tierney. "Did you and Robert do it? A lot?"

Tierney sat bolt upright. "No! What are you talking about?"

"I thought you said you shared his tent."

"Yeah, but it wasn't like that." Tierney rubbed her face. Unable to see Trish's expression in the darkness, she nevertheless felt her keen curiosity. "We traveled together because it was convenient, that's all."

"He never came on to you?" Trish was leaning on her elbow. "He must have tried to kiss you, right?"

"No." Tierney hesitated. "He did take off his clothes once, but it wasn't like that."

Trish whooped. "Took off his clothes! Sounds like it was like that to me. How about you? Did you take yours off, too? Did you guys fool around?"

Tierney felt confused now, unsure what Trish was after. "I told you it wasn't like that."

Trish patted the bed, inviting Tierney to lie down again. "Just trying to make conversation," she said. "Do you have a boyfriend—back home, I mean?"

"No," Tierney said after a moment, sliding between the covers again.

"No, never—or no, not right now?"

Geez, she was relentless! "Does seventh grade count?" Tierney couldn't help laughing when she remembered how persistently Stevie Boyer kept trying to French kiss her that year while she kept her jaw clenched against his probing tongue.

"Depends," Trish said. "Did you two have sex?"

"Of course not! We were only twelve."

Trish seemed a little stumped. "Don't tell me you're a virgin."

"You guys are so focused on sex," Tierney complained. "Is that all you can think about?" She turned onto her side, away from Trish.

"It's okay if you are." Trish paused, but Tierney didn't speak. "So, are you?"

"I'm going to sleep. Good night." Tierney's heart was beating hard, for some reason.

At least Trish knew when to quit. She rubbed Tierney's back, nuzzling close again. She even kissed the back of her head before wrapping Tierney in her arms. "Sweet dreams." Tierney tried to sort out what had just happened. Was Trish testing her or something? She wanted the older girl to like her and not think she was a baby, but Tierney wasn't about to lie about her lack of experience with boys. And anyway, why did it matter if she was a virgin or not? Even though Trish was only three years older, she clearly had a lot more experience than Tierney did. A lot could happen in three years, Tierney thought, but guessed that no matter how much time went by, she was never going to be the kind of person who liked to talk about sex.

When she awoke in full daylight to the crowing of a rooster, Trish was still spooning her. The bird's raucous, slightly hysterical cries sounded as if they came from the other side of the wall, directly behind their heads, but despite his continuing urgent proclamations, Trish slumbered on even as Tierney extricated herself from her embrace. Dressing quickly, Tierney stepped outside. There was that amazing fragrance again. After she'd emptied her bladder, she wandered around the storybook setting and in the daylight could fully appreciate how much work had gone into creating this picture-perfect homestead: in addition to the assorted buildings, one of which appeared to be under construction, there was a sizeable garden, newly planted and entirely surrounded by a really tall fence. The bases of many if not most of the birch trees were for some reason wrapped with chicken wire. Rounds of firewood were stacked almost as high as Tierney was tall in various locations close to the main house, and many cords of split wood formed a kind of wall cornering the wide deck. It was a heck of a lot of firewood, making Tierney marvel that the Alaska winter might pose an even more daunting challenge than North Dakota's. She noticed a black VW bug parked in a clearing beside the house, a narrow dirt road parting the bushes behind it. Across from the toolshed where she and Trish had slept, in a stand of large-trunked trees, several handmade benches and an assortment of folding lawn chairs surrounded a fire pit. A long, wide plank that upon closer examination appeared to have been milled from a single tree rested on a pair of sawhorses, serving as a table. The incomparable heady perfume that suffused the valley smelled particularly potent here.

"Good morning," Cleo greeted her from a short distance away. When Tierney turned, she saw the older woman carrying a small wire basket of chicken eggs. "Are you hungry?" Cleo was wearing knee-high rubber boots, last night's schoolmarm outfit replaced by worn denim overalls and a flowered blouse. A different headband encircled her forehead this morning, this one a thin strap of suede decorated with a pattern of red-and-blue beadwork. Tierney wondered if the headband was Cleo's signature fashion accessory; with her dark hair in twin braids today, she bore a distinct resemblance to Pocahontas.

"I think I could eat a horse," Tierney said as she followed Cleo back to the house on a low wooden boardwalk that crossed a small side-creek. A kind of dock halfway along the boardwalk extended to a rock-encircled pool. Tierney saw the brightly painted tops and glass shoulders of what turned out to be maybe fifteen jars of various sizes standing in the shallow pool. "What is this?" she asked.

"My refrigerator," Cleo said, squatting to pluck out an orange-lidded pint jar containing a creamlike liquid. "Orange is for dairy. Half and half—for our coffee." Wiping water from the bottom of the jar with her hand, she led the way to the house and showed Tierney the rack outside the door where she was to leave her shoes.

Stepping inside in her socks, Tierney smelled fried potatoes and bacon—her favorite meat. Her stomach growled loudly in response. Cleo laughed. "I guess you really are hungry."

Directly opposite the thick wooden front door was a very tall arched window that perfectly framed the triangular snowy spire behind the house. Cleo and Gavin had apparently cleared the trees from the back of their home to channel this dramatic view, like a living work of art. Tierney could see a waterfall plummeting over a cliff halfway down the mountain. A barrel woodstove sat in the middle of the open floor plan, emitting just enough heat to take the chill off the morning. On one side of the house, the kitchen blended into a dining area where the table, situated beneath another window that overlooked the rambunctious creek and the morning sun, was already set for three. The sitting room opposite ended in a short staircase in the corner that evidently led to the den-like bedroom; Tierney glimpsed fabric-covered walls and ceiling, an avocado-colored shag carpet covering the floor. The overall effect of what she could see there reminded her of magazine pictures of the kinds of homes that nomadic people created.

The high-ceilinged house felt a little like a museum. Most of the window ledges and a number of shelves displayed baubles, decorative items, and things brought in from out of doors: a piece of driftwood, sea shells, an empty bird's nest. Photos literally covered the walls of the sitting space, a few in frames, but most of them snapshots thumbtacked directly into the painted drywall. Cleo was saying something about the heat loss from the height of the ceiling, explaining that they'd used a "double-wall" construction to compensate because they had really wanted the airiness. When she realized that Tierney was either too distracted to understand or just plain didn't know what she was talking about, Cleo stopped in mid-sentence and instead tied a red apron around her waist and set to work breaking eggs into a bowl in the kitchen.

Tierney continued to gaze about in wonderment. The interior of the house was painted in some pastel color that the morning light rendered golden, and the thick walls gave the space a feeling of silent sanctity, like a church. She heard Cleo whisking the eggs before pouring them into a preheated frying pan with a soft sizzle.

"Smells good," Tierney said, shaking herself out of her trance. "How can I help?"

"Nothing yet." Cleo smiled. "I've got a list of chores as long as my arm, but not 'til after breakfast, so make yourself at home."

Tierney found herself gravitating to the bookcase that formed one wall of the short staircase. She recognized about half the titles as being the kinds of books her dad would read, Norman Mailer, Alistair McLean, and Ian Fleming among them, but there were also lots of books by authors she'd never heard of: Woolf, Vonnegut, LeGuin, and Didion. One title particularly caught her eye. *Bury My Heart at Wounded Knee*. Tierney slipped the worn paperback from between its neighbors and looked at the cover, which had an old-timey photo of an American Indian on it. The author's name was Dee Brown. Was that a man or a woman? She knew she'd heard of this book—possibly from Mr. Palmer, her history teacher—but couldn't remember what he'd said about it. She carried the volume over to the drop-leaf table, where Cleo was setting down two plates containing home fries and bacon strips.

"You like to read?" Cleo said, turning back to the kitchen.

"As long as it's not for school."

Cleo returned with a cast iron skillet of scrambled eggs flecked with some kind of vegetable. "I added some spinach to keep us strong," she said. "Green eggs and ham." After fetching a plate of thick slices of buttered toast that looked like they were cut from a loaf of homemade bread, she pulled out her chair. "Sit," she said to Tierney, reaching across the table to set small spoons into three opened jelly jars, each one containing a different vividly colored preserve.

"This looks incredible," Tierney said. "Thank you so much." She could barely taste the spinach in the eggs, which were surely the freshest she'd ever eaten. She silently counted her blessings. The setting here was like something out of a dream, Cleo had to be one of the most interesting ladies she'd ever met, and for once Tierney wasn't facing the prospect of yet another day of hitchhiking to yet another new place.

Cleo wanted to know Tierney's "story," so she filled her in on her dad and Helen, how her mom had died from an infection after surgery for "some female-related kind of thing." Despite the fact that she was doing all the talking, Tierney was embarrassed that she had completely cleaned her plate while Cleo was still only halfway through her meal. The older woman didn't seem to mind. "I guess you weren't kidding about being hungry," she said, indicating the stack of buttered toast. "Try some of my prize-winning preserves. The rose-petal won a blue ribbon last year at the state fair."

Rose-petal jelly? Tierney had never heard of such a thing. She stared at the light-pink contents of the jar closest to her before picking it up to hold under her nose. Sure enough, it smelled exactly like a big bouquet of roses. "Peach?" she guessed, pointing to the jar filled with orange jam.

"Apricot," Cleo said.

"What's this one?" Tierney asked, picking up the last jar to marvel at its deep red color, through which the morning sunlight smoldered.

"Salmonberry."

"From fish? Really?"

"Just try it." Cleo set her silverware on her plate. "So you decided to fly the coop and head north. Good for you. You made the right choice. Our country's getting crazier and crazier what with Tricky Dick's Watergate shenanigans."

"My dad calls him that, too!"

"He's got a screw loose, that man. Talk about abuse of power."

In the end, Tierney ate three slices of toast, each spread with a different jelly. "It doesn't taste fishy at all," she said of her final slice. "They're all delicious."

"Later in the summer, I'll show you what salmonberries are."

Again, Tierney liked it that Cleo talked as if Tierney would be around for a while. Cleo handed her a small wooden coffee grinder that reminded Tierney of a music box and asked her to grind the beans while she put a kettle of water on to boil. She showed Tierney

308

how to empty the ground coffee from a little drawer in the box into the filter paper and red plastic funnel she'd set over a ceramic pitcher.

"I forgot how much Trish likes to sleep in," Cleo said as she poured boiling water into the filter, unleashing a familiar bitter aroma. Tierney's dad loved fresh-brewed coffee; she had to be sure to remember to make that phone call.

"You better go wake her so she doesn't sleep all day," Cleo said.

Tierney discovered Trish still fast asleep. She shook her shoulder, explaining that Cleo wanted them to get to work soon.

"That's the only trouble with this place," Trish grumbled as she set her feet on the floor. "You can never just relax and enjoy it."

Tierney hovered while Trish dressed, even following her when she stepped outside to pee. She heard herself burbling about how "magical" everything was.

"Just wait 'til your hands are covered in blisters and you're so tired you don't even want to eat," Trish said drily.

When they pushed open the door to the house, Cleo was sipping from a cup of creamed coffee and browsing *Bury My Heart at Wounded Knee*. "Nice of you to join us," Cleo said to Trish. "There's a plate of food for you on top of the stove."

"Thank you," Trish mumbled.

"Are you going to read this?" Cleo asked Tierney, closing the book and setting it down on the table.

"Could I borrow it from you?"

"If you want to. It's pretty heavy." When Tierney reached to heft the paperback in her hand as if to weigh it, Cleo said, "I mean it's really intense. But probably every American should read it. I think what we did to the Indians is even worse than slavery. Well, as bad as, anyway." She peered into Tierney's face. "You've got some Indian blood, don't you?"

"Not that I know of."

"You don't know?" Trish had carried her plate to the table and was crumbling her bacon over her scrambled eggs. "How can you not know something like that?"

"Well, I'm one-eighth Cherokee. Or is it Chippewa?" Cleo said. "I get the two of them confused."

Tierney tried to do the calculation. "One of your grandparents was American Indian?"

"Great-grandmother, but I never knew her."

Trish looked up from her plate. "Is that what inspired you to develop your Indian princess dance routine?" Tierney glanced at the other girl, detecting sarcasm.

"Sort of." Cleo seemed unaffected by Trish's tone. "That and the messed-up history of the so-called settling of the West, which is what this book is all about. I swear, it's truly heartrending: one broken treaty after another and what can only be called cold-blooded massacres. Genocide. They don't teach this stuff in school."

Tierney leaned forward in her chair. "What I want to know is, where are all the Eskimos? I thought Alaska was supposed to be full of them."

"You've probably already seen a few," Cleo said, "without knowing it. It's not like they dress in sealskins and carry harpoons. Not in this part of the state, anyway. They look just like all the rest of us."

Before Tierney knew it, she was telling them about Maggie-Magpie and how the two roustabouts had said they "shared" her, how they'd carried her from their car and left her lying on the ground outside the bar. "Me and Robert didn't know what to do," Tierney finished. "For some reason, I can't stop thinking about her. But she wasn't Eskimo," she remembered. "She said she was Indian."

"Do you know where she was from?" Trish asked. Tierney shook her head, feeling a little breathless. "Probably Athabascan," Trish continued. "I imagine she either woke up and went inside to join them, or they put her back in their car when they were ready to leave. She's probably fine."

"I don't know about that." Cleo wore a grim expression. "There's some real unsavory characters coming north these days because of the pipeline. You know that chick who went missing up near Eagle River?" Both Trish and Tierney nodded. "Well, another one's disappeared. Just a few days ago. They're saying that both of them are Native girls. I heard this one is a dancer."

"Where?" Trish asked, her mouth full of food.

"Downtown. Fourth Avenue." Trish and Cleo exchanged a look that Tierney couldn't read. Cleo's clipped tone matched the somewhat angry expression on her face. "I guess this one's on the petite side, too. They're saying there could be others."

"What do you mean?" Trish stared at her.

"There's at least one missing girl from last winter that nobody's talking about. I just wonder if that Seattle serial killer isn't operating up here now."

"But how could he be in two places at once?" Trisha said. "I thought another girl just went missing down there, too."

Cleo stood. "I don't know." She carried their breakfast things into the kitchen. "It's freaky, though. That's for sure."

Wide-eyed, Tierney flung her gaze from Cleo to Trish and back to Cleo. "What do you mean, serial killer?" she said. "How do you know those girls didn't choose to disappear? I mean, I just kind of disappeared from Williston, but it was on purpose. How do you even know they're dead?" Neither Cleo nor Trish said anything, but they glanced at each other in a way that made Tierney feel childish.

When Trish had finished her food, she pulled two round metal washtubs from under the woodstove. "Say, Cleo. After we do the dishes, would it be okay if I took Tierney to the waterfall?" Even though she barely knew her, Tierney could tell Trish was striving for a casual tone.

"Maybe later," Cleo said, wiping off the counter. "Right now, there's a lot that needs doing. Come join me in the garden once you get things cleaned up in here." With that, she pushed through the front door and presumably pulled on her rubber boots; in a minute they heard her descending the steps from the deck.

Trish showed Tierney how to sprinkle powdered soap into one of the washtubs and ladle hot water from the full cauldron that sat atop the woodstove. "We can do them out on the deck," she said, freeing a dish rack from its nail on the end of the kitchen counter and carrying it and some tea towels outside.

Standing on the ground, the surface of the deck was the perfect height for the job. Tierney thought she wouldn't mind washing dishes every day if she could do it like this, outside in the fresh air. It was a far cry from the steamy, narrow, windowless room in which she'd sprayed numberless dirty plates and glasses before feeding them into the giant dishwasher at Milly's.

When they were done, and the dishes were arranged to air-dry outside, they joined Cleo in weeding the rows of seedlings that were sprouting in the garden. When Tierney asked about the height of the fence, Cleo explained that moose were capable of clearing anything less than eight feet tall. Cleo gathered up the small piles of spindly weeds and tossed them into the nearby chicken coop, where the birds scrambled to eat them. After that, there was firewood to stack, and kindling to split with an ax and a hatchet. Cleo showed them how she wanted rocks hauled from the bend in the creek to create a wall around the fenced-in chicken coop; she thought it might help to deter the fox or coyote that had recently found its way into the pen. And she wanted more chicken wire wrapped around the base of more birches, which apparently was an effective defense against the tree-felling habits of the local beavers.

Cleo went inside at some point, reappearing at lunchtime with grilled cheddar cheese and tomato sandwiches on homemade bread, a large plate of still-warm peanut butter cookies, and tall glasses of a pink drink with a mint-leaf garnish that she identified as rhubarb juice. She set down the tray of food on the long slab table at the fire pit, near where Trish and Tierney were splitting kindling, and announced she was going back inside to sew.

"By hand?" Tierney asked.

"I have a treadle," Cleo said simply, turning away, and Tierney had a hazy memory of her mother pedaling her foot on just such a machine way back when.

As they washed their hands beside the creek with the bar of soap that Cleo had presented to them along with a stack of towels, Tierney could feel the beginnings of blisters forming on her palms. "I wonder if Robert got that job," she said. "I wonder if I'll ever see him again. Can you believe I don't even know his last name?"

"And I wonder if I'll ever see Sir Lancelot again."

Tierney splashed some water at Trish. "Don't forget he's a homo."

Trish tried to push her into the creek, but Tierney escaped without getting wet.

After they ate, Trish produced a new, tightly rolled joint. "Ta da!" she said with a flourish.

"Not for me," Tierney said. "I'll fall asleep."

"I wish you weren't so uptight," Trish complained, striking a match and sucking hard on the joint. "Lighten up and light up!" she quipped, but for once she seemed content to smoke alone.

Glancing toward the house, Tierney raised first her own plate and then the plate that had held the cookies, licking them both clean.

"Hey," Trish took another long sip from the joint, held it, and exhaled slowly. "It's 'later.' We can go to the waterfall!"

"I don't think we should. I get the feeling Cleo wants us to get a lot done today. Maybe we could go tomorrow?"

Trish shook her head. "Her bark's worse than her bite. She pushes, but it's almost like she expects you to push back." She extinguished what was left of the joint. "Anyway, it's not like we're getting paid. She can't exactly fire us." As she'd done yesterday, Trish tucked the roach behind the matches in a matchbook and put it in her sweatshirt pouch. "Come on," she said, heading into the woods.

Tierney looked at the house indecisively. "Hurry up!" Trish hollered, already almost out of sight. Tierney scrambled after her, telling herself that the outing would provide a break from the chores, that they wouldn't be gone long, and that in any case, there was no shortage of daylight in which to get work done. If necessary, they could stay up late. Besides, she thought, weaving through the trees, it was high time she sampled the Alaska wilderness.

But the excursion to the waterfall proved to be much more involved than the leisurely walk in the woods that Tierney had pictured; the trail snaked through spruce and birch forest, seldom running straight, and required the precarious crossing of two plunging creeks on fallen logs slippery with moss and rotting bark. By the time half an hour had passed and they still seemed closer to where they had started than to where they were trying to go, Tierney knew they had made a poor choice, but by then she was too worried about getting lost to turn back without Trish—especially after they encountered a startlingly large pile of what Trish matter-of-factly said was bear shit. "Most likely from a grizzly."

Once she decided it was too late to change course, Tierney gave herself over wholeheartedly to the adventure. They clambered over fallen trees, waded shin-deep through a marshy bog that Trish called "muskeg," and skittered across the sloping pile of jagged scree that made up the base of the mountain they had to skirt to reach the falls. Tierney had done a fair amount of car camping with her family and had even gone on some overnight hikes, but she'd never done anything like this.

They drank whenever they were thirsty from one or another of the countless cold rivulets that Trish said were snowmelt from the still-frozen patches high above them. Her companion seemed so at home in these surroundings that it inspired Tierney to think that one day she, too, might learn to be equally comfortable in the wild. "I've never met a girl like you," she told Trish admiringly.

Trish turned to her with a grin. "This is the best, isn't it?"

"Darn right."

"It's nice to have some company for a change. I've only done this hike by myself, because no one else will ever go with me."

Trish had made this trip by herself? And more than once? She must be fearless, Tierney decided, watching Trish pull herself up onto a rock ledge. She was beginning to think Trish was the coolest girl she'd ever met. She was like a more grown-up version of Pippi Longstocking: uninhibited and funny and strong, someone who could care less what others thought of her. The waterfall, when they reached it, was almost anticlimactic. The best part, Tierney thought, was exploring a wild place with someone she was beginning to like. A lot.

By the time they swaggered back into the homestead hours later, they were muddy, sweaty, tired, and full of themselves. The sun had moved behind the mountain, casting Raven Creek valley into shadow. Cleo was weeding in the garden again; she scarcely glanced at the two girls as they apologized sheepishly for their long absence. "It's not a resort," she said quietly. "If you want your supper, you'll have to earn it." She returned her gardening tools to the shed before retiring into the house.

So Tierney and Trish resumed the work of filling the wheelbarrow with rocks from the creek, taking turns laboriously wheeling the load over uneven ground to the chicken coop and dumping it in a growing pile. They worked together to cut lengths of chicken wire, awkwardly wrapping birch trunks with the springy metal fencing until it grew too dark to see. As they discussed whether or not they should just go to bed without supper, Cleo called out from her doorway, inviting them inside for bowls of creamy salmon chowder, salad, and squares of savory cornbread slathered with butter, the house lit with candles in the absence of electric lights so that Tierney once again felt as if she were inhabiting some kind of fairy tale.

That night, while Trish fired up her roach in their sleeping quarters, Tierney dug out her last fresh T-shirt and only pair of clean underpants from her backpack, and carried them, along with the bar of soap and a bath towel, to a secluded spot beside the creek. Although it was dark and she was completely alone, she still felt shy about undressing, so she quickly peeled off pants and underpants to wash her bottom half as fast as she could in the cold water, dressing again before peeling off her sweatshirt and shirt to wash her upper body.

"I didn't know where you went," Trish complained, already shedding her own clothes. "Why didn't you wait for me?" She sounded hurt.

"Sorry." Tierney hurriedly reached for her towel, using it to shield her bare chest. Had Trish really missed her, or was she just joking? While Tierney kept her back turned to put on her clean shirt, Trish stripped without a shred of self-consciousness and waded waist deep into the creek, ducking into the water before lathering her entire body at record speed and reimmersing herself to rinse off. "Shit!" She pranced out of the creek yelping, grabbed her towel, and dried herself frenetically, hopping from foot to foot to warm up.

It wasn't that Tierney thought there was anything wrong with nudity; it was just that she had never learned to feel comfortable with it. She wasn't even all that relaxed in a bathing suit, although once she got into the water, of course, it no longer mattered. But as she seemed to be with lots of things, Trish was casual about her own nakedness. Tierney watched her towel herself dry, admiring Trish's long, slim trunk and strong legs. Trish maybe wasn't glamorous in the conventional Elizabeth Taylor or Marilyn Monroe sense of voluptuous curves and melon-sized breasts, like Pearl, but Tierney thought she could definitely be considered a beauty.

"Quit staring at me!" Trish said. "Pervert."

Tierney immediately turned her back, which made Trish laugh.

"Do you have any clean clothes I can borrow?" Trish asked.

Tierney picked up her sneakers. "Sorry, I just put them on." She sat on the ground to wipe off her feet. "I had big plans for Cleo's washing machine and dryer."

"Ha ha." A moment later, Trish crept up to Tierney silently, tapping her on the shoulder and making her jump.

Tierney swatted her. "You brat."

"So, I noticed you have a great body," Trish said, wrapping herself in her towel. "You're a foxy lady."

Tierney stared at her, her pulse beginning to race. She remembered how she had awoken to find Trish spooning her. She recalled last night's back rub, the goodnight kiss on the back of her head. Was it possible that Trish was as drawn to her as she was drawn to Trish? Was all that talk about sex last night supposed to be a buildup to something else, and had Tierney disappointed Trish by failing to reciprocate her displays of affection?

"Your breasts are much bigger than mine," Trish continued. "Sexier." She leaned a hand on Tierney's shoulder for balance as she brushed off the soles of her feet to step barefooted into her sneakers.

Tierney knew this was the moment to tell Trish that she was attracted to her, too, that in fact she was pretty smitten. She felt herself tremble, heart pounding, as she cleared her throat to speak.

"You should seriously think about dancing at the Majestic," Trish continued. "The money's really good. Better than cannery work or waitressing or the only other jobs that are available to girls." She glanced at Tierney. "Don't look like that. It's not so bad." A moment later, she added, "Too bad Lance isn't here tonight, with me all nice and clean. I would definitely show him a good time." Trish laughed, tousling Tierney's hair.

Even though it was too dark for Trish to see her cheeks burning, Tierney ducked her head. Thank God she hadn't said anything! Her heart continued to hammer, but now it was for a different reason. She couldn't believe she had come so close to declaring her feelings for Trish. What could she possibly have been thinking? Tierney quickly reviewed what she had said, reassured that, no, she had given nothing away. She would make sure to eradicate these feelings until no trace of them remained. No one must ever suspect how close Tierney had come to falling for another girl.

4.

The next morning, the crowing rooster again woke Tierney, and also as before, Trish slept right through the bird's ruckus. Tierney slipped carefully from beneath Trish's arm and studied the other girl's face, which seemed even prettier when she was asleep. She shivered to think how close she had come to ruining everything last night. Despite her relief, however, she felt as heavy hearted as if someone close to her had died.

Her neck and shoulders tightened when she stood; the muscles in her legs and arms protested movement. She would have been happy to stay in bed, but knew they owed Cleo a full day of work after yesterday's ill-timed, albeit outstanding, trek to the waterfall.

When she knocked softly and pushed open the front door, Cleo was rolling pastry on the kitchen counter, three pie tins at the ready to receive their bottom layers of crust. "Good morning. Where's your partner in crime?"

"We're really sorry about yesterday. We want to make it up to you today."

"I can tell you're a good worker." Cleo never paused in her pastry-rolling activity. "And Trish can be, too, but sometimes I don't much care for her attitude." She asked Tierney to crank the handle of the cast-iron grain mill that was clamped to the edge of the counter and already filled with brownish wheat berries. Tierney discovered that she had to use both hands for the task; it took longer than she would have expected to grind two cups of flour.

"Did you see the rhubarb plants at the far end of the garden?" Cleo asked when she had finished. Tierney nodded. "Pull me off about ten cups' worth of stalks." Cleo handed her a paring knife. "Put the leaves in the compost bin next to the chicken house."

When Tierney returned with the leafless rhubarb stems, she was glad to smell more bacon sizzling on the stovetop. She chopped the rhubarb into half-inch pieces at Cleo's instruction, putting them into a large stainless steel bowl. Cleo meanwhile had mixed up a batch of pancakes with the freshly ground flour and was already flipping the first flapjacks in the skillet. They sat down to eat without discussion, Tierney spreading her pancakes with plenty of butter before drizzling them with what Cleo said was homemade birch syrup, which was denser than maple syrup and tasted, Tierney decided, of Alaska. She asked for seconds of everything and drank two cups of what Cleo said was her own blend of peppermint, rose-hip, and spruce-tip tea.

"You are the best cook I ever met," Tierney said.

"Thank you. How'd you like the waterfall?"

It took Tierney a moment to realize it wasn't a trick question. "Amazing. The hike there was really fun." She remembered Trish flinging her arms up in triumph when they finally reached the falls. Magnificent Trish. She lowered her head for a minute then raised it with an effort, forcing a smile. "I love it here!" she blurted.

"Here, Raven Creek? Or here, Alaska?"

"Both."

Cleo smiled. "I've only been up to the waterfall once."

"But I thought you said you've lived here for five years."

Cleo shrugged. "Gavin and I hiked to it before we bought the property. Since then, seems like we're always too busy."

Tierney pondered this information, hoping that she would live the kind of life where there'd always be time for adventure.

"I guess you're going to have to wake Trish again," Cleo said. "Tell her to get her ass in gear."

But Tierney returned shortly with the message that Trish wasn't feeling well, that she thought she was PMS, and did Cleo have any pot she could smoke since that would relieve her cramps?

"That's it," Cleo said tightly, removing her apron and flinging it over the back of a chair. She pushed open the door and Tierney watched through the window as Cleo marched to the shed in her rubber boots. She decided to make herself useful by doing the dishes, and was ladling hot water into the washing pan when Cleo returned just a few minutes later.

"I asked Trish to leave," Cleo said. "And she shouldn't hitchhike alone, so that means you've got to go, too. Sorry. I'm counting on you coming back, though, because I've enjoyed your company, and you really are a good worker."

"At least let me do the dishes."

Cleo nodded, handing her the drying rack. Then she disappeared into her bedroom, and soon Tierney could hear the rhythmic percussion of the treadle sewing machine.

By the time she'd finished washing the dishes on the deck, Trish still hadn't emerged. Tierney figured that her pride was wounded and that she had chosen to forego breakfast. "Okay if I take Trish something to eat?" she called to Cleo.

Cleo emerged from her bedroom to tear off a sheet of paper towel onto which she made a sandwich of two pancakes with three strips of bacon layered in between. She handed it to Tierney. "There's something I want you to have," she said, retrieving a paperback book from the sitting room. Tierney glanced at the title. *Giants in the Earth*. "It's about the settlers in the Dakotas. I think you might like it," she said. "Pass it on when you're done."

"Thank you for everything," Tierney said. "I'm sorry about—"

"Don't you worry," Cleo smiled. "I'm already plotting how to bring you back here. I could really use a reliable worker." She squeezed Tierney's shoulder. Adopting a serious tone, she said, "Promise me you two will hitchhike together. If you get even the slightest bad vibe from any of your drivers, *do not* get into the car. And if you're already in a vehicle, you demand that he put you out immediately. I don't care if it's the middle of nowhere, you hear?"

Tierney promised. By the time she reached the toolshed, Trish had already buckled the strap of Tierney's backpack around her own waist and was waiting for her behind the building.

"Are you really on your period?" Tierney asked, handing her the food.

"No," Trish said irritably. "Let's blow this pop stand." She ate hungrily while Tierney stuffed the book into an outer pocket of her pack and checked their sleeping quarters to make sure they hadn't left anything behind.

Their hike out to the highway was uneventful; they got a ride within minutes, and the white-haired couple who picked them up decided in short order to take them all the way to Seward, since as they said, it would make for good sightseeing. Although they scolded the girls for hitchhiking, claiming it was unsafe, they also bought them lunch at the Sea Breeze café and waited while Tierney made a long-distance call from the pay phone outside the restaurant.

She had decided to call her sister rather than her dad, since the honeymooners weren't due home until late that night. In truth, it was a relief to know she wouldn't have to talk to her father, wouldn't have to try to explain to him why she'd left without saying goodbye.

When Rita answered the phone in Rapid City, sounding as frazzled as usual, Tierney was caught off guard by the lump that suddenly formed in her throat. Her voice came out sounding a little strangled. "Hey, it's me, Tierney. I need you to do me a favor."

"Hello, dear sister. How are you and your family?"

"Yeah. Sorry. Everybody okay?"

"Do you have a cold? We're hanging in there. Wes likes his new job. I'm still barefoot and pregnant," Rita laughed. "Where have you been? I've been trying to reach you. They'll be home tonight, right?"

"That's why I'm calling. I'm in Alaska. On a pay phone."

"Very funny."

"No, really." Tierney tried to explain.

"Tierney, stop. It's not funny." Tierney could hear her younger nephew fussing, followed by Rita telling the older boy to leave his brother alone.

"It's the truth, Ree. I'm in a place called Portage. It's on the ocean. I'm sorry I didn't tell you."

Rita was silent.

"Seriously," Tierney continued. "It's south of Anchorage."

"How'd you get there?" Rita still sounded skeptical.

"Hitchhiked. I left right after they did. I'm telling you the truth, but I can't talk too long because these people are waiting for me. They're giving me a ride to Seward."

"You're serious, aren't you?" Rita's tone changed. "Holy cow."

"We need to talk fast."

"Geez, I can't believe you did that. Just up and left. Didn't think you and Helen were going to work out, huh? I didn't either, tell you the truth. Even so, this is quite the statement, missy."

"It's an adventure, not a statement. Tell Dad I'll get in touch with him once I get settled, okay? Tell him I'm doing fine. Better than fine. Tell him not to worry."

"You know darn well he's going to worry."

Tierney felt like crying again. "Tell him it's really beautiful here, really wild. He'd love it." She swallowed hard. "And you guys take care, okay? Tell Gus not to pick on Ben."

"Promise you'll call me again as soon as you can."

"Okay." Tierney wiped her dripping nose with the back of her hand. "One more thing, Sis. Do we have Indian blood, you and me?"

"Sure do." Tierney could hear one of the boys demanding Rita's attention. "I thought you knew that. Mom's mother was half Sioux."

Tierney caught her breath. "Really? Okay, thanks. Gotta go; everyone's waiting for me."

"Love you."

"You, too."

Tierney was glad when Trish and the wife fell asleep in the car shortly thereafter, and their driver switched on the car radio. In no mood for talking, she pretended to snooze. She felt as far from her home and family right now as she thought it was possible for her to feel, but still lacked any desire to go back. Tierney also felt strange about knowing she was part Indian, one-eighth, and wondered why it should make such a difference in the way she thought of herself. But it did somehow. Wait 'til she told Cleo.

Mostly though, now that she was on the road again, Tierney had a lot of anxiety about finding work. She'd have to ask Trish what kinds of jobs she might be able to get in Seward—anything but topless dancing. A deep male voice on the radio stated that the House Judiciary Committee's request for Nixon's secret tapes and the White House's countering claim of executive privilege were now going to be argued before the Supreme Court. What did that mean? She heard the driver sigh audibly.

Still feigning sleep, she followed their journey through the landscape between lowered eyelids: more nameless mountains and frothing glacial streams. The car slowed when they entered a small roadside community, at which point Tierney sat up and rubbed her eyes as if she'd just woken. The driver greeted her with a kindly smile in the rearview mirror. "Moose Pass," he said, and pointed out a wheeled whetstone that stood beside a flume of water at the side of the road, a hand-lettered sign nearby declaring: "If you have an axe to grind, do it here." The road continued to wind its way alongside a serpentine turquoise lake, train tracks appearing and disappearing beside them, until they arrived on a kind of floodplain at the head of a long, narrow bay.

Seward was as green and pretty as a postcard, boasting the kind of charm that Anchorage had lacked. The town itself appeared to be arranged in a tidy grid; the small old-style wooden houses appealed to Tierney for their tidy sense of order. The entire community was enclosed on three sides by massive snow-smeared mountains, opening onto the ocean at its front. It felt to her like the opposite of flat, dry, land-locked Williston. By now Trish was awake, too, and directing the driver to the home she shared with Pearl, Angela, and Donna Sue, as his wife continued to doze in the front seat. When they drove down the main street, Trish elbowed Tierney to look left and she saw the marquee for the Majestic Bar and Grill, sandwiched between two other storefronts. Flashing red lights on one side of the entrance advertised "Girls! Girls! Girls!" while on the other, a spot-light was angled to illuminate the words "Exotic Dancers" painted in dark script on white signboard.

No one was home when they arrived at the two-story house in the center of town. The dwelling was old, but clean, and furnished with comfortable if slightly shabby furniture, carpet, and window coverings. Trish gave Tierney the tour: small kitchen, tiny downstairs bathroom, Pearl's bedroom off the living room, the steep narrow staircase that led to the two slope-ceilinged bedrooms and bathroom on the second floor. Trish showed her the bunk bed in the smaller bedroom shared by Donna Sue and Angela. "They want it to look like they sleep separately, but they always sleep together," she smirked.

"Maybe they sleep together because they're lonely," Tierney retorted. "Did you ever think of that?"

"What's *your* problem?" Trish said, pushing open the door of her own bedroom, in which a frameless double mattress lay on the floor, flanked by a dresser on one side, and a single ladder-back chair on the other. Trish's dirty clothes were piled on the floor in the corner. "You can sleep with me, or you can sleep downstairs on the couch. Suit yourself." Tierney leaned her pack against the wall, retrieved the book that Cleo had given her, and without another word descended the skinny staircase to the living room, where she stretched out on the couch while Trish showered upstairs.

She woke up to the sound of many voices in the kitchen. Trish had gone shopping while Tierney was napping, and now she, Pearl, Donna Sue, and Angela were busily grating cheese, slicing onions, chopping lettuce, and cooking hamburger meat for a taco supper.

"Hi, Sleepyhead!" Pearl greeted her brightly when Tierney appeared in the doorway. "Feel like dicing some tomatoes?"

"Is it okay if I shower first?"

"I put a towel out for you," Trish said without turning around from the stovetop.

"Thanks."

They were all excited to show Tierney where they worked, so after dinner the group walked together the half-dozen blocks to the Majestic, Pearl and the blondes wearing their dance costumes under their clothes since, as they explained, they weren't even provided with lockers, let alone any kind of dressing room. Tierney relieved Pearl of the bulky satchel she carried over her shoulder and found it surprisingly heavy. "What do you have in here?" she asked.

"Props."

As Tierney soon discovered, the windowless interior of the grandiose-sounding Majestic was basic and plain, the walls largely undecorated, the lighting dim, and the bar, bar stools, small tables and chairs utilitarian rather than stylish. The "stage" on which the girls performed was nothing more than an eight-foot-square, raised plywood platform aligned against one wall, and it stood only a foot or so off the floor. At least the Majestic did have a real floor, Tierney thought, unlike the Funny Bone's hard-packed dirt and peanut shells.

An old jukebox was backed against the wall a few feet from the stage, and when they arrived there was only a smattering of customers—almost all male. The lady bartender, Freddie, clearly adored the dancers, making each her favorite drink, whether it was cherry coke (the blondes), a Tequila Sunrise (Trish), or a margarita (Pearl). She poured Tierney a big glass of milk "on the house."

The five of them took a table directly in front of the stage, and Trish entertained everyone with her version of the events that had taken place at Raven Creek, which included a description of Cleo as having "no sense of humor when it comes to her precious homestead." The bar slowly filled; at nine, Donna Sue and Angela went to work serving drinks. Apparently, Pearl's contract did not require her to wait tables, and Trish was still on her days off.

At ten o'clock sharp, Pearl beckoned to Angela, and the girl nodded, set down her empty serving tray, and plucking the wad of bubble gum she had been chewing from her mouth, she squashed it with her thumb and forefinger onto the rim of her soda before making her unhurried way in socks to the jukebox. She wore a faded T-shirt over her jeans, her hair in a long blonde ponytail. When Tierney peeked under the table, she saw Angela's empty sneakers where they'd been kicked off. Without pausing to study the song menu, Angela proceeded to punch in some music selections and then, with a begrudging reluctance, mounted the small platform, unceremoniously removed her T-shirt to exhibit an orange swimsuit top that was not at all revealing, and stood slouched and seemingly bored, waiting for the music to begin. Even Tierney, who barely knew her, could see how uncomfortable the girl was.

Someone dimmed the house lights. A floodlight above the stage bathed the area in a garish tint.

Angela was not much of a dancer, doing little more than sway through Barbra Streisand's "The Way We Were." The music did not exactly fit the context, Tierney noticed, not that the audience seemed to be paying the performer much attention. When the song clicked off abruptly at its end, Angela came to a standstill. Continuing to avoid eye contact with anyone, she took off her socks and affected boredom again while waiting for the next song to begin. Tierney noticed that the conversations in the bar had become somewhat more subdued and expectant.

At the first strains of "Seasons in the Sun," Angela stepped out of her jeans, seemingly with as little fanfare as if she were getting undressed for bed in the privacy of her own room. After dropping her pants to the stage, she used her foot to push them over toward her socks and T-shirt. Now she wore only the orange bathing suit—top and bottom. As before, there was nothing about either her posture or facial expression that could have been construed as even remotely sexy or suggestive, Tierney thought. As Angela continued to sway back and forth, some guy at the bar emitted a piercing whistle followed by a loud, "Yeah, baby!"

At their table, Trish laughed. "You're slaying 'em, Angela," she called to her housemate. In return and still without expression, Angela flipped her middle finger at Trish. The audience laughed appreciatively. Tierney noticed that Donna Sue, waitressing alone, had gotten busier as more customers arrived.

Finally, while the jukebox recalibrated for the next song, Angela unceremoniously unhooked her bathing suit top and dropped it on top of her other clothes, standing with her hands at her sides looking pale, vulnerable, and rib-thin under the unflattering spotlight. The tips of her nipples resembled the erasers on new pencils. If I really am a lezzie, Tierney thought, shouldn't I be attracted to Angela right now? But all she felt was sorry for her. It was true that Tierney's skin had prickled with goose bumps when Angela removed her top, but it was only because she wanted to protect her.

Again she "danced," this time to the strains of Eric Clapton's "I Shot the Sheriff." The customers loved it, or at least responded to this topless number more noisily than they had previously. As soon as the song ended, Angela, still without expression, took a bow to widespread applause then turned her back as she hastily pulled on her T-shirt. She bundled her other clothes and carried them with her to the table her friends shared. Tierney smiled at her, with both sympathy and respect. "You were great," she said. As artless as the performance had been, Tierney was pretty sure she could not have done what she'd just watched Angela do.

Angela pulled on her jeans and laced up her sneakers, picked up her serving tray, and resumed the work of clearing empty glasses from tables and taking orders for drinks. Donna Sue was up next, and Tierney was surprised to discover that the small, somewhat mousy girl was at heart an exhibitionist. In contrast to Angela, who had never looked at anyone the whole time she was on stage, Donna Sue's eyes never stopped surveying the crowd, seeking approval. When she found it, she fixed the person with a gap-toothed grin and gyrated her hips in poor imitation of a striptease artist. The fact of the matter was that she was a young girl who danced like a bouncing teenybopper, but her energetic performance made Angela's seem even more wooden and awkward in hindsight.

Was it possible that Donna Sue actually enjoyed this? When she unhooked her bathing suit top, she swung it around her head, causing the audience to clap and hoot. "Take it all off!" some guy yelled, and Donna Sue wagged a finger at him like he was a naughty boy. It was too bad she was so flat-chested, Tierney thought, because she might have had a real future as a topless dancer had she been better endowed. Still, Donna Sue knew how to connect with the crowd; when she finished her set, the audience whistled and cheered loudly. A few men even rose to their feet in a standing ovation. Tierney thought that maybe, just maybe, she might have been able to fake her way through the kind of performance Angela had offered, but knew she could never convey enjoyment, as Donna Sue had done. "You were really good," she told Donna Sue when the girl returned to the table, took up her serving tray, and joined Angela to serve drinks.

There was a fifteen-minute break before Pearl went on, the main act. Pearl left to use the restroom to make adjustments to the costume she was wearing. When she returned, it was in a silk chiffon robe that barely concealed the fact that she was scantily clad underneath it. The bar was almost silent when "Let's Get It On" by Marvin Gaye began to play and Pearl started to slink and dip, slowly and sensually. If Angela's and Donna Sue's dancing were leagues apart, Tierney thought, Pearl's was in a class of its own. She was clearly a pro—from her sequined bikini to her precise, well-rehearsed, and impeccably timed movements. Tierney felt the atmosphere in the bar shift into a new gear. Unlike Angela, Pearl didn't seek to avoid eye contact with her audience, but unlike Donna Sue, she was not soliciting anyone's approval. "What I do is an art form," her movements seemed to say. "I offer it to you as a gift."

Trish caught Tierney's expression. "She's good, isn't she? She makes the rest of us look pathetic, but what the heck."

Unlike the others, Pearl danced a total of four numbers before she left the stage. Tierney knew that never in a hundred years could she perform with the elegance and grace that Pearl had just exhibited.

The three each danced one more set apiece that night and that was it. They walked home together in the dusky night, dawn already lighting the mountaintops.

"How much do you get paid?" Tierney asked Donna Sue.

"Forty a night, but fifty if we dance on Friday or Saturday. Plus we get tips on the drinks we serve." Donna Sue glanced at her. "Of course, Pearl and Cleo make a lot more than we do."

It sounded like a heck of a lot of money to Tierney, especially when you considered that it was for only about four hours' worth of work. But when she tried to picture herself half-dressed on that plywood platform, her mind balked. No way, she thought. Not me.

Once they got home, they ate up the leftover tacos and played cards for a couple of hours. It was fully light by the time they finally went to bed, Tierney choosing to sleep on the couch in her sleeping bag. Trish looked a little miffed about this, but she didn't say anything.

The next day, Trish went with Tierney to several restaurants, but none of them were interested in offering Tierney a job. They weren't hiring, she was repeatedly told. When they left the third establishment, Trish said, "You should go by yourself. They all know I'm a dancer."

"What do you mean?"

"They're family businesses. They think we're immoral." Trish shrugged as if it didn't bother her, but Tierney could tell that it did.

So Trish went home, and even though Tierney made a point of systematically visiting all the eateries in Seward, she failed to turn up a single lead. "I even walked out to the cannery, but it's closed," she said to Trish, who had showered and was wrapped in a towel, perched on the edge of the tub shaving her legs for work later that night. She was smoking a fat joint that smoldered on the lip of the sink.

"Want some?"

Tierney shook her head.

"Cannery won't be hiring for a while yet. I should have warned you, saved you the trip. Sorry."

Tierney tried to read the book Cleo had given her, but kept getting distracted by her anxiety that she would never find a job—any job—and would have to borrow money from these girls in order to pay her way home.

That night, Trish danced while Angela got a day off. Not surprisingly, Tierney thought, Trish was good at it. Not on a par with Pearl, of course, but good at it in the sense of making the dancing seem like fun. She had a sassy, teasing air that many of the men seemed to appreciate, hamming it up through "You're So Vain." When the music started for her last number, "Dueling Banjos," the crowd roared at Trish's song selection: she danced faster and faster as the banjo pickers' tempo accelerated, finally collapsing in a histrionic heap on the stage. When she returned to the table after her set, she was laughing. Donna Sue swung by with a tray full of unserved drinks, to let them all know that their boss Donald, the elderly owner of the bar, had just fired the dishwasher and was in the back with his sleeves rolled up, elbow deep in soapy water. The others took turns tiptoeing to the kitchen to see for themselves. It was a cause of great merriment, Tierney noticed, apparently because the girls disliked Donald and thought he was sleazy.

It took Tierney half of Pearl's dance set to recognize the opportunity, but when she did, she pushed her chair back from the table so abruptly that it fell over. "Where are you going?" Trish said.

Tierney entered the kitchen, approaching the stoop-shouldered, gray-haired man she found rinsing plates before an industrial-sized stainless steel sink. "I can do that," she said. "I have experience."

Donald looked at her in surprise. "No kidding?" he said, already stepping back and shaking water off his hands.

"No kidding." Tierney stepped forward, pulling up her sweat-shirt sleeves.

"Five an hour?" He dried his hands on a towel and reached to shake hands with her, looking her up and down, appraisingly.

It was double what Milly had paid, but then again, Alaska was expensive. "Okay." Tierney shook his hand and stepped toward the sink.

"Wait a second," Donald said. "Can you dance?"

Tierney shook her head. "Nope."

For an hour or so, she felt triumphant, proud of having taken the initiative to score the dishwashing job, like it was some kind of major feat. But it didn't take long before the familiar isolation and drudgery of washing dishes reminded her that this was the only thing that she knew how to do, that she was completely lacking in other marketable skills. She was relieved to be earning money again, it was true, but it was discouraging to find herself once more standing in front of an oversized sink. Wasn't Alaska supposed to be her fresh start, her brand-new life?

Cleo arrived the next day, Saturday, in her black VW bug. Apparently, she had developed quite a reputation and following as one of Alaska's top exotic dancers, having performed all over the state for more than a decade. She had wrangled a special contract out of

Donald, dancing only one night a week as a kind of star attraction. And either because it was the weekend and/or because of Cleo's popularity, the bar was packed that night with pipeline workers in cowboy boots, sporting gold-nugget jewelry and belts with over-sized buckles. Trish, Donna Sue, and Angela scurried around from the get-go, taking drink orders, serving, and clearing the tables of empty glasses.

Cleo had real acts: the Schoolmarm was one; another was the Lion Tamer (with a stuffed lion that she'd brought with her). The men went crazy every time she cracked her leather whip while standing near-naked in a pair of high-heeled black boots. Of them all, Cleo was the most like a stage actress, inhabiting her various roles with real conviction.

Tierney was disappointed to have to miss most of Cleo's act. This was another problem with dishwashing; you were always far from the action. By the time she was able to take another break, she was thoroughly disenchanted with her tedious, humid job. Trish hauled her outside into the alley and for once Tierney was happy to get high with her. Anything to spice up the monotony of washing dishes. Once they returned inside, Trish coaxed Tierney to taste her drink, a Tequila Sunrise, which mostly just tasted like fruit juice. Since Tierney was thirsty and due back in the kitchen, she downed the whole thing.

Half an hour later, Trish found Tierney at the sink in tears. "What's wrong?"

"It would be one thing if I were at Cleo's. At least then I could do the dishes outside in the open air. But this," Tierney blubbered as she gestured to her windowless corner, "this just sucks." Donna Sue and Angela arrived to unload trays of dirty glasses, and the three huddled around their new friend, seeking to console her.

"You should try dancing," they chorused. "It's easy. The money's good. The guys get to look but they're not allowed to touch."

Soon Cleo and Pearl came looking for them, and the two professionals also persuaded Tierney to give it a try. "Nothing ventured, nothing gained," Pearl said. Donald showed up next, glaring at everyone, and the three younger cocktail waitresses slunk back to work. Donald's expression quickened the moment the two older dancers explained to him that Tierney was going to give dancing a try.

"I'm all in favor of that," he enthused, ogling Tierney's chest.

"I have the perfect swimsuit for you," Cleo said. "It's not very revealing at all. With your coloring, they're going to think you're Hawaiian. Exotic! And this is the perfect night for your first time, because it's actually much easier when the house is full."

So they got her ready, Pearl digging an artificial flower hibiscus from her satchel of props and clipping it to Tierney's hair. Cleo beamed and clapped her hands. "Aloha!" Trish proffered another Tequila Sunrise, urging Tierney to chug-a-lug, before Cleo helped her make three song selections at the jukebox. Then Tierney mounted the little stage wearing her jeans and T-shirt over the tropical pattern bathing suit that Cleo had loaned her, her face feeling hot. She stared at her feet, her arms locked rigidly across her front, and found herself utterly incapable of taking off her shirt. The music kicked in, one of her favorite songs, "Crocodile Rock," and being careful to look only at Cleo and Pearl, seated at the front table with encouraging smiles on their faces, Tierney managed to shuffle jerkily, arms still crossed.

"Take it off," one of the men in the audience yelled. Another yelled, "Take it all off!" It was like waking from a trance; Tierney froze. She knew she could no more take her clothes off in front of all these people than she could fly to the moon. She hung her head and mewled, distinctly hearing Trish intone, "Uh oh," from somewhere out on the floor.

Cleo and Pearl came to Tierney's rescue at the edge of the stage, both reaching out a hand to help her down, sitting her between them at the table and consoling her as best they could while the song finished. By the time Jim Croce had sung a few bars of "Bad Bad Leroy Brown," Pearl was scrambling to get herself ready to start her act early, reaching into her bag for the scarves and hats that were part of the costuming for her performance. Tierney covered her face with her hands, aware of the commotion she had stirred. She wanted to hear Trish crack a joke and say it was no big deal, happened all the time, but she knew Trish had to keep working or she would be fired.

Tierney couldn't look at anyone. She mumbled something into her hands. "What?" said Cleo. "Can't understand what you're saying." Suddenly the three younger girls all converged at the table.

"I said I didn't come all this way to be a stripper!"

"We're not strippers!" Pearl hissed, flustered and offended.

"I mean, nothing against any of you, but it's just not for me."

No one said anything, but they all moved away from her, the other girls returning to work and Pearl mounting the stage with no choice but to dance to Tierney's final song selection, Paul Simon's "Kodachrome." Not a very Pearl-like song, Tierney realized. She knew she had disgraced herself—not by her failed attempt to join their ranks as a dancer, but by her awful comments. When she was finally composed, she returned to the kitchen, still wearing the fake hibiscus blossom in her hair and the swimsuit underneath her clothes.

By the time Tierney had put all the clean dishes away, Donald was ready to lock up. The others had already departed, but Trish waited, though she had a decidedly frosty air about her. The two girls walked home without speaking, and just before they reached the house, Trish muttered hotly, "I wish you hadn't of said what you did." She stopped before the front door.

"I know. I'm sorry."

"It sounds like you think you're too good for what we do."

Tierney couldn't bring herself to look at her. "I know. I'm sorry," she said again.

"Anyway, you're supposed to be at least nineteen, so you couldn't have done it anyway."

Tierney's mouth fell open. "Why didn't you say something earlier? Why'd you let me make a fool of myself?"

Trish shrugged. "It never occurred to me until right this minute. Listen, you have to sleep in my room tonight; Cleo always gets the couch when she's here."

"Okay, but I'm sleeping on the floor."

"Suit yourself."

The following day, a Sunday, was the only day of the week that the Majestic was closed, so everyone was off duty. After some awkwardness in the house—she could tell the others were doing their best to avoid her—by midafternoon it felt to Tierney like she'd mostly been forgiven. It probably helped that she'd walked to a store and paid a small fortune for a pound of bacon and a dozen eggs, cooking them up for everyone's brunch. Later, in celebration of the solstice, Cleo and Pearl bought picnic food; they all piled into the Lincoln and drove out to Lowell Point, where they built a fire on the beach. It was a warm day, perfect for sunbathing, roasting hot dogs, toasting marshmallows, and wading in the ocean as the tide went out. Tierney was thrilled to find a bald eagle feather, determined that it should prove her lucky talisman.

Trish lit a joint that no one else wanted to smoke. Cleo and Pearl shared a bottle of red wine. The sunlight never dimmed. Finally, Pearl stood and brushed the dark sand from the seat of her pants. "If someone wants to give me a ride home, the rest of you can stay here."

Tierney noticed that Cleo had a pained look on her face; soon the others had noticed it, too. They waited for Cleo to explain. "Last night was my last night," she finally burst out, her voice quavering. "I already told Donald."

The others gaped at her. "What do you mean?" Pearl said, looking stunned.

"I promised Gavin I'd quit," Cleo explained tearfully. "He's earning good wages on the pipeline now. We don't need the extra money. He made me promise." She cried copiously. "I never thought it would be this hard to tell you." After an initial flurry of concern and consternation, wherein they all converged around their queen,

Tierney noticed that Pearl had withdrawn from the circle. She looked slightly ill, her hands held together in front of her mouth as if she were praying, her eyes flitting from Cleo to the ocean and back again.

By midnight, it was decided that Cleo would take Tierney home with her to Raven Creek the next day, where Tierney would be her "right-hand girl" in exchange for room and board and spending money. Cleo promised her that it wouldn't all be work, that they'd find ways to have fun as well. She offered to teach Tierney how to sew, and even though Tierney had absolutely no interest in sewing, as much out of gratitude to Cleo for taking her in as out of politeness, she murmured her thanks.

"Don't let her take advantage of you," were Trish's parting words. She told Tierney she always had a place to stay in Seward. "You can sleep on the floor as much as you like." Trish promised to show up at Raven Creek sometime soon so they could further explore the valley. "You can help me find the abandoned gold mine that's supposed to be up there."

Tierney quickly fell into the rhythm of life at Raven Creek, and it never lost its enchantment. She kept in touch with her dad through her sister, until the day Rita told her he'd calmed down over Tierney's unannounced departure, at which point she called him directly.

"Where are you, exactly?" he asked.

"I don't want to tell you."

"Why not?"

"I'm scared you'll try to come find me and take me home."

He said nothing for a whole minute, and then he sighed. "I know you had to leave," he said, "but I wish you didn't have to go so far."

"But it's *Alaska*," Tierney told him somewhat boastfully. "Sometimes it's worth it to go the distance to get what you want. You've said so yourself."

"I know, missy," he said—a little sadly, Tierney thought. "But sometimes people go too far and forget where they came from."

"I promise I won't do that."

The truth of the matter was that even though she'd come a long way, Tierney knew she still had a long way to go to become the person she hoped to someday be.

Another young woman disappeared, this one a diminutive Filipina dancer who had recently moved to Anchorage from Kodiak. Immediately following her vanishing, the Alaska State Troopers announced they'd located human remains they had identified as those of Karen Ann McMasters, missing since spring, near the Knik River. They determined that she'd been shot in the back of the head. A few days later, Trish and Pearl showed up at Cleo and Gavin's homestead. They were on their way to the Anchorage airport, Pearl explained. She had broken her dance contract at the Majestic and was flying home to Vegas.

"Whoever's going after little brown-skinned girls might decide to come after me," Pearl said.

"It can't be that Seattle killer because they just had another disappearance down there, too." Trish looked at the others. "Although I guess they're also getting shot in the head. What is the deal, anyway? When did it get to be open season on girls?"

"When has it ever not been?" Cleo said.

"So far, up here, it's only colored girls," Pearl said a little bitterly. "Anyway," she continued, glancing pointedly at Tierney, "it was never my intention to be a career dancer—no offense, Cleo. I've been saving up for nursing school next year."

Both she and Trish commented on how long Tierney's hair had grown and, over tea and homemade oatmeal cookies, the two of them took turns styling Tierney's locks into various hairstyles, her favorite of which was multiple little pigtails sprouting all over her head. Pearl and Trish spent the night, everyone staying up late and then sleeping in Cleo's house. When it was time for Trish to take Pearl to the airport the next day, Cleo and Pearl hugged each other and cried.

In late July, the US Supreme Court unanimously voted for the president to turn over his secret tapes. Cleo said it was the beginning of the end for Richard M. Nixon. A week or so later, stepping out of the toolshed in the middle of the night to pee, Tierney realized it was pitch dark. And cold. She saw stars glittering overhead, the first she'd seen in Alaska. On August 8, while on a shopping trip to Anchorage, she and Cleo were surprised to find many of the customers in the Prairie Market gathered around the boxy radio at one of the cash registers. As they joined the group, Tierney could hear a familiar voice intoning, "I have always tried to do what was best for the nation."

"Is that Nixon?" Cleo asked, and several people nodded, but no one spoke.

"I have concluded that because of the Watergate matter, I might not have the support of the Congress . . ."

Tierney heard a man gasp, "Oh, my God. Is this what I think it is?"

"Therefore, I shall resign the presidency effective at noon tomorrow."

"About time," another man muttered, while a woman burst into tears and began to cry noisily. "What will become of America?" she sobbed.

"Good Lord," a bespectacled older man said. Nixon's voice continued to drone. A young mother with a kerchief over her head began to hyperventilate, which caused her little girl, whom she was holding by the hand, to whimper. Some of the women held their hands to their faces; most of the men looked angry. Cleo was shaking her head, her lips tight. Holy shit, Tierney thought to herself. What's happening?

Although the group remained rooted in place until the speech was concluded, Tierney found it hard to attend to anything else the president said as he rambled on, seemingly repeating himself. A few people exchanged reactions in subdued voices, apparently sharing the opinion that Nixon should have hung on and not let himself be pressured into resignation. "He's the *president*," one of them said. "He shouldn't let anyone tell him what to do."

But in the privacy of the store's produce section, Cleo told Tierney flatly, "He went too far. I hope he gets all the punishment he deserves; I have no sympathy for him. None. He has really damaged this country."

"Good riddance," Tierney said, practically hearing her father's voice in her ear. She said it with bravado, like she actually knew what she was talking about, but in fact she felt queasy.

"I'm just glad I live in Alaska and not in the U.S. of A.," Cleo said.

Tierney glanced at her. "But Alaska is a state. It's part of the US."

"It is and it isn't," Cleo said. "You'll see."

Cleo helped Tierney get her records from the Williston School District and accompanied her to registration at West Anchorage High School, having arranged for Tierney to live with an old dancing friend in exchange for providing occasional childcare. Marie and her twin toddlers lived right around the corner from Tierney's new school. On the day she helped her move into town, Cleo presented Tierney with an envelope containing five crisp one-hundred dollar bills.

"It's too much!" Tierney protested.

"You earned every penny of it," Cleo said, repeating her highest praise. "You're a good worker."

Tierney made friends at school more easily than she had any right to expect, perhaps because there were a lot of new kids, most of them the offspring of recent pipeline hires. She met a boy, the co-captain of the school's winning football team, who loved to go hiking on the many nearby trails as much as she did. Noah, a kind person with an easy smile, came from a religious family.

Tierney was drawn to him instantly, and loved it that he seemed to enjoy her company as much as she enjoyed his. She'd never had a close friendship with a guy before, so in this sense he was a true boy-friend, but as time went on she began to wonder if she was ever going to feel about him the way she thought girls were supposed to feel about guys. She planned to talk to him about it when the time seemed right.

338

One night just before homecoming, he solemnly informed her that they could not have sex because he was "saving himself" for marriage. Tierney was struck by how nervous he was; apparently, he was afraid that she might not want to keep going out with him. She reached for his hand, relieved and happy that—at least for now—she was free to care for him as much as she did. It still scared her to think how close she'd come to going too far in her feelings for Trish that night beside Raven Creek. She decided she would just enjoy Noah's company and focus on keeping her grades up. A counselor at school had told her that she might be eligible for a scholarship to the University of Alaska next year.

Tierney's father flew to Anchorage over the Thanksgiving weekend for two days and nights; he met and approved of Noah, thanked Marie copiously for sheltering his daughter, and tried to give Tierney some money. "Keep it," she said, taking pride in the fact that she was able to turn his offer down. "I'll let you know if I need it, okay?" She and Noah took him up to Glen Alps, where they saw sixteen antlered bull moose congregating in a snowy bowl, and her dad agreed that Alaska was a pretty special place. Still, he had tears in his eyes when she kissed him goodbye at the airport.

Over their winter break, Noah and Tierney went to see a new movie, Grizzly Adams, at the Fourth Avenue Theater. By the time they had used the restrooms and purchased their popcorn and drinks, the lights had already gone down in the theater, so they stood for a moment just inside, letting their eyes adjust.

"We can sit here," Tierney whispered, motioning to the uppermost row of seats.

"No way," said Noah, nudging her to keep moving. "That's where the fairies sit." He led them toward seats on the aisle about halfway down.

"What did you say?" she asked.

"Fairies. Homos. They always sit in the last row."

Tierney yanked his arm. "Is that what your church teaches you?" she challenged in a loud whisper.

Taken aback, Noah stared at her in surprise. He reached to hold her food so that she could sit more easily, mumbling his apology.

By the end of the movie, which they both loved, all was forgiven, and as they made their way out of the theater, Tierney looked curiously at the remaining occupants of the highest seat row, to see if there could possibly be any truth to what Noah had said.

Only two patrons remained there, two youngish guys with long hair and beards, who both somewhat resembled Grizzly Adams. She smiled, wondering if Noah had noticed them. With a shock of recognition, Tierney realized that one of them was Robert and that the other was the same guy Robert had left the Funny Bone with that long-ago summer night. What was his name? Lance. She remembered how infatuated Trish had been with the good-looking boy, but also recalled what Cleo and Pearl had said about him. Were he and Robert homos? Even as she stared, she saw Robert reach over to brush something off Lance's beard and heard Noah snort. Normal men didn't touch each other like that, did they?

Lance and Robert were laughing over something one of them had said and looked to be in no hurry to leave. Tierney ducked her face behind Noah's shoulder. For some reason, she didn't want Robert to see her. Soon they were out on the street, walking toward Noah's car, and after the initial flood of relief at having escaped detection, Tierney became aware of how boring and regular she and Noah looked: his crew cut and letter jacket, her own dopey outfit consisting of Shetland sweater and pressed woolen slacks.

She still didn't know Robert's last name. What if she never saw him again, never had a chance to thank him for traveling to Alaska with her, for his good-natured companionship over hundreds of miles? If Robert and Lance really were homosexuals, Tierney thought, and if being homosexual was such a bad thing, why did they look so happy to be in each other's company?

"Wait!" she said to Noah, pivoting suddenly to run back to the theater. "I saw someone I know."

"Where are you going?" Noah yelled, uncertain whether or not to follow her.

The theater was completely empty; Robert and Lance were gone. Tierney felt inexplicably desolate as she hurried back out to the street, searching the sidewalks frantically as Noah arrived and demanded to know what was going on. After concealing herself from him earlier, it now felt like a matter of life and death that she identify herself to Robert. She stepped out into the street, a car swerving to avoid hitting her, Noah exclaiming and trying to pull her back.

A few blocks down Fourth Avenue, headed east toward the mountains, she spotted two figures walking side by side. It was them. She felt so happy she hugged Noah.

"Come on," she said to him, taking off again at a run, cupping her hands around her mouth to holler Robert's name, watching him stop and turn toward her.

WORKS CONSULTED

Carter, Steven. *Outrage: The 1993 Australian Gay and Lesbian Short Story Anthology.* Sydney: Designer Pub, 1994. Print.

Claycomb, Ryan. *Lives in Play: Autobiography and Biography on the Feminist Stage.* Ann Arbor: University of Michigan Press, 2012. Print.

Drake, Robert, ed. *The Gay Canon.* New York: Anchor Books, 1998. Print.
Evans, Mei Mei. "'Nature' and Environment Justice." The Environmental Justice Reader. Eds. Jonie Adamonson, Mei Mei Evans, and Rachel Stein. Tucson: University of Arizona Press, 2002. 181–193. Print.

Evans, Mei Mei. "Queer(y)ing 'Nature.'" *Journal of Interdisciplinary Studies: A Journal of Criticism and Theory* 7, no. 1 (2005): 27–35. Web.

Kleinberg, Seymour, ed. *The Other Persuasion: The Homosexual Theme in Fiction.* London: Macmillan Publishers, 1977. Print.

Manguel, Alberto, and Craig Stephenson, eds. *The Flamingo Anthology of Gay Literature: In Another Part of the Forest.* London: HarperCollins, 1994. Print.

Mellor, Mary. *Feminism & Ecology.* Cornwall: Hartnolls, 1997. Print.

Patchett, Ann, ed. *The Best American Short Stories.* New York: Houghton Mifflin Company, 2006. Print.

Ruff, Shawn Stewart, ed. *Go the Way Your Blood Beats: An Anthology of Lesbian and Gay Fiction by African-American Writers.* New York: Henry Holt & Co, 1996. Print.

Timmons, Stuart. *The Trouble with Harry Hay.* Brooklyn, NY: White Crane Books, 2012. Print.

White, Edmund, ed. *The Faber Book of Gay Short Fiction.* London: Faber and Faber, 1991. Print.

Williams, Amber M., and Poet on Watch, eds. *G.R.I.T.S. — Girls Raised In the South: An Anthology of Southern Queer Womyns' Voices and Their Allies.* Seattle: CreateSpace Independent Publishing Platform, 2013. Print.